The American History Series

SERIES EDITORS
John Hope Franklin, *Duke University*
Abraham S. Eisenstadt, *Brooklyn College*

Arthur S. Link
Princeton University
GENERAL EDITOR FOR HISTORY

David R. Goldfield
UNIVERSITY OF NORTH CAROLINA
AT CHARLOTTE

Promised Land

The South since 1945

HARLAN DAVIDSON, INC.
ARLINGTON HEIGHTS, ILLINOIS 60004

This book, or parts thereof, must not be used or reproduced in any
manner without written permission. For information, address the
publisher, Harlan Davidson, Inc., 3110 North Arlington Heights
Road, Arlington Heights, Illinois 60004-1592.

Library of Congress Cataloging-in-Publication Data

Goldfield, David R., 1944–
    Promised land.

    (The American history series)
    Bibliography: p.
    Includes index.
    1. Southern States—History—1951–   . 2. Southern
States—History—1865–1951.   I. Title. II. Series:
American history series (Harlan Davidson, Inc.)
F216.2.G64   1987   975   86-16243
ISBN 0-88295-850-X
ISBN 0-88295-843-7 (pbk.)

Manufactured in the United States of America

91 90 89 88 87 EB 1 2 3 4 5 6 7

for Erik
and his generation of Southerners

CONTENTS

FOREWORD

Every generation writes its own history, for the reason that it sees the past in the foreshortened perspective of its own experience. This has certainly been true of the writing of American history. The practical aim of our historiography is to offer us a more certain sense of where we are going by helping us understand the road we took in getting where we are. If the substance and nature of our historical writing is changing, it is precisely because our own generation is redefining its direction, much as the generation that preceded us redefined theirs. We are seeking a newer direction, because we are facing new problems, changing our values and premises, and shaping new institutions to meet new needs. Thus, the vitality of the present inspires the vitality of our writing about our past. Today's scholars are hard at work reconsidering every major field of our history: its politics, diplomacy, economy, society, mores, values, sexuality, and status, ethnic, and race relations. No less significantly, our scholars are using newer modes of investigation to probe the ever-expanding domain of the American past.

Our aim, in this American History Series, is to offer the reader a survey of what scholars are saying about the central themes and issues of American history. To present these themes and issues, we have invited scholars who have made notable contributions to the respective fields in which they are writing.

Each volume offers the reader a sufficient factual and narrative account for perceiving the larger dimensions of its particular subject. Addressing their respective themes, our authors have undertaken, moreover, to present the conclusions derived by the principal writers on these themes. Beyond that, the authors present their own conclusions about those aspects of their respective subjects that have been matters of difference and controversy. In effect, they have written not only about where the subject stands in today's historiography but also about where they stand on their subject. Each volume closes with an extensive critical essay on the writings of the major authorities on its particular theme.

The books in this series are designed for use in both basic and advanced courses in American history. Such a series has a particular utility in times such as these, when the traditional format of our American history courses is being altered to accommodate a greater diversity of texts and reading materials. The series offers a number of distinct advantages. It extends and deepens the dimensions of course work in American history. In proceeding beyond the confines of the traditional textbook, it makes clear that the study of our past is, more than the student might otherwise infer, at once complex, sophisticated, and profound. It presents American history as a subject of continuing vitality and fresh investigation. The work of experts in their respective fields, it opens up to the student the rich findings of historical inquiry. It invites the student to join, in major fields of research, the many groups of scholars who are pondering anew the central themes and problems of our past. It challenges the student to participate actively in exploring American history and to collaborate in the creative and rigorous adventure of seeking out its wider reaches.

John Hope Franklin
Abraham S. Eisenstadt

ACKNOWLEDGMENTS

The South* is like the tar baby. The more you delve into it, the more difficult it is to let go. If detached perspective is a prerequisite for sound scholarship, then the Southern historian faces an awful dilemma. Living in the region compounds the problem since you either love it or hate it (perhaps at the same time), but are seldom indifferent to it. As the title of this book implies, my emotions tend toward the affectionate side. My admiration stems not only from what the South is today, but also from what its people have gone through to get to this point. In a sense, it involved a journey through the desert, a revelation akin to the parting of the Red Sea, and a deliverance of sorts, if not into the promised land just yet, then at least within hailing distance.

The book represents a personal odyssey as well. Coming from a people accustomed to desert treks as well as to numerous other wanderings, I am at last settled in. I have a stake here and one of my objectives in this book is to encourage that commitment among my fellow Southerners, and an understanding among those not blessed with birth or residence in the region. In this task, I have had the incalculable assistance of novelists, scholars, and journalists whose work precedes mine and for whose insights I am grateful. Equally inspirational have been my history department colleagues at UNCC,

---

*I define the South as the eleven former Confederate states plus Kentucky.

(continued)g

especially Dave Patterson, Harold Josephson, Paul Escott, and Julia K. Blackwelder, and my close associates in the university community, Ed Perzel, Schley Lyons, and Tom Turner. Their good humor and encouragement helped me to maintain the proper perspective on my work and life.

To list my colleagues in the historical profession whose conversations and readings of the manuscript in whole or in part were invaluable to me would test the indulgence of my publisher. But I must mention three scholars who were particularly helpful in shaping this book: Dewey Grantham, John Hope Franklin, and especially Abe Eisenstadt.

It is difficult to pinpoint the role Blaine Brownell played in this work, except to say that whenever I thought about the South at its best, I thought of this native Alabamian. His ideas and friendship are enmeshed in its pages more than I know.

The pages would have come more slowly were it not for Connie Higginbotham and Mary Bottomly. They did more than process words; they offered advice and generally kept me from getting too sure of myself. I am also indebted to Barbara Lisenby, head of our Interlibrary Loan staff, for her prompt and efficient attention to my numerous requests. Anita Samen performed superbly as copyeditor. And Maureen Gilgorc Hewitt was a patient and supportive executive editor.

I am especially indebted to my benefactor, Mrs. Sanford Davenport, for her support of our department in general, and me in particular. In this connection, the indefatigable Dr. Bonnie Cone, UNCC's founder, has been a model for all of us here. I appreciate her encouragement of and interest in my work. The University supported my research and writing on this book with a timely summer grant.

My family—my parents, my wife, Marie-Louise, and my son, Erik—provided the stability and foundation for whatever creativity appears in these pages. Though this book was a labor of love, it took time away from those I love. I am grateful for their understanding.

This book is especially for Erik, a first-generation Southerner, who is most fortunate to be in this place at this time.

Aside from its economic and physical attributes, the South has the potential for moral leadership as well. The region's history and especially the years since the Second World War have made it so. I am hopeful that Erik and his generation of Southerners will fulfill that potential.

World War II and the Seeds of Change

The South in 1940

The South in 1940 was a region caught by time. The past—its memories and practices—dominated regional life. The present and the future were merely stations on the continuum of the past. Southerners cultivated their fields much as they had a century earlier, expending prodigious amounts of fertilizer and sweat to grow mainly cotton. The demanding staple had leeched the soil and the economy, yet had stubbornly persisted despite this and despite the capricious world demand for the fiber. The South was still a rural, agrarian region in the midst of an urban, industrial nation. Its cities were modest and the characteristic urban settlement was the small town. It seemed as if the South and its people had always been poor, or at least since the Civil War, and had failed to share in the prosperity that accompanied this nation's emergence as a world power. The South in 1940 also remained a biracial society; since slavery days race had dominated the thoughts and politics of the region.

The resulting sharply segregated society, predicated on white supremacy, occasionally boiled over into violence.

This was not only the way things were, but to many Southerners, especially to white Southerners, this was the way things ought to be. In a form of intellectual alchemy, Southerners transformed these regional debilities into attributes. Defeat became the hallowed Lost Cause, a strong sense of place and kinship ties overcame the reality of rural poverty, and race pride obscured, for whites, the tragedy of a biracial society. Moreover, Southerners felt that this was God's design; the devout evangelical Protestantism that distinguished the region sanctified the existing order, the order of the past, and emphasized individual salvation and the afterlife, implying man's helplessness, even blasphemy, to tamper with the status quo. It was a fatalistic perspective that generated, according to Southern writer, John Crowe Ransom, "a vast quantity of inertia."

Yet, as we know, in the generation after 1940, the South underwent a startling metamorphosis. From the nation's number one economic problem, the South transformed itself into the epitome of the urbanized, postindustrial Sunbelt. And the region synonymous with racial separation and exclusion made significant progress toward attaining a racial accommodation that other regions could envy. How and why this transformation occurred is the major focus of this book.

But there is another theme implicit in the following pages; although Southerners were successful, for the most part, in throwing off the double yoke of racial separation and economic weakness, they did not necessarily abandon other elements of regional life that set them apart from the rest of the country. John Shelton Reed, a Chapel Hill sociologist, has discovered that Southerners remain more likely than other Americans to express a strong attachment to their localities; they are more family-oriented than other Americans and maintain a continued reverence for the past, frequently expressed by their veneration of ancestors and love of regional history; and they are more church-going than citizens elsewhere. Southerners have fashioned a new society while adhering to some old traditions. Even more interesting, perhaps, is that these traditions once supported and reinforced the old rural, biracial order.

This latter point is not surprising because Southerners' strong sense of past and place and their abiding religious faith contained liberating as well as constricting elements. In a nation where the past is quickly devalued or forgotten, the Southern sense of the past could act as an antidote to the overweening pride that often accompanies a presentist mentality; ties with families, with historic structures and events, impart a stability and continuity to a society. Southerners also savor place; they love their land. In this temperate region, Nature extends the riot of colors and fragrances into months when much of the country suffers a gray barrenness. Southerners have translated their relationship with the land into environmental protection, the copious use of landscaping and country flora in urban environments, and a less hurried, more relaxed lifestyle.

Southern religion offered a path less encrusted with regional mores and more reflective of the ancient Judeo-Christian theology of love and brotherhood. The fatalism over present circumstances can be countered by the optimism of eventual salvation for the Southerner and for a reunited region regardless of past sins.

This does not imply that Southerners, as they approach the last decade of the twentieth century, have attained a promised land of prosperity and equality. The disparate elements of regional tradition still compete for the Southern mind. But at least now the positive aspects of these traditions are visible and active, thanks to the basic transformation of Southern society over the past forty years.

In 1940, the basic outlines of this transformation were yet invisible. True enough, New Deal legislation had disrupted venerable cultivation and labor patterns, but mules still walked the cotton rows and cotton remained the region's leading cash crop. In Mississippi, for example, the number of cotton bales produced in 1939 was roughly the same as in 1930. The small farm, inefficient and unproductive, still reigned as well: the average cropland harvested in 1939 was thirty acres. More important, with the notable exception of the Tennessee Valley residents, the lifestyle of the South's farm population altered little, and perhaps deteriorated, during the 1930s. Housing, health care, and education continued to be shockingly substandard.

Though New Deal legislation facilitated labor union organizing, aside from some success among rubber and steel plants, particularly in Alabama, the South's workforce remained unorganized. In terms of race relations, the visibility of blacks in the Roosevelt administration and the well-publicized activities of Eleanor Roosevelt kindled hope among some Southern blacks, but New Deal programs in the region adhered to the color line. Such New Deal projects as government buildings, roads, dams, parks, and sewer systems altered the physical landscape of the region, but the social and economic framework of Southern society remained intact.

And then the war came. Southerners in 1940 probably had an inkling that they were to embark on another war, but they could not have been expected to fathom that the effect of the forthcoming fury upon the South would be as great as, if not greater than, that of the Civil War. For future generations of Southerners there would still be only one War; but memories and feelings from that conflict would be refracted through the prism of another war that, in many respects, would fulfill the dreams of the first.

War and Prosperity: Costs and Benefits

During the New Deal the South had been more or less a reluctant patient, and purported cures fell far short of the mark. World War II was quite another matter. Here was an opportunity for the South to demonstrate its commitment to American ideals, as it had done in World War I. Ever striving for legitimacy in national opinion, the Southerner characteristically threw himself into the war effort. Moreover, the region, imbued with the legends of valor from "The War," perceived the battlefield as considerably more than a killing ground. It was a stage for redemption and an affirmation of regional ideals.

National economic priorities and strategic military considerations coincided with Southern desires to contribute significantly to the war effort. The federal government had recently identified the South as the nation's major economic problem area, as a region plagued by, among other handicaps, a huge labor surplus and chronically low wages. The government had targeted the South for special treatment with respect to military training centers and contracts for shipyards and aircraft plants. Also, prior to American entrance into the war in 1941, the Northeast possessed the greatest concentration of defense contractors. It made good sense from a strategic standpoint to decentralize defense work.

Southern ports, dormant under economic depression, sprang alive with infusions of federal money. Naval and private shipyards in Newport News, Norfolk, Charleston, Pensacola, Mobile, Pascagoula, and Houston issued calls for workers and more workers. Interior cities maintained the rapid regional cadence of wartime development as focal points for aircraft plants. Consolidated-Vultee in Fort Worth undertook construction of B–24 Liberators in 1942 and Bell Aircraft of Marietta, Georgia, secured the contract for the B–29 Superfortress. Tulsa, Nashville, and Birmingham firms received components contracts to supply the mushrooming Southern aircraft industry. The region's climate was another factor in attracting federal funds, especially for training bases. The armed forces desperately needed large numbers of trained recruits quickly in the early months of 1942, and the South's moderate climate facilitated outdoor maneuvers and training of troops as well as their rapid deployment. Military bases generated spin-off activities in adjacent towns and cities that further accelerated economic development. Eventually, the federal government spent $4 billion, or more than one-third of the national total, on military facilities in the South, as well as a like amount on defense contracts awarded to public and private installations in the region.

The transformation occurring in some of the states and cities as a result of wartime expenditures was staggering. During the war the massive Ingalls shipyard facility at Pascagoula, Mississippi, employed three times as many people as had resided in the town prior to the war. By 1944, the village of 6,000 inhabitants four years earlier had become a small city of 30,000 people. Incomes rose throughout the impoverished state during the war years: per capita income increased 100 percent during this period and bank deposits grew fivefold. The establishment of national uniform wages at defense installations proved a bonanza to Southern workers, traditionally the lowest-paid regional labor force in the country. Women, when they worked before the war, typically earned no more than five dollars a week; during the war years, forty dollars a week was the norm. As for men, especially those but recently chained to a deteriorating agrarian economy, a cash income of $500 a year would have been considered a windfall; now, some men earned that sum in a week. A reporter for *Fortune* magazine interviewed an erstwhile cropper, now a defense worker in a Panama City, Florida, plant, whose newfound affluence had created an unanticipated dilemma: "Hit's got me right bothered," the worker allowed, "how I'm a-goin' to spend it all."

Indeed, the human costs of rural displacement and the general persistent underemployment in the region seemed to dissipate overnight. The steady cash income represented a major change in lifestyle for those Southerners accustomed to periodic, subsistence incomes and onerous credit arrangements whose obligations never seemed fulfilled from one year to the next. Now it was possible to plan, to buy, to hope, and to dream. And it was there merely for the asking. As the touring *Fortune* correspondent concluded: "For the first time since the 'War Between the States' almost any native of the Deep South who wants a job can get one."

The employment opportunities generated by war resulted in a mass shuffling of the Southern population. Mobility within and out from the region reached an all-time high during the war years and, for the first time in decades, there was a detectable migration into the South. With war industries absorbing so many Southern workers, the revolution on the farm continued and accelerated. Shortages, strategic shifts to soybeans, truck crops, and livestock production resulted in a general agricultural prosperity throughout the region, enhanced by the removal of the excess rural population. The region's farm population declined by 22 percent during the war, a migration that stimulated mechanization and crop diversification, which in turn spurred income upward. Between 1940 and 1944, farm income in the South more than doubled from $2 billion to $4.7 billion annually, representing a per capita cash income jump from $150 to $454. This significantly lessened the gap with the rest of the nation's farmers, who earned $530 per capita in 1944.

Just as defense industries altered lifestyles, renewed agricultural prosperity enabled remaining farmers to enjoy the technological benefits of modern America, from electricity to indoor plumbing to automobile ownership. By 1945, nearly one in three Southern farms possessed electricity, compared with only one in six just five years earlier. Isolation decreased and a wider variety of consumer goods were within reach of farmers, despite wartime restrictions. Equally important, from a psychological perspective, the presence of viable industrial employment alternatives meant that family farms could stay that way now that younger sons and daughters could go off to the factory while parents or other kin maintained the farm. In fact, while the farm population dropped drastically during the war, the number of farms remained roughly intact, indicating that migration was selective within families.

But maintenance of the family farm over the short term obscured more basic changes occurring in the Southern countryside as a result of the war. The men and women going off to war or to the industries that fueled the war were the South's agrarian future—they were mostly under thirty-five years of age, restless, and ambitious for a better life than the uncertainties of the soil. They left behind an aging population that would less carry on the region's venerable rural traditions than preside over their declension. In such rural regions as Calhoun County in the northern Alabama Piedmont, suddenly thrust into the national economic mainstream with a defense installation, the accompanying introduction of paved roads, electricity, and better schools implied a future for the next generation, though the breakdown of isolation inevitably signaled an encounter with the rest of the world—a meeting that would prove jarring. For the moment, the war produced a mixture of past, present, and future jostling for attention and, for the first time in decades, there existed a discernible difference between the three time frames. Writer H. C. Nixon observed that, in his native Calhoun County, Alabama, toward the end of the war farmers used "three kinds of power for plowing: tractor, mule, and ox," and went to town "in wagons, buggies, and autos." That winter, farmers were heating their homes with "pine knots, oak wood, coal, oil, gas, and electricity."

Time advanced even faster for Southern cities, the prime beneficiaries and, in some cases, victims of the wartime bonanza. Southern urban population increased by more than one-third during the 1940s, with most of that advance occurring during World War II. The telescoping of this increase between 1940 and 1943 created particular difficulties for Southern cities accustomed to a pace of growth that was much more leisurely, if not nonexistent. Mobile was the fastest-growing city in the country during this period, experiencing a 61 percent population increase, with Norfolk, another major coastal defense installation, close behind with a 57 percent jump.

But mere population figures, however impressive, do not convey the impact of such growth on relatively slow-paced Southern cities. Agnes Meyer, a reporter for the *Washington Post,* entitled her 1943 tour of the urban South "Journey Through Chaos." The population crush overwhelmed Mobile, a city heretofore known mainly for its oysters and its Mardi Gras. Now, with two major shipyards in addition to an Alcoa plant, the city turned into a dense makeshift campground al-

most overnight. Rooming house boarders slept in shifts and
any multiple-unit structure became a tightly packed dormitory.
Author John Dos Passos visited the city in 1943 and the scene
shocked even this veteran observer of disorder. Mobile looked
"trampled and battered like a city that's been taken by storm.
Sidewalks arc crowded. Gutters are stacked with litter. ...
Garbage cans are overflowing. Framehouses on treeshaded
streets bulge with men. ... Cues [sic] wait outside of movies
and lunchrooms." The nineteen-member police force was inadequate to challenge the street gangs, vandalism, and looting
that accompanied the frontier conditions. City services, never
a strong suit of Southern urban governments, disintegrated
before the population crush, with refuse collection and water
supply disappearing altogether at too-frequent intervals. By
1944, however, the federal government had assumed the task
of providing housing and services to a stressed population.

If Mobile, a city of over 100,000 inhabitants in 1940, was
unable to cope with its newfound reality as a boom town,
smaller Southern cities and towns experienced even more chaotic conditions. In 1940, Pascagoula was a quiet fishing and
farming town on the Mississippi Gulf Coast. As the site of the
sprawling Ingalls shipyard after 1941, the town's population
quintupled in three years. Most of the newcomers arrived from
the Mississippi countryside and were unfamiliar with urban
densities and lifestyles that soon characterized the town. "In
the grocery stores they are lost," one observer wrote, "because
they do not know what to buy, cannot make up their minds
quickly in the crowd, and get jostled around by the others."
They crowded into trailers and tents in areas of inadequate or
absent services, sewage facilities, and roads. Overworked medical and social service personnel provided sporadic assistance
when possible, but frequently it was not. A young mother whose
husband worked at Ingalls expressed the human costs of this
situation in a resigned country drawl, as if her story were not
extraordinary but something that had happened so often that
it was expected, even if it shocked the listener unaccustomed
to the trials of life in a Mississippi that had merely shifted

scenery—rural to urban—but not conditions. Her two-year-old son, she explained, "was sleeping and he waked up and began crying, so I carried him in the living room, and his hands began drawing, and his feet, and I thought he was going into convulsions. ... My husband ... went to call the doctor ... and told him the baby was going into convulsions, and the doctor told him to give him the medicine ... and he thought the baby would be all right. And my husband told him he was vomiting it up just as fast as we gave it to him, and the doctor said he was tired and had to go to bed and get some sleep, and he didn't come." The baby died.

Not all Southern cities and towns, of course, collapsed under the pressures of population and economic development. In addition to receiving the benefits, but few of the costs, of nearby military installations, Dallas and Atlanta became regional federal administrative centers that built upon a diversified economic base to produce significant, but relatively orderly, growth both during and after the war. But the migration to and the conditions in Southern cities touched off an uneasiness among many Southerners, who were ambivalent at best about the benefits of urban civilization. Bloated cities such as Norfolk and Mobile lacked simple urban services but catered to a bold variety of prurient tastes. The very disorderliness of urban life, its threats to family and faith, the jostling and breezy informality yet anonymity of these wartime cities were incongruent with the Southern way of life. Perhaps some Southerners dismissed such deviance as a temporary aberration brought on by war. But white Southerners knew war meant change, and peace, from their own remembered past, was no guarantee of status quo ante. Above all, the migration to the cities, as well as the war itself, raised concerns about the maintenance of white supremacy.

War and Race: Dreams and Realities

Virginius Dabney, member of a prominent Virginia family and respected editor of the Richmond *Times-Dispatch,* confided to his friend W. T. Couch, director of the University of North Carolina Press, that when the war began, he—Dabney—was convinced that while Southern blacks would seize the opportunity of war to seek improvement in their condition, they would be content to do so within the established framework of segregation. Dabney admitted, however, that his initial impression had been off the mark. "The dead cats which have been mine during the past couple of years," he wrote, "have made me realize all too vividly that the war and its slogans have roused in the breasts of our colored friends hopes, aspirations and desires which they formerly did not entertain, except in the rarest instances."

Indeed, the American war propaganda machine produced daily reminders that we were fighting for freedom and liberty against the evils of fascism. It was unlikely that Southern blacks would fail to make the connection between the war against fascism abroad and the war against discrimination at home. And for those white Southerners who allowed themselves perceptions of the race issue beyond supremacist symbols, the meaning of the war for blacks was obvious too. In July 1943, William Faulkner wrote to his soldier-stepson, predicting that "A change will come out of this war. If it doesn't, if the politicians . . . who run this country are not forced to make good the shibboleths they glibly talk about freedom, liberty, human rights, then you young men who have lived through it will have wasted your precious time, and those who don't live through it will have died in vain."

From the outset of American entrance into the war, blacks were intent on "mak[ing] good the shibboleths," as they adopted "double victory"—at home and abroad—as their official slogan. In 1942, the National Association for the Advancement of Colored People (NAACP) convened in Los Angeles and issued a ringing declaration pledging the organization to eliminate segregation in the armed forces, discrimination in education and employment, and obstruction of voting rights. The agenda was unremarkable for a group that had been in the vanguard of the fight for racial equality since the second decade of the century. They had promoted these specific causes nearly that long, but had heretofore operated in a moral vacuum. Now with the nation raised to an ideological fervor, the NAACP sought to seize the opportunity and act quickly.

More unusual, in terms of precedent, was the newfound voice of Southern blacks. Doubtless their agenda matched and exceeded the list of the New York-based NAACP, but regional conditions had imposed a harsh silence on their aspirations. If the war did not moderate racial culture, at least it emboldened blacks to connect the fight for freedom abroad with their own battle at home. Touring the South during the summer of 1942, writer and Georgia resident Lillian Smith noted the eagerness with which young blacks signed up for the armed forces "to prove to white Americans their willingness to die for a country which has given them only the scraps from the white folks' democracy." But she also noted a new sentiment, something darker, and stronger, "a quiet . . . resentment, running like a deep stream through their minds and hearts," that would not quell until they attained justice. A few months later, a group of Southern black leaders met in Durham, North Carolina, and issued a simple statement that they were "fundamentally opposed to the principle and practice of compulsory segregation in our American society." The declaration paralleled NAACP concerns, but both the location and its public promulgation were precedent-shattering.

The association of overseas and domestic objectives encouraged W. T. Couch and his University of North Carolina Press to undertake a project to gather together leading blacks, such as Rayford Logan, Roy Wilkins, and W. E. B. DuBois, for an anthology on wartime and postwar goals especially for Southern blacks. But Couch was stunned by the strident tone of the manuscript presented to him by Logan late in 1943 and considered withholding publication. The deep current perceived by Lillian Smith was bubbling to the surface, dispelling any doubts that blacks sought modest, incremental gains. Couch reluctantly published *What the Negro Wants* in 1944, and Logan's summary in the book encapsuled the tenor and nature of the reform agenda it presented: "In the name of democracy for all Americans we ask these irreducible fundamentals of first-class citizenship for all Negroes: 1. Equality of opportunity. 2. Equal pay for equal work. 3. Equal protection of the law. 4. Equality of suffrage. 5. Equal recognition of the dignity of the human being. 6. Abolition of public segregation."

In subsequent decades, when desegregation became the leading priority for Southern blacks it obscured the fact that when the movement for racial justice accelerated during the war years, blacks pursued both economic and civil rights together. The combination reflected differences of opinion among Southern blacks on regional racial priorities. Some, particularly those in middle- and high-status positions within the black community, preferred to work for economic equality within the framework of segregation, at least for the time being. Others believed that an assault on segregation was a prerequisite for economic equality. In any case, blacks felt sufficiently hopeful to advance a comprehensive array of proposals designed to secure the rights for which Americans of every color were fighting and dying.

But Southern blacks in particular were not only encouraged by the war itself, but also by signals from the federal government that there existed in Washington at least tacit approval of the regional racial agenda. Besides the tireless campaigning of Eleanor Roosevelt in behalf of racial equality, there was substantive civil rights legislation in the form of the Fair Employment Practices Committee (FEPC). Responding to a threat from black union leader A. Philip Randolph to stage a massive march on Washington, the Roosevelt administration established the FEPC in 1941 to ensure that neither labor unions nor firms engaged in defense-related work would discriminate against black workers. The committee received and reviewed complaints and passed along its recommendation to the Department of Defense for action. That such a measure was necessary in the midst of a growing labor shortage indicates the depths of racial exclusion not only in the South, but in the rest of the country as well.

While the FEPC provided a glimmer of economic opportunity for blacks, the United States Supreme Court advanced racial equality along the political front. From outright intimidation to more subtle methods involving complicated literacy tests and obscure hours and locations for voting registration, Southern white leaders had effectively circumscribed or, particularly in rural areas, eliminated the black vote. These measures dated back to the late 1890s, when the threat of the Populist party and widespread vote fraud hastened black disfranchisement at the hands of the ruling Democratic party. Black voting dropped precipitously, though the disfranchisement statutes never mentioned race, thus complying with the letter of constitutional prohibitions against suffrage discrimination based upon color. In the process, the South evolved into a one-party region in which the general election became a mere formality that attracted as little as 10 percent of the eligible voters. Whatever electoral excitement existed in this one-party system occurred in the primary to choose the candidate for the general election. But the Democratic party openly barred blacks from voting in the primary.

Courts had upheld challenges to the white primary on the basis that the Democratic party was a private organization with a consequent right to limit membership on a variety of criteria including race. A black dentist from Dallas, Texas, Lonnie Smith, nevertheless challenged the legality of the white primary in Texas in 1940. The case, *Smith* v. *Allwright,* eventually reached the United States Supreme Court and, in 1944, Justice Stanley F. Reed, a Kentuckian, held for the eight-person majority in favor of Smith. The Court declared that, despite precedent to the contrary, political parties are agents of the state in holding primaries. The white primary, therefore, violated the right to vote secured by the Fifteenth Amendment to the constitution. The decision not only opened the most important election in the South to blacks, but also indicated that the Supreme Court was amenable to the possibility of breaking precedent when that precedent conflicted with American ideals. And the war had placed those ideals front and center.

The federal government continued to respond to those ideals during the war in areas under its immediate purview, thus avoiding direct confrontations with influential Southern political leaders. The army, for example, integrated its officer-training program, and the navy and marines liberated blacks from kitchen work by offering duties in higher-status and skilled positions—opportunities more appropriate for advancement when black servicemen returned to civilian life.

Similar opportunities for skill and income upgrades existed in defense plants for blacks outside the armed forces. Federal contracts and federal strictures against discrimination opened up an array of employment for a population that had been confined to menial "nigger work" occupations. The life-style impact for the black defense worker was "blinding," as writer Maya Angelou remembered. "For the first time," she continued, "he could think of himself as a Boss, a Spender. He was able to pay other people to work for him, i.e., the dry cleaners, taxi drivers, waitresses, etc. . . . the war let him know that he was appreciated." With greater confidence, the Southern black raised his expectations of what was possible in his region. The question and objective was no longer merely survival, but, as black writer Alice Walker put it, "to survive *whole.*"

The potential of changing fortunes for the black Southerner alarmed whites. The white Southerner had, of course, confronted change before and, unlike other Americans, had long associated change with decline and the loss of a cherished way of life. The Lost Cause had taught him that and he had learned that lesson well. So, regardless of the improbability of controlling the effect of far-off events, the white Southerner was not likely to offer up his way of life to the federal government as part of the regional contribution to the war effort. Southerners measured well the impact of war, better than most Americans; now that another war was intruding the outside world into Fortress South, they steeled themselves for their own regional conflict.

The first indication of heightened white awareness was

the proliferation of rumors concerning violations of racial mores. These rumors were reminiscent of the slave insurrection scares during the antebellum era and the periodic surfacings of racial fear during Reconstruction and the 1890s—times of stress and change similar to the early 1940s. Though most of these rumors remained unsubstantiated, the accuracy of the charges was less important than the salutary function of the rumormongering itself. Besides reflecting the uncertainty of whites over the security of regional racial mores in a time of flux, the rumors closed the ranks of Southern whites. Dissenters from the racial status quo existed throughout Southern history, but their presence was not threatening until a perceived crisis. World War II and resultant black aspirations and federal policies precipitated such a crisis. The rumors served to demonstrate the seriousness of the situation to those whites who may have needed such a reminder.

Most of the stories of racial transgression involved violations of racial etiquette, innocuous in themselves, but ominous as part of a general pattern of racial insolence aimed ultimately at toppling the structure of white supremacy. Rumors abounded of blacks arming themselves, taking advantage of the camouflage of war; of black insults, especially those of sexual innuendo, to white women; of blacks jostling whites and exhibiting general obnoxious behavior; and of flagrant black disregard of segregation. Worse than what allegedly had occurred already were the potential dangers lurking in the near future. As white men went off to war, one such speculation went, "every Negro man will have a white girl." The general prediction was that, unless checked quickly, blacks would "become impudent, unruly, arrogant, lawbreaking, violent, and insolent."

The rumors shortened white tempers. When a white MP berated and assaulted a black soldier in Centerville, Mississippi, for losing a button on his uniform, an onlooking sheriff, at the MP's behest, fired into the black's chest at point-blank range and asked the MP, "Any more niggers you want killed?" In Hampton, Arkansas, a deputy sheriff shot and killed a black soldier protecting his sister from an attack by an inebriated white man. And, in June 1943, authorities in Beaumont, Texas, arrested a black day laborer for allegedly raping a white woman whose husband worked at a local shipyard. The 2,000 white workers at the yard, already agitated by reports of impending black employment there, marched to the city jail, where the police chief convinced them that the alleged rapist was not yet in custody. Thus frustrated, the workers, at this point joined by 2,000 whites from the city, invaded black neighborhoods and vented their vengeance for six hours, destroying property, killing two blacks, and injuring hundreds of others in the process. The Beaumont riot had a postscript: a medical examination of the alleged victim revealed that not only was there no evidence of assault, but she had not engaged in sexual activity for at least twenty-four hours prior to the purported rape.

The trigger-quick attacks on blacks in uniform and the strong racial sentiments at defense installations underscored the fact that the armed forces and the workplace were flashpoints for violence. For blacks, the armed services and the plant were arenas to demonstrate their worthiness to full citizenship rights as well as forums to attain those rights. White Southerners were quick to perceive these chinks in the regional armor and to attack them. When the Roosevelt administration extended the suffrage to Southern black GIs through the absentee ballot, white Southerners protested vigorously. Virginia Durr, a noted civil libertarian from Alabama, recalled that when the absentee ballot provision went into effect in 1942, her father informed her that "all white people in Alabama are buying pistols and other ammunition in preparation for the race war which is coming."

If white Southerners could become so exercised over the prospect of black soldiers who were mired in the mud of southern Italy casting ballots that could not possibly affect the outcome of any Southern election, it was not surprising that the Supreme Court's decision negating the white primary received universal condemnation in the South, from demagogue to Democrat. South Carolina's Senator Cotton Ed Smith, long a

Roosevelt nemesis, implored "All those who love South Carolina and the white man's rule [to] rally in this hour of her great Gethsemene to save her from a disastrous fate." And the usually supportive and liberal senator from Florida, Claude Pepper, warned the Court that "the South will allow nothing to impair white supremacy."

But it was the FEPC and its promise of equality of opportunity for blacks that most provoked white Southern vitriol. Mississippi Senator Theodore G. Bilbo and Congressman John Rankin, among the most vociferous articulators of regional racial ethics, denounced the committee in unequivocal terms. The FEPC was dangerous in itself, to be sure, but it portended a more diabolical federal assault on regional prerogatives. As Bilbo noted, "every Negro in America who is behind movements of this kind . . . dream[s] of social equality and intermarriage between whites and blacks." Sexual subversion was not the only catastrophe lurking behind federal machinations. The FEPC, Rankin warned, was "the beginning of a Communistic dictatorship the like of which America never dreamed." Not only in Mississippi, but throughout the South, and not only among venerable race-baiters, but among the moderates, FEPC became anathema to white Southerners.

In practice, the FEPC proved to be not much of a threat to whites and a considerable disappointment to blacks. The committee relied on local officials' interpretations of its mandate to protect against job discrimination, and it did not challenge segregation. The wartime employment bonanza in Southern defense industries was primarily for whites only. Local defense contractors argued that white employees would refuse to work alongside blacks, so in order to avoid production delays or worse, they hired blacks, if at all, for only the most menial work. By November 1943, for example, the Southern Welding Institute in Memphis had trained and graduated 180 black welders, none of whom was able to secure employment in that craft in the South, though many received offers from defense installations in other parts of the country.

The Southern white reaction to FEPC, far out of proportion to the committee's influence, demonstrated the sustaining power of symbols in the region. Southerners measured their lives in symbols, in intangible patterns of belief—the Lost Cause, evangelical Protestantism, and race—all much larger than what they seemed, to an outsider at least, to represent. It was not merely a war, but a Cause; not only a theology, but a way of life; not merely a set of rules governing relationships and behavior between races, but a historically and religiously sanctioned distinction. And white men judged each other by their fealty to these symbols, so even silence was evidence of doubt and an indication of heresy.

Those Southern whites who saw beyond the symbols despaired. Since the formation in 1919 of the Committee on Interracial Cooperation, an integrated group of Southerners dedicated to the improvement of regional race relations, the hope had been that a gradual erosion of the biracial edifice was possible until, eventually, it would fall of its own weight. But the storm of opposition to racial concessions that broke over the region during the war years made the edifice seem impregnable yet again. Chapel Hill sociologist Howard W. Odum concluded sadly that during World War II race relations in the South had reached the lowest ebb "since the period a hundred years earlier, which led to the War between the States."

While the war failed to shake concessions from white supremacy, it did penetrate the region's persistent poverty and insularity. Southerners had cash in their pockets for the first time, perhaps, in their lives; they had been to different parts of the world—before a journey to town was something to savor and discuss for days; they had moved about, uprooted, and been exposed to new experiences; and, white and black, they had for the first time in a century a future to go along with and maybe challenge their burdensome past.

H. C. Nixon remarked in 1945 how the world had intruded on his small town in the Alabama foothills with discussions about world affairs, avid reading of dailies from Birmingham and even Atlanta, listening to the radio, and receiving letters and observations from soldiers far away. For those who would soon return to their native places, it would be even more difficult to recapture the isolation and security of the past. They would agree with William Alexander Percy, returning to Mississippi after World War I, that "You can't go back to the old petty things without purpose, direction, or unity." But Percy returned to an impoverished, rural South that had been fleetingly brushed by wartime prosperity. The sons of his generation would confront quite different prospects; and therein lay the promise and the problem of the postwar South.

CHAPTER ONE

A Southern Spring: The Postwar Years, 1945–1954

Ever since the Civil War, which seemed like today to Southerners, regional spokesmen had periodically promised and proclaimed the coming of a new South. Like the Second Coming of Christ, the new era would redeem the region's faithful from the awful burdens of the past; and, like the Second Coming, the new South was inevitable. But how many times had the prophets erred? How many testimonials of progress, epics of industry, and tales of cityhood had proved false? When President Roosevelt parted the cotton curtain and revealed an economic civilization in ruins, it was not a recently attained status, but a condition locked away from the rest of America for at least two generations. So when Atlanta journalist Ralph McGill proclaimed from the bully pulpit once occupied by the visionary snake-oil salesman, Henry W. Grady, that henceforth in the postwar South the symbol of progress would be "a test-tube rather than a cotton field," it seemed that here was yet another iteration of the patent-medicine rhetoric the

South had been receiving in large doses with little effect since the other war.

But there was a difference this time. The rhythm had changed. For returning GIs and for those who waited at home, the customary inertia of the place had seemingly given way to movement: "Yankees coming South; Negroes going North; cotton going West; livestock coming East; money coming in." The accelerating tempo of life seemed to portend something good at last for the region. But Southern history taught caution. There had been numerous false starts before, and even if the movement was somehow more purposeful now, its ultimate course could leave Southerners bereft of past and place, even as they entered the national mainstream. W. J. Cash had predicted at the start of World War II that "In the coming days [the South] . . . is likely to have to prove its capacity for adjustment far beyond what has been true in the past." With the war over and the whirlwind of activity underway, Cash's prophecy was about to be tested.

Up on the Farm: The Green Revolution

Nowhere was the potential for change greater than on the Southern farm. For decades, the region's rural monoculture had drained natural and human resources. The South was poor not necessarily because of its dependence on agriculture, but because of the nature of that agriculture—its land and labor patterns, its overproduction, and its consequent debt. The cotton culture was a devastating cycle of poverty only partially broken by Depression policies and war. By the 1980s, however, a drive though the Black Belt of the Deep South, where fields of white once moved lazily in the humid August breeze, would reveal more often than not a sea of green. Off State Highway 167, riding into downtown Enterprise, Alabama, in the heart of the erstwhile cotton empire, there is an even stranger sight. There, in the center of town, is a bronze statue of a boll weevil—probably the only place in the country that has seen fit to honor an insect. The community folklore states that the weevil came, the cotton left, and soybeans and peanuts and prosperity arrived. It wasn't all that simple, of course, though it summarizes a generation of social and economic change in the Deep South's agricultural heartland.

It was difficult to wean Southerners from their dependence upon cotton. Although the Agricultural Adjustment Act (AAA) of 1933 effectively reduced acreage, farmers retired marginal land and stepped up yields on remaining cultivating areas. By 1937, cotton production had already reached the disastrously high pre-New Deal figures, so the Roosevelt administration resorted to allotments in 1938 in order to keep a tighter rein on cotton production. Though the government eased allotments during the war years, Southern farmers showed little inclination to cultivate the staple to traditional levels. Several major alternatives had emerged in the interim to make cotton a less attractive cash crop.

The labor situation was a major factor in accelerating the search for alternative crops in the South. The AAA, of course, stimulated farm migration inadvertently by reducing farmed acreage. The war absorbed the remaining surplus labor and then some—in the armed services and in factories. Discharged servicemen, their families, and defense workers discovered quickly that the end of the war did not signal an end to options away from agriculture. H. C. Nixon reported in 1946 from his rural community that the area's greatest export had become its labor—to the industries converted to peacetime production in Anniston, the Calhoun County seat; to nearby Fort McClellan; to Gadsden, twenty miles to the northwest, with its steel and rubber factories; and to the rest of the country.

It was this last alternative that was especially appealing to the many Southerners whose war experiences and travel had broadened their horizons. Nearly one out of five Southerners left the region during the 1940s, compared with one out of seven in the previous decade, and one out of ten during the 1920s. The accelerated outmigration was especially evident among blacks. As they were the most rural Southerners with the fewest opportunities, this was hardly surprising in a region undergoing the equivalent of an agricultural enclosure movement. More than 1 million blacks left the South in the 1940s.

During the war years alone, the farm population dropped by more than 20 percent, reflecting a portion of this outmigration. Between 1940 and 1960, the decline was nearly 60 percent. Although the South had suffered from a chronic labor surplus in its agricultural sector, the exodus from the farm more than depleted this reserve and necessitated major alterations in cultivation patterns both during and after World War II. Enter the green revolution.

The soybean is a marvelous crop. It is a food for both humans and animals, and it is an important ingredient in products as diverse as detergents and paint. Since the war threatened traditional sources of oil and feed supplies, the soybean fulfilled both needs. Roughly more than 50 percent of the bean was usable in some form, making it the most versatile crop in existence. But equally important for the Southern farmer in the 1940s, it required considerably less labor than cotton and was more amenable to available machinery (mechanical cotton pickers were expensive, cumbersome, and appropriate only for the largest plantations). A Louisiana State University agronomist reported in 1943 that "The average man labor requirements for producing an acre of cotton in the ... Delta are 183.6 hours; ... an acre of soybeans, 9.6 hours."

As cotton production declined, soybean cultivation soared. The major shifts, in terms of acreage diverted directly from cotton to soybeans, occurred initially in Arkansas, Mississippi, Tennessee, and North Carolina, which harvested 739,000 bushels of soybeans in 1943, nearly triple the amount of the 1940 yield. By the mid-1970s, the transformation of Southern agriculture from cotton to soybeans was nearly complete. In 1940 the South had produced 7.6 million bales of cotton and 5.4 million bushels of soybeans; by 1975, those figures were 3 million bales and 523 million bushels, respectively. The West by then had become the premier cotton-producing region, while the South had taken the lead in soybeans.

Southern agriculturists responded to labor shortages and

price supports in other ways. Idle cotton land not given over to soybeans or too eroded for the profitable cultivation of cash staples grew grasses that required relatively little tending and that stimulated livestock farming. Soybean meal was an especially successful feed for livestock and poultry, so production of one complemented the others. As early as 1944, farmers in Montgomery County, Alabama, in the Black Belt, derived more than one-half of their income from livestock and only 22 percent from cotton. By the mid-1970s, Georgia was less appropriately the Peach State than the Chicken State, leading the nation in that category, and leading Ohio and Indiana in the number of cattle.

The shift in agricultural production and government farm programs resulted in a tripling of per capita farm income during the war. The injection of cash into the regional economy not only enabled farmers to purchase automobiles and refrigerators despite wartime shortages in durable goods, but also accelerated mechanization.

The McLemore brothers owned a 7,000-acre plantation in Montgomery County, Alabama. Unlike many of their neighbors, the McLemores were not so eager to abandon cotton as their major cash crop. In 1946, the brothers set aside a 150–acre tract to determine the feasibility of mechanizing cotton cultivation, a necessity given the dwindling labor resources at their command. Their objective was to produce cotton from seed to market without the assistance of human hands. During the course of the season, machines successfully planted, fertilized, chopped, weeded, defoliated, and picked every cotton boll on that plot.

The McLemores' successful experiment portended a time when the sharecropper and the mule would be relics of a bygone agricultural era in the South. Cotton mechanization was a complicated business, however. International Harvester had developed a mechanical picker by 1942, but early generations of this model required a uniformly maturing crop for the machine. This necessitated, in turn, new breeds of cotton, whose bolls would open higher on the stalk and more evenly. To

ensure that the machine picked clean cotton for ginning, farmers had to apply chemicals to control weeds. These and other
adjustments in cotton cultivation were not yet in place during
the immediate postwar years; but by the mid-1950s, machines
picked nearly half the cotton crop in the region, and a decade
later cotton farming was totally mechanized.

While the science of cotton farming caught up with the
technology of harvesting the crop, farmers throughout the South
were purchasing a more immediate mechanical aid—the tractor. The tractor was a mechanized mule that required less
maintenance and possessed a greater range and work capacity.
The farmer was able to cultivate more land with fewer hands.
Tractors also facilitated adjustments to crops other than cotton. As early as 1948, the Georgia Agricultural Experiment
Station observed that tractor farms were larger and farmers
had generally abandoned such row crops as cotton and corn
in favor of small grains, pasture, and livestock.

Since machines were more efficient on larger landholdings
and since they reduced the need for human labor, as farm
owners mechanized, sharecroppers and tenants were displaced.
One tractor could accomplish the work of twenty-five sharecroppers and, over several years, generate lower costs. The
farm chores that remained after mechanization were seasonal
and an available pool of laborers resided in nearby towns and
cities anxious for the temporary work. So a new generation of
Southerners lost their historic contact with the land but not
their dependence on it.

A tour through the rural South, especially in the Black
Belt, confirmed the labor revolution generated by mechanization. Some areas resembled rural versions of ghost towns,
with a lonely chimney marking the spot where a ramshackle
wooden cabin once stood, home to a poor sharecropper and
his family. Remnants of the cabins themselves, that had once
contained the laughter, conversation, and sorrow of a way of
life now gone, stood with boards askew, as if the structure
itself were anxious to get on with the dismantling of an era.
Sometimes nothing at all remained, all traces having been wiped

out and ploughed under by the now-ubiquitous tractor, obliterating the past so the future could proceed.

But most visitors passed quickly over this bittersweet rural landscape. Those who had visited the region in its doldrums now marveled at its altered aspect. In 1945 *Collier's* magazine ran a feature on the "Revolution in Cotton," and the same title appeared at the head of a more detailed discussion one year later in the *New Republic.* In the 1930s, *Life* magazine had sent photographer Margaret Bourke-White to the rural South to capture its misery on film. Her poignant depiction of the stoic, impoverished sharecroppers of the region spoke more than any New Deal report on economic conditions in the South. She returned in 1949 and presented the nation with a different portfolio: contoured ploughing and extensive peach orchards near Spartanburg, South Carolina; a mechanical cotton picker in the Mississippi Delta; and green pastures reclaimed from erosion.

For more than a century, Southern leaders had devised sometimes-elaborate schemes for economic development; and always agriculture inhibited their fulfillment: too little capital, too much illiteracy, too many unskilled laborers, and not enough consumer demand. This was changing now and the prospects for catching up suddenly seemed more realistic. The words most often heard in chamber-of-commerce board rooms, corporate lunch rooms, and university classrooms throughout the region were "growth" and "balance." Growth—how to achieve it; and balance—how to develop an industrial sector to complement the new vigor of the farm economy. "The principle to be served," geographer Rupert Vance wrote in 1943, "is one of balance. While we seek to improve agriculture, we shall also seek to make the best use of industrial . . . opportunities."

The Quest for Economic Development

During the 1930s, the state of Mississippi under Governor Hugh White had proposed such a program—Balance Agriculture with Industry. But depression and then war, as well as a crippled agricultural sector, scuttled the scheme. Conditions had changed after 1945, and Southern economic boosters revived the Mississippi plan as a regional model to develop an industrial capability. Here emerged the latest version of the South's frantic scramble after economic respectability. In fact, it was more than a question of growth. As journalist H. Brandt Ayers noted at the height of Sunbelt hyperbole: "In the South's long trek down through history it has sought something even more important than material comfort; it has sought self-respect."

Yet, with an irony endemic to the region, the quest for self-respect as embodied by prosperity revealed the insecurities of the region and its people. But who can blame them after so many unfulfilled searches for the American Dream? Being an American and being a Southerner was more a contradiction than dual citizenship. Stephen Suitts, director of the Southern Regional Council, a longtime critic of the booster mentality, asks nevertheless for understanding: "Southerners don't have any rich relatives. . . . Without a heritage of anything except denial, Southerners, given a chance to improve their standard of living, are doing so, and they do it largely without concern or perception of ultimately whether it's good or bad. To not have the problems of your parents is to not have problems."

So Southerners were bound by their past to duplicate "every vast Yankee excess," as Willie Morris put it, because that was the only success model they knew. Soon after the war, Southern states began issuing industrial development bonds, a Mississippi innovation, to finance land acquisition and subsidize plant construction to lure Northern firms. Local taxpayers incurred minimal obligation since the firm using the facility paid rent that amortized the bonds. Although several states outside the South adopted this recruitment scheme, by the early 1960s Southern states accounted for 87 percent of the industrial development bonds issued in the nation.

Communities also offered tax incentives deferring or reducing tax payments, occasionally for as long as twenty years after the firm began operations in the locality. This strategy was more questionable than the bond issue, since the town or city usually absorbed some infrastructure costs—roads, sewers, and water connections—involved in the factory's relocation, without sufficient tax revenues to finance these support services. Local taxpayers either found heavier tax burdens or a reduction in the level and quality of services as the price for recruitment. Some Mississippi towns discovered, as their counterparts elsewhere soon learned, that the subsidies and incentives tended to attract the more footloose and marginal operations that could and did leave when the tax deferment period expired or when managers complained about declining services and increased taxes. As early as 1941, W. J. Cash warned in dramatic fashion against these recruitment schemes. He argued that they gave "away the wealth of the South on a scale hitherto unprecedented in a region which has always eagerly given away its wealth. And it exacts no adequate advantage." Cash went on to charge that the "people who mainly gain from it are the merchants and bankers. And that gain is purchased at the price of the virtual enslavement, the constant degradation, of masses of the common whites." He concluded by acknowledging that "The South desperately needs new industries . . . but not at this price."

Of course Cash was not only referring to the tax and service burdens on working-class Southerners, he was pointing out their exploitation by both recruiters and the firms recruited by them. Since the days of Henry Grady, local boosters had offered the native Anglo-Saxon work force as a prime lure. The major difference in the postwar South from these earlier efforts was that now recruiters could boast of not only docility and low wages, but the relative absence of labor unions at present and for the foreseeable future. Federal legislation during the Depression and the labor shortage through the war years facilitated union efforts, though the South generally resisted the intrusions of organized labor. For labor-intensive activities such as textiles, furniture, or paper milling, the higher wages and fringe benefits demanded by unions could reduce profits

sharply. A union-free South became an attractive alternative
for these types of operations. And Southern boosters capital-
ized on this advantage. "No Hostile Union Here and None
Desired," proclaimed a Clanton, Alabama, industrial recruitment brochure. Recruiters in Williamsburg County, South
Carolina, promised potential recruits that there were "no unions
or union activity in the area" and that "the appreciation of
fair play and genuine spirit of cooperation inherent in the
people make such activities an extremely remote possibility."

Southern entrepreneurs also pointed out that their labor
force was predominantly rural. The revolution on the farm
had provided an eager labor surplus imbued with rural values
that would not look kindly upon such outside agitators as
union organizers. And, indeed, CIO organizers during and immediately following World War II encountered workers' vig-
ilante groups.

Southern boosters were also careful to note the less tangible, i.e., noneconomic, benefits of Southern life. The South,
after all, is a beautiful region, a fact that would not be lost on
entrepreneurs hailing from the gritty cities of New England or
the Midwest, where the snow was dirty and the elements of
the other seasons either too brief in duration or so overcome
by industrial effluvia as to be ignored. "Beauty is Our Money
Crop," a Flannery O'Connor character boasted about his Georgia town, and it was not long before boosters elsewhere picked
up the refrain. In the Peach State during the early 1950s, the
Georgia Power Company, the Georgia Municipal Association,
and Georgia Tech's Engineering Experiment Station combined
to sponsor the Certified City Program, designed to assist local
leaders with necessary civic improvements ranging from the
town's esthetic appearance to educational and recreational facilities in order to enhance the attractiveness to outside industries. Of course, Southern localities had always paid attention to the esthetic dimension—the climate and rural
background of many town residents predicted this emphasis.
But here now was another important selling point: this middle
landscape, this cross between urban and rural, could be en-

joyed by those for whom such advantages had long ago disappeared if, in fact, they had ever existed. The irony was that the types of firms attracted by the combined recruitment package were often polluting industries that could potentially reduce the very quality of the Southern landscape promoted by the recruiters.

It became clear to local boosters by the early 1950s that the growing sophistication of financial and advertising schemes required some coordination through a permanent organization dedicated solely to industrial recruitment in particular and to economic development in general. Accordingly, numerous communities across the region formed Local Industrial Development Corporations (LIDCs) and by the early 1960s, the South accounted for one-third of these bodies nationwide. The LIDCs took on responsibility for working out subsidy agreements and, as nonprofit organizations, they could assume higher-risk investment responsibilities than commercial lending institutions. In addition, they could offer below-market interest rates on development loans. Since the South was a capital-poor region, these corporations were essential to provide potential relocators with flexible and generous financial packages. They also served as models for state development agencies that emerged by 1960.

Southerners pursued not only local development but also sought to maintain their influence with the federal government. The region's leading academics, particularly the group at Chapel Hill working with Howard W. Odum, fervently believed that regional parity was essential for national economic health. And a conscious redistribution of national wealth, coupled with vigorous local development efforts, was the surest method to attain that objective.

At the close of World War II, the national economy was still highly skewed in favor of the Northeast. Although comprising less than 8 percent of the nation's land area, the Northeast and a portion of the Midwest accounted for 90 percent of the value of industrial production. Financial and commercial dominance characterized this region as well, advantages that were self-perpetuating and reinforcing. Even the more prosperous areas of the South fell under Northeastern control. As one journalist put it in 1946, "Texas is New York's most valuable possession." Economic development required credit, access to national and international markets, and informational services; thus as the South would become more integrated into the national economy, its dependence on these elements and on the Northeast would necessarily increase.

Wartime expenditures in the South, however, loosened the economic grip of the Northeast to a small degree, at least enough to elicit hope from Southerners advocating a redistributionist policy. After the war, the South sought to maintain this flow, not at the expense of other regions, but as a complement to balanced national growth. Though Southerners eschewed federal involvement in all other areas, they courted federal funds with great ardor.

And they were well-placed to do so. A half-century of one-party rule left Southern Democrats dominant in the Congress, especially in the Senate. The seniority-rich delegations from the South occupied key positions on major committees. Presidents seeking to fulfill their legislative agendas discovered that cajoling and compromising with Southern politicians was a necessary part of the governmental process. During the years immediately following World War II, Senator Richard B. Russell, chairman of the Senate Appropriations Committee, was probably the most powerful individual in that body. Fellow Georgian Carl Vinson headed the Armed Services Committee in the House of Representatives. By 1960, these two Georgians were instrumental in securing fifteen military installations for their state that employed more than 40,000 people, as well as funneling lucrative defense contracts to Lockheed in Marietta, making that firm the largest nongovernmental employer in the state. By 1960, these facilities contributed $2 billion annually to Georgia. Charleston's congressman, L. Mendel Rivers, performed similar services for his constituents, leaving one journalist to express wonder that the weight of all those military installations had not caused the genteel seaport to sink.

Other aspects to the South's postwar economic development required less lobbying and advertising to attain. The South had been, historically, a prolific land, occasionally too much so, but one with a vast natural resource potential. The land itself, though much abused, was one such prominent resource, and the relative facility with which Southern agriculturists changed cultivation patterns owed in part to the resilience of the soil. The climate was another God-given element that, though violent at times, proved to be a natural attraction for the region. Florida had benefited from its balmy locale since early in the century, but as roads improved and as retirement there became economically more feasible for greater proportions of the population after the war, the Sunshine State enjoyed an unprecedented boom.

The development of the petrochemical industry was a relatively new phenomenon of Southern natural resource endowment. Texas followed Florida as the regional pacesetter in economic advance largely on the strength of this natural-resource-based activity. By the mid-1950s the Texas-Louisiana area was producing one-half of the nation's oil, with the richest deposits not yet tapped. The abundance of oil and gas, sulphur, and fresh water was ideal for the development of petrochemicals.

The burgeoning economic activity, whether of natural or man-generated origin, reinforced the population mobility that characterized the region by the mid-1940s. While the South continued to lose population to other sections of the country during the 1940s, a perceptible trend of population retention and even of in-migration occurred. Even in some rural districts, traditionally vast reservoirs of labor, the influx of industry helped stem the flight of young and ambitious Southerners. More important, however, in terms of magnitude was the growth of the region's cities.

Urbanization, Southern Style

"People have moved to town," was how Lillian Smith summarized regional demographic change in 1949. The population of Southern cities grew by 36 percent during the 1940s to lead the nation in urban growth. Of the South's forty-nine metropolitan areas, forty-three gained population; in the North, only twenty-five of seventy-four metropolitan areas experienced an increase in population.

The nature of Southern urbanization began to change as well. The region typically possessed the nation's largest share of urban places with under 10,000 inhabitants. Prior to 1940, these centers had grown faster than the South's larger cities. After 1940, however, the region's pattern of urbanization matched the national trend as large city growth accelerated and small-town population advance declined proportionately. While Southern cities merged with their Northern counterparts in some statistical categories, the result of this convergence looked quite different on the Southern landscape.

Experiencing a major spurt of growth in the second quarter of the twentieth century, southern cities essentially grew up with the automobile. Though the auto's greatest impact was on the rural South—breaking isolation, improving access to health, education, and market services, and, through truck gardening, altering some cultivation patterns—the internal combustion engine left an indelible impression upon Southern cities. Low densities, even in the central business district, sprawling developments linked by ribbons of roads, commercial strips, shopping and office malls, rigid separation of land uses, and poorly developed mass transit were all symptoms and causes of automobile dependency. The Southern city became the quintessential suburban city, with roads and discrete subdivisions the basic landscape.

These were not only new cities, in spatial terms, but they were located in new places, that is, in places heretofore not at the center of major urban development in the South. Cities along the coast and on major navigable rivers had long dominated the Southern urban hierarchy: Norfolk, Charleston, Savannah, Mobile, New Orleans, and Memphis, to name the more prominent examples. As the nation depended less on water in commerce and more on the railroad, the urban pattern shifted in the South, especially to the Piedmont region, where the terrain and soil composition were well suited to railroad building and convenient to Northern and Deep Southern points. By the late 1940s, Charlotte had already surpassed the seaports of Charleston and Wilmington as the Carolinas' leading urban center and had expanded its railroad network, which, in turn, generated major highway and airport development. Moreover, as a financial, administrative, and retail center, Charlotte possessed the type of diversified, service-oriented economy that would characterize the national economic trend by the 1960s.

But Atlanta was the brightest star in the Piedmont constellation of cities in the late 1940s. Atlanta had always figured prominently in the numerous versions of the New South that had appeared since the Civil War. The city was the launching point and shining example for journalist Henry W. Grady; it was the birthplace of Coca-Cola; and it was the focal point for the boosterism of the 1920s. Atlanta's central role is not surprising given, among other advantages, its strategic location. A line drawn from Boston through New York to New Orleans, and another line extended from Chicago to Miami will intersect roughly in the vicinity of Atlanta. As early as the 1840s, the city parlayed its locational advantage into railroad connections that in the twentieth century transferred to highway and airport focal points. After World War II, Atlanta reinforced its role as the region's major distribution center, attracting wholesale and retail firms and branch plants of leading manufacturers.

Atlanta's aggressive mayor, William B. Hartsfield, exemplified a new type of urban and regional leadership emerging after 1945. The booster was nothing new in the Southern city, of course, but the new version soft-pedaled white supremacy and displayed an appreciation for urban services that the civic-commercial elite of an earlier era lacked. Also, the new men were likely to be involved in activities, such as finance and business administration, that brought them into frequent contact with counterparts elsewhere, making them less parochial and more cosmopolitan in perspective. Their priorities were

efficiency in government and development in the urban economy, and they were not chary about utilizing governmental
institutions to further these obligations.

In New Orleans, a young returning veteran, De Lesseps
Morrison, was elected mayor in 1946. Morrison introduced
budgetary reform, established recreation and housing depart-
ments to serve both races, and extended streets and sewers
into new neighborhoods. Once a political cesspool, New Orleans became a national example, with Morrison symbolizing,
as *Time* magazine put it, "as well as anyone . . . the postwar
energy of the nation's cities." Similar business and service-
oriented elite, young and more representative than before, took
control in Dallas and Charlotte as well. The emphasis on efficiency meant that trained administrators and planners were
filtering into the local bureaucracy to provide continuity and
expertise.

Though the new urban administrations were nominally
Democratic, even if they bore such neutral names as the Citizens Council in Dallas, there was increasing evidence after
1945 of Republican sentiment in the urban South, especially
among the business leadership. This was understandable, considering the nature of the Democratic party in the region at
that time, top-heavy with elderly rural or small-town politicians and notoriously parsimonious. Democrats controlled state
legislatures that were mighty engines of inactivity and served
the interests of a few well-heeled lobbyists rather than the constituency of the state.

The power of the state political structure resided primarily
in the county courthouses and secondarily in the state legislature, and neither institution was especially disposed to urban
causes. The state legislatures particularly were unique bodies,
combinations of sedate gentlemen's clubs and barbecue pits.
Journalist Harry Ashmore described the Southern legislatures
of the early 1950s as "the happy hunting grounds of the interests. The typical member is a small town lawyer who makes
no secret of the fact that he has accepted a part-time job that
pays little . . . in order to run errands for his clients . . . do the

bidding of utilities, liquor dealers, insurance companies, banks, labor unions." In some state legislatures, members from rural rotten boroughs who retained their influence through longevity and patronage held the reins of power. Perhaps the most complete oligarchy of this kind existed in South Carolina, where Edgar A. Brown and Solomon Blatt from sleepy Barnwell County ran the state for more than a quarter of a century. Both men rose from poverty. Brown's parents were small farmers, and Blatt's father was a Russian Jewish immigrant who sold combs and corsets. They successfully blocked measures that threatened the twenty-five predominantly rural counties around Barnwell, and they were assiduous in their attention to planters, utilities, textiles, and banks.

The condition of Southern state government was incongruous with the new service-oriented and efficiency-minded entrepreneurs of the urban South. And state government was likely to be more of an obstacle than an ally for some time to come due to the political system and the dominance of one party. The control of party and state politics by a tight coterie of men from rural counties and towns had reduced democratic politics to an occasional formality attended by relatively few constituents. In the 1940s, the white electorate participating in state-wide contests ranged from below 10 percent in Virginia to 18 percent in Georgia. In the latter state, the incentives for Atlantans to vote in such elections were minimal considering the county unit system, which virtually disfranchised the city's voters. Candidates for state-wide office, including U.S. senator and governor, entered the Democratic primary (the only election of import in Georgia prior to the 1960s), and for every county they won, they received two votes for each representative of the legislature from that county. The most populous county—Fulton, the location of Atlanta—could cast six votes, since it sent three representatives to the legislature. So three sparsely populated counties equaled the vote of the state's largest county. In practical terms, a vote in Atlanta was worth about one-seventieth of a vote in a rural county. Governor Eugene Talmadge boasted that he never campaigned in a county

with a streetcar, i.e., an urban county; under the unit system
he could avoid population concentrations and still coast to
victory in the primary.

Other Southern states did not possess such an obvious
deterrent to popular government, but they nevertheless ensured rural dominance by avoiding reapportionment. Tennessee, for example, still operated under legislative district lines
and quotas drawn in 1901. Alabama too had not undergone
a reapportionment since 1901, so Jefferson County, where Birmingham was located and which comprised one-sixth of the
state's population in 1940, received representation from only
one of the thirty-five state senators and seven of 106 representatives. On the other hand, Lowndes County in the Black
Belt, with a declining population of 22,000, three-quarters of
whom were disfranchised blacks, was entitled to one senator
and two representatives.

Urban leaders often railed against this rural oligarchy.
Ralph McGill tangled with the Talmadges on more than one
occasion, and he perceived the rural counties that returned
such politicians to office time and again as the locus of "the
most hidebound political thinking, the most corrupt county
government and justice, the most friction and race violence,
and much of the drag on the South's general progress." On
the other hand, in the countryside, residents looked upon Atlanta as a Yankee city, and in Black Belt Alabama, Birmingham was "up North."

Little wonder that these urban outcasts occasionally voted
Republican. The business orientation of Southern urban leaders also comported with Republican philosophy. The first major break occurred in the 1952 presidential election, in which
several Southern cities cast their ballots for the Republican
nominee, Dwight D. Eisenhower. In Atlanta, for example, 64
percent of the upper-income precincts favored Eisenhower. In
Florida's emerging "urban horseshoe," extending from Sara-
sota in the west to Orlando in the central area to Broward and
Dade Counties on the Atlantic coast, Republican sentiment

waxed strong and contrasted sharply with the Democratic politics of the rest of the state.

In short, urban politics in the South reflected a flexibility and an openness rarely experienced beyond city borders. Competing factions, often under various labels, debates over public policy, responsible journalism, and even black political participation characterized the urban political scene in the years immediately following World War II. This was so even in the cities of the Deep South, such as Montgomery, Alabama, where in the aftermath of *Smith* v. *Allwright* blacks voted in Democratic primaries, not in huge numbers but sufficiently to be courted by local politicians. And in Jackson, Mississippi, NAACP officials organized blacks into a voter's league in 1944 and, indeed, by 1953, Henry Allen Bullock reported that "Practically every southern city has a Negro voter's league." Better drainage, paved streets, and more convenient bus routes were some of the measures secured through league efforts. There was even a scattering of black officeholders in the urban South, including a black city councilman in Richmond in 1948, and two black councilmen in Nashville in 1951.

The events swirling in and about Southern cities in the late 1940s seemed to signal a new departure for the region: the maintenance of wartime prosperity after the war, the industrial recruitment successes, the progressive political leadership, and the moderating racial climate generated optimism even among those cognizant of the numerous historic disappointments. With cities in the lead, per capita income in the South rose from approximately one-half the national average in 1940 to more than two-thirds by 1960. Bank deposits nearly doubled during the 1940s, and individual income increased by 223 percent in that decade, compared with a 119 percent rise in the North. Editor Ralph McGill ventured in 1950 that, at last, a genuine Southern spring—a blossoming of economic prosperity and urbanization with all their social and political implications—was nigh: "For a generation now, the South has talked and written of a 'New South.' The birth pains are at last beginning." This seemed especially so with respect to race.

Race: Expectations

Southern blacks emerged from World War II with reasonable expectations that life would be better. A great many assumed that a change in scenery would invariably enhance their prospects; it was not so much to obtain a fresh start as it was to step on the first rung of the American Dream ladder for the first time. There were no ladders in the countryside; mechanization, crop diversification, and government policies were precluding agrarian options for blacks even if they were so inclined, and many were not. However mystical the tie with the land, farming also represented the heritage of slavery and, in recent times, subservience. Some expressed their preferences by leaving the region altogether. The war had taken black veterans to a world considerably less restrictive and demeaning; at least, from their brief and often superficial contacts, it seemed that way. So they sought that world. More than 1.5 million blacks departed from the South during the 1940s, and over 1 million of those came from Southern farms. Those blacks deciding to remain in the region, less certain of success in the North, perhaps having no kin or neighbor there, or perhaps even a bit timid about dislodging venerable roots, often selected Southern cities either as staging areas for the eventual journey to the North or as final destinations. In 1920, roughly 27 percent of Georgia's white inhabitants resided in cities, compared with 23 percent for blacks. By 1950, blacks had become more urbanized than whites—44 percent to 39 percent. The state's five largest cities absorbed most of the black urban population increase. By 1950, these cities contained nearly one out of every three blacks, compared with only one out of six in 1920.

In view of the limited opportunities in agriculture and the expanding Southern economy in other regional locations, the cityward migration of Southern blacks is not surprising. But in the aftermath of World War II, Southern cities offered other attractions for blacks. Living standards, especially the basic amenities such as water, sewers, and electricity, had improved.

In some cities, such as Atlanta, public housing was an improvement, at least initially, over the sharecropper's shack. There were also a few basic liberties afforded by an urban residence, within the boundaries of segregation to be sure, but nonetheless tangible improvements over a more restrictive life in the countryside. This was especially the case with respect to voting, as mentioned earlier. And blacks saw additional signs of encouragement beyond city borders.

A new group of white leaders was emerging in the postwar South to challenge the old politics based upon racial and social inequities. These men were hardly a postwar version of the Populists—they supported economic development as much as, if not more than, their establishment adversaries, and their proposed experiments with Southern government were modest, even in the political context of the region. They were not racial egalitarians by any means, but they shared a sense of fairness and believed that the white South would never move forward without Southern blacks also advancing.

Such was the philosophy of Alabama's James E. ("Big Jim") Folsom, a sprawling man with a fondness for women, alcohol, and liberal politics. Elected governor in 1946, Folsom promoted an ambitious program including reapportionment, the appointment of registrars amenable to enrolling blacks, the removal of a state constitutional prohibition against women serving on juries, and an array of educational and social service reforms. He sought the elusive coalition of the Populist era—blacks and poor whites. "As long as the Negroes are held down by deprivation and lack of opportunity," he declared in 1949, "the other poor people will be held down alongside them." Nor was Folsom a political oddity in Alabama: Senators Lister Hill and John Sparkman shared his views, though they were not as outspoken, especially on racial matters.

In Arkansas, Marine veteran Sid McMath won election as governor in 1948 and fought to keep the state loyal to President Truman in the midst of Southern discontent. He also espoused a social and educational program similar to Folsom's. The ubiquitous Longs retained control of Louisiana, and while their reign provided good entertainment, they also diverged from the regional biracial norms and espoused social programs and tax structures considerably beyond the consciousness of the old-line Southern political leaders. Earl Long was elected governor in 1947 and fought for increased black voter registration and state-supported health and transportation programs. He once retorted in his inimitable style to political foe and staunch segregationist Willie Rainach, "you got to recognize the niggers as human beings!" And Tennesseans launched a trio of progressive politicians after the war, Senators Estes Kefauver and Albert Gore and Governor Frank Clement. In the 1948 senatorial race, Kefauver successfully built a coalition of academics, working-class whites, and newly enfranchised blacks to secure the seat. Ralph McGill rejoiced at the end of the 1940s that "The South is freer of ranters and demagogues than it has been for a generation or more."

As prospects for Southern blacks brightened at the local and state levels, there was a corresponding shift in their favor in Washington. The reconstitution of the Democratic party continued as Northern urban blacks swelled party ranks and held the potential balance of power in several key industrial states. President Harry S. Truman, a Missourian whose vice-presidential candidacy in 1944 received little enthusiasm from blacks, was aware of the changing political arithmetic; but he also maintained a simple faith in basic American ideals that had recently emerged from a period of crisis. If white Southerners looked hopefully to this undistinguished border-state politician to stem the erosion of biracial norms, Truman's actions almost immediately after assuming the office quickly disabused them of that notion.

In June 1945, Truman protested the cut-off of funds for the FEPC and succeeded in restoring the funds and maintaining the committee's existence, at least until the following year. Then, in December 1946, concerned by increasing violence against blacks in the South, Truman appointed the fifteen-member President's Committee on Civil Rights, which included two prominent liberal Southerners, Frank P. Graham, president of the University of North Carolina, and Atlanta race relations activist and Methodist lay leader Dorothy M. Tilly. Truman charged the committee to prepare a report recommending legislative remedies for the biracial system, particularly in the South. The report, *To Secure These Rights*, issued the following year, proposed a broad array of measures, most aimed at the South, including antilynching legislation—a measure that had periodically and unsuccessfully appeared before Congress since the late 1920s; abolition of segregation in the armed forces and in the District of Columbia; elimination of the poll tax—a levy designed to limit political participation; ending of racially segregated seating in interstate public transportation; and the withdrawal of federal funds from those institutions practicing segregation. The Southern members of the committee agreed on all points except the suggestion to cut off funds from offending institutions, arguing that such a measure would cause Southerners to run up the flag of the Lost Cause, mount the ramparts, and eventually destroy the entire program. And, as the region was struggling to upgrade its lagging educational system, the measure would hurt black and white children, not the real culprits in the biracial drama.

The president agreed with Graham and Tilly, and he soft-pedaled that recommendation, but incorporated the rest into a major civil rights legislative package and presented it to the Congress in February 1948. He embroidered upon the original report by also advocating the establishment of a civil rights division within the Justice Department and a Joint Congressional Committee on Civil Rights to report to the president at regular intervals. Though Southern-dominated committees in both houses made short work of Truman's civil rights agenda, he reintroduced the package in 1949, and for the next two decades the civil rights issue remained an important part of congressional business. Blacks rewarded Truman by turning the vote in Illinois and California to his favor in his 1948 upset victory over Republican Thomas E. Dewey. Truman also demonstrated that in the new Democratic party it was possible to achieve a national electoral triumph without significant support from leading Southern politicians.

While Southern blacks received few substantive victories from the Truman administration, the United States Supreme Court continued to scratch away at the Southern biracial edifice. Blacks, especially the legal division of the NAACP, sensed that the high Court was increasingly open to challenges to segregation and discrimination. The abolition of the white primary encouraged blacks to utilize litigation as a means of ultimately ending their second-class citizenship in the South.

Next to the ballot, access to decent education was the most important item on the NAACP's legal agenda. Although the Supreme Court had ruled in 1896 in the case of *Plessy* v. *Ferguson* that separate facilities for blacks and whites were constitutional so long as they were of equal quality, a brief survey of black public schools in the South during the late 1940s would confirm that these schools were manifestly inferior to white schools. This was especially so in rural areas, where white county politicians viewed education for blacks at best as time away from field work, and at worst as creating the potential for disaffection. Funding levels reflected these attitudes: for every dollar expended on black public schools, counties and localities spent four dollars on white facilities. Ratios were higher in rural districts, where total expenditures were low to begin with. Scott's Branch School in Summerton, South Carolina, was typical of black rural schools in the 1940s, with more than 100 children to a class, outdoor toilet facilities, no running water, kerosene lamps instead of electricity, inadequate heat from a wood stove, and a dirt playground. And some black children had to walk nine miles around a lake to this cabin, or else rowed across to it. When Navy veteran Harry Briggs requested a school bus for these children in 1947, R. W. Elliott, the school board chairman, denied the petition with the comment: "We ain't got no money to buy a bus for your nigger children." The denial provoked a lawsuit, *Briggs* v. *Elliott*, alleging that black schools in Clarendon County were inferior to white schools and therefore violated the separate-but-equal precept of the *Plessy* case. Eventually, the plaintiffs broadened their argument to charge that segregated facilities were inherently unequal, and civil rights attorneys merged the *Briggs* action with several other school segregation cases, which resulted in the *Brown* v. *Board of Education* decision in 1954.

But the *Brown* decision was actually the culmination of several Supreme Court rulings on school cases as far back as 1938, with *Missouri ex rel. Gaines* v. *Canada,* where the Court held, for the first time, that racial discrimination in education was unconstitutional. The case involved Lloyd Gaines' unsuccessful attempt to gain admission to the University of Missouri Law School. The state offered to pay his tuition at a law school in a nonsegregated state, but the Court declared that "equal protection can be afforded only within the jurisdiction of the state."

The *Gaines* case left unresolved the separate-but-equal formula, but the Court responded directly to that precedent in two subsequent cases, both decided in 1950: *Sweatt* v. *Painter* and *McLaurin* v. *Oklahoma State Regents.* In the former case, the plaintiff was denied admission to the University of Texas Law School on the grounds that an equally competent law school for blacks already existed in the state. Although not overturning *Plessy* explicitly, the Court ruled unanimously that Texas had deprived the plaintiff of equal protection of the laws and ordered him admitted. The justices extended this principle in the *McLaurin* case, in which the plaintiff had already been admitted to the Oklahoma University graduate school but officials had barred him from participating in school activities. In another unanimous ruling the Court held that segregation was itself a denial of equal protection because it affected the successful pursuit of the plaintiff's graduate studies.

It took no legal scholar to discern the drift of the Court's opinions as the *Briggs* case and its companions wended their way through the judicial system. In fact, several Southern states sought to salvage the badly battered *Plessy* precedent by pumping prodigious sums into black school systems. South Carolina's Governor Jimmy Byrnes, for example, spent two-thirds of the state's $124 million allocation to education over a four-year period beginning in 1951 on black school facilities, though blacks comprised little more than 40 percent of the school population. The *Brown* decision rendered such frantic reparations irrelevant and completed the first phase of the Southern black assault on segregation.

If Southern blacks took heart from their political and legal advances after World War II, the increased willingness of Southern whites to speak out in their behalf was at least as encouraging. Though opinions on race were never monolithic among the white South, the regional culture offered compelling incentives toward maintaining at least the facade of orthodoxy. But as some white political leaders in the heady postwar atmosphere ventured tentatively toward conciliatory racial rhetoric, the long-silent white liberals of the region offered their support for regional racial adjustments. The impetus for racial reform among liberals had religious roots. Though Southern religion complemented restrictive elements within Southern culture, like those elements it possessed liberating qualities that had emerged briefly in the past but were generally submerged under the stifling regional conformity. Southern religious institutions provided the background and personnel for the Social Gospel movement at the turn of the century (aimed primarily at improving the educational and social conditions of poorer whites) and for subsequent efforts, however modest, at interracial cooperation.

The Southern Conference Education Fund (SCEF), formed in 1946, included two seminary-trained individuals among its leadership, James Dombrowski, who served as director in 1947, and New Deal veteran Aubrey Williams. The fund was an interracial organization dedicated to improving "the educational and cultural standards of the Southern people in accordance with the highest democratic institutions and ideals." Translated into policy, this meant advocating integrated schools. To this end, the fund published a journal, *Southern Patriot*, to document the negative influence of segregation on

Southern life, and, not incidentally, to indicate the diversity of racial views among Southern whites.

The Southern Regional Council (SRC) was a less militant, though thoroughly interracial, body established in 1944 with Howard W. Odum among its leadership. The Christian roots of the SRC were less evident, as membership included a significant proportion of academics, but the same sense of fair play that permeated the work of the SCEF characterized the council's activities. Council members arrived at an integrationist viewpoint gradually; it was not until 1949 that the council issued a statement through its publication, *New South*, that segregation "in and of itself constitutes discrimination and inequality of treatment." And in the following year, the council offered its vision of the New South, quite different from the whirring turbines and steel skyscrapers that denoted more typical versions of a resurrected region. The council proposed a moral foundation upon which to build the superstructure of a revitalized and redeemed society, relieved of its historical burdens:

The South of the future . . . is a South freed of stultifying inheritances from the past. It is a South where the measure of a man will be his ability, not his race; . . . where all can feel confident of personal safety and equality before the law; where there will exist no double standard in housing, health, education, or other public services; where segregation will be recognized as a cruel and needless penalty of the human spirit, and will no longer be imposed; where, above all, every individual will enjoy a full share of dignity and self-respect, in recognition of his creation in the image of God.

The commonalty of all Southerners with God was a popular theme of liberal whites and blacks in a region where such connections were likely to be understood, pondered over, and ultimately acted upon. The Southern Baptist Convention, one of the region's most influential organizations, had not in its long history been in the forefront, or even visible for that matter, in the area of racial reform. World War II and the rekindling of Christian spirit in the few interracial bodies extant in the region prodded the Baptist group to action.

Accordingly, after the war, the SBC moved immediately to implement a program of racial reconciliation, especially with black Baptists. The Convention's Home Mission Board increased the budget for its ministry to black Baptists from $33,000 in 1944 to $109,000 in 1945. A year later, T. B. Maston of the board enthusiastically reported that "There is a stirring in the hearts and consciousness of Southern Baptists. There are signs of a new day and a new attitude. Many Southern Baptists . . . are overcoming their racial prejudice." As if to underscore Maston's observation, North Carolina Baptists that same year passed a resolution declaring that "Segregation of believers holding the same tenets of faith because of color or social status into racial or class churches is a denial of the New Testament affirmation of the equality of all believers." The following year, the convention itself promulgated an agenda of racial reform to be followed by all Southern Baptists. Though the principles were relatively mild compared with the statements issued by the SCEF or the SRC, they represented a major departure for the group in the area of race relations and were supposed to serve to prepare members for the inevitable day when the South's biracial system would no longer exist:

- We shall think of the Negro as a person and treat him accordingly.
- We shall continually strive as individuals to conquer all prejudice. . . .
- We shall teach our children that prejudice is un-Christian.
- We shall protest against injustice and indignities against Negroes. . . .
- We shall be willing for the Negro to enjoy the rights granted to him under the U.S. Constitution.

The words of the Southern Baptists reflected the optimism that all things were possible in this, the newest South; that the ancient racial shibboleths could dissolve in prayer and good works. If the region could demonstrate signs of throwing off its traditional poverty and political debilities, why not its racial perspectives? And, if the South could do all these things—physical and spiritual—it would be redeemed from its burdensome past and could not only assume its place as an American region at last, but because it had been cleansed, washed in the blood so to speak, the South could lead the nation to a promised land. As lawyer Gavin Stevens argued in Faulkner's *Intruder in the Dust* (1948):

We—he and us [black and white]—should confederate: swap him the rest of the economic and political and cultural privileges which are his right, for the reversion of his capacity to wait and endure and survive. Then we would prevail; together we would dominate the United States; we would present a front not only impregnable but not even to be threatened by a mass of people who no longer have anything in common save a frantic greed for money and a basic fear of a failure of national character which they hide from one another behind a loud lipservice to a flag.

But the journey to redemption would be a painful one. Along the way, white Southerners would need to confront their sin, and especially their past. They would need to see, in the words of James McBride Dabbs, "the universal meaning of failure and defeat." And the teachers of this hard lesson would be the blacks. It was apparent in the years immediately following World War II that some white Southerners, willing to follow Christian ethics and their consciences, were prepared to embark on this arduous odyssey through the deserts of their souls and society. But as writers, from the ancient Hebrew prophets to, more recently, Flannery O'Connor, have observed, violence often precedes grace. There were also Southerners for whom the status quo was comfortable and right; why seek out pain and the unknown? The racial reforms touted by President Truman, black litigants, the Southern Baptist Convention, and even fictional protagonists, represented not only a threat to racial etiquette, but to a way of life in the seamless web of Southern culture. Southern blacks and their white allies, flush with the enthusiasm of positive signs in the region and in Washington, mistook this newest South for the New South. The struggle for a redeemed region had merely begun.

CHAPTER TWO

Reaction and Resistance, 1945–1956

It was to be a false spring. The Americanization of Dixie could occur on one level, while regional traditions prevailed on another. Southerners were comfortable living in tomorrow and yesterday because for so many years time had been immaterial and undefined. But the racial implications of postwar prosperity and politics threatened to disturb the comfort of timelessness. For race was a crucial element of Southern society: it provided the basis for white political solidarity; it shaped manners and defined place; it infected religion; it was a strong link to a distinctive history; and it served to command unity of white thought and action. A threat, even if only potential, to white supremacy would likely provoke a strong reaction. And it did.

Politics and Race

The flashpoint occurred initially in the political arena, where Democratic party leadership had historically fended off challenges to its control by raising the flag of white supremacy. As political scientist V. O. Key, Jr., explained in his pathbreaking analysis, *Southern Politics in State and Nation* (1949), "In its grand outlines the politics of the South revolves around the position of the Negro." The appeal to race not only brought independently inclined whites back into the fold, it stunted reform by diverting attention away from substantive problems. It was not surprising that Key concluded by warning that "The race issue . . . must be considered as the number one problem on the southern agenda. Lacking a solution for it, all else fails."

The political thaw in the South immediately following World War II was not as imminently threatening nor as focused as the Populist revolt a half-century earlier. There were brush fires of reform and change here and there however that if left untended could flare up and engulf the heirs of the Redeemers. The aggressive entrepreneurs of the cities, the emerging black electorate, the growing federal presence, and the political advance of individuals (such as "Big Jim" Folsom, Frank P. Graham, Claude Pepper, and Sid McMath) concerned the county courthouse crowd, the hail-fellow-well-met legislators, and such ancient political institutions as the Byrds of Virginia, Theodore Bilbo of Mississippi, and the Talmadges of Georgia. Their day seemed to be passing, at least until they seized upon the methods of their political ancestors and rode race and history to power once again.

Several aspects of regional life in the late 1940s assisted the modern Redeemers in securing Fortress South against change. First, there was segregation itself. Though segregation was an ever-evolving institution of racial accommodation, white Southerners had grown accustomed to the etiquette of race. Segregation was an anchor in the midst of buffeting winds of change and dislocation; it defined and maintained place in an insecure society. Lillian Smith wrote, "The white southerner" was "not a proud man, . . . but one torn by feelings of inferiority, . . . [and] continually driven to assert his superiority to the Negro and his identification with the 'gentleman.' "

Another factor worked in favor of the postwar Redeemers,

and that was the nature of the opposition. The progressive leaders were never a unified group and, after the war, two issues increasingly fragmented their ranks. First, there existed strong disagreement over the question of segregation. For those such as James Dombrowski and Aubrey Williams, segregation was an evil in itself and had to be rooted out before meaningful racial reform could occur. Others, such as journalists Hodding Carter and Virginius Dabney, whatever their private beliefs, felt that a public attack on segregation would retard even reverse racial progress. Also, some in this group genuinely believed that segregation was too entrenched in Southern society to consider its extinction, at least for the time being. Ralph McGill wrote in the *Atlanta Constitution* in September 1948 that "Only a fool would say the Southern pattern of separation of the races can, or should be, overthrown." Fellow liberal journalist Hodding Carter agreed: "I cannot emphasize one point too strongly," he declared that same month. "The white South is as united as 30,000,000 people can be in its insistence upon segregation."

Some of this posturing may have been to deflect criticism against these journalists for their racially moderate views and to reassure readers that, at base, they adhered to Southern traditions as much as anyone. The difficulty was that in pronouncing the immutability of segregation, these editors were both raising their readers' expectations and promoting a false sense of security, especially during a time of increased federal activity in the field of civil rights. This latter point was the second dilemma confronting Southern white liberals, and it illuminated the inner conflict of maintaining Southern loyalties while at the same time supporting basic changes in the regional way of life.

Since the late 1930s a growing Southern chorus had expressed concern about the expansion of the federal government. Historically, the augmentation of federal authority had boded ill for the South, and suspicions of Washington reached through all segments of white Southern society. Even such seemingly neutral legislation as a federal antilynching statute evoked vigorous opposition in the South, not because Southerners condoned lynching, but rather because the proposal involved federal intrusions into state matters. Such constitutional distinctions generated little interest in the rest of the country, but in the South, as part of the hallowed past, they were very much present in contemporary thought. Further, the South cherished its insularity, ever suspicious of the foreign because of its potential to disrupt the regional culture. Southerners in postwar America were already in the midst of significant changes, so the regional culture was the lighthouse in the stormy sea of uncertainty, and Southerners headed instinctively for that beacon, shunning all other shores.

The feeling was general in the white South, with some accuracy, that outsiders could not begin to understand the nuances of regional culture. Policies devised to rectify perceived Southern inequities, therefore, were bound to fail and, in fact, could create more problems. Accordingly, Southern white liberals cautioned their Northern counterparts against tampering with regional racial institutions. That could only generate antagonism, erase the already considerable progress underway since 1940, and promote a vicious backlash. Hodding Carter in 1950 warned off "uninformed" outsiders and added that "any abrupt Federal effort to end segregation [would] dangerously impair the present progressive adjustments between the races."

The Northern record of implementing policies to reform Southern society was not encouraging to Southern liberals. Northerners either abandoned the policies at crucial stages, leaving liberals and blacks in extremely vulnerable positions, or they intervened heavy-handedly, unmindful of the cultural context. As Gavin Stevens noted in *Intruder in the Dust*, "That's what we are really defending: the privilege of setting him [the black Southerner] free ourselves, which we will have to do for the reason that nobody else can, since going on a century ago now, the North tried it and have been admitting for seventy-five years now that they failed. So it will have to be us. . . ."

But there was little agreement as to the nature and pace

of self-help nostrums. When the Southern Regional Council denounced segregation unequivocally in 1949, the group lost some support, most notably Virginius Dabney, who retreated so far that, only a few years later, he was lending his editorial support to the Byrd regime. On the other end of the spectrum, Charleston's controversial federal Judge J. Waities Waring, who in 1947 had presaged the *Brown* decision by ruling in the *Briggs* case that segregation was inherently unequal, rejected the Jim Crow liberalism of Hodding Carter and the "dangerous and insidious doctrine . . . of gradualism."

While the liberals squabbled amongst themselves, the old-line political leaders seized the platform and utilized President Truman's civil rights initiatives to regain control in the region. White Southerners were, generally, not particularly exercised by impending legislation, perhaps because they felt its passage was far-fetched and perhaps because of the continued postwar optimism. Building a new South and the tools with which to get on with this task occupied regional energies. Indeed, the elections of 1946 indicated that white Southerners were attracted to politicians who were surprisingly forthcoming on racial and social rhetoric. But it was precisely this attraction that so alarmed the old-liners, and they sought to counter it with the traditional methods of subduing divisions within the white South.

Race-baiting accelerated after 1946, with such perennial practitioners as Mississippi's Theodore G. Bilbo showing the way. Of the FEPC extension, Senator Bilbo warned that it was "nothing but a plot to put niggers to work next to your daughters." When the president presented his civil rights package in February 1948, Southern hostility reached its postwar zenith. Virginia Senator Harry F. Byrd termed the program a "devastating broadside at the dignity of southern traditions and institutions," that would inevitably result in bloodshed. When the moderate newspapers picked up the refrain, it was possible to hear the door to the already rickety house of Southern liberalism and free thought slam shut, shaking the structure to its very foundations. The Nashville *Banner* referred to the "vicious planks" in Truman's legislative package and allowed how "the people of the South are tired of being pushed around, subjected to abuse." In fact, the change by 1948 was that not only the Bilbos, but a broad range of Southern leadership perceived the Truman-led Democratic party as groveling "on their bellies through the dirt to kiss the feet of minorities." There was even discussion about boycotting the 1948 national Democratic ticket, or even voting for the Republicans. The Southern Congressional leadership generated such intense heat that a Truman ally and old Southern liberal, Kentucky Senator and Majority Leader Alben W. Barkley, refused to shepherd the civil rights program through the Senate.

As the door slammed on Southern liberals, it closed shut on potential dissenters in general. It had always been the case that when running up the symbolic Stars and Bars you would need to salute or suffer the consequences. For Judge Waring, the penalty was isolation from lifelong friends, periodic cross burnings, and garbage dumped on the lawn. When he died in 1968, only twelve whites attended his funeral. One of the few white mourners, a man who shared the judge's beliefs but maintained them in silence, explained to a reporter, "We all can't do like him. We can't all be crucified." Will Alexander, a Southern pioneer in interracial cooperation, retired to a farm outside of Chapel Hill in 1948 and became the subject of vicious rumors that prominent Jews and Eleanor Roosevelt were bankrolling a clandestine attempt by Alexander to purchase land in the area to give to blacks. Even old university colleagues were avoiding him by the time he died in 1956. Indeed, the Tar Heel state, which had enjoyed a modest reputation for fostering interracial groups, uniting labor, blacks, and white liberals, experienced the rapid denouement of this experiment. As state AFL-CIO President Wilbur Hobby recalled in dispirit: "the race thing killed it."

"The race thing" was coming to dominate Southern politics and Southern life in general. The old-liners' manipulation of the president's initiatives, coupled with well-intentioned but nonetheless self-righteous declarations from some Northern politicians, rekindled the regional obsession with race. As the 1948 presidential election campaign opened, the old-liners perceived the opportunity to redeem the region yet again. Their reaction to Truman's program was carefully staged histrionics, since the likelihood of its passing Congress was nil. Both sides were guilty of posturing for effect: the Truman coterie, who realized the negligible chances of passage but who utilized the opportunity to gain Northern support in a tight election, and Southern congressional leaders, who also recognized the futility of the program, but who viewed the occasion as a rhetorical platform to rally sentiment at home and stave off the growing independence of the Southern white electorate.

Led by Governors Strom Thurmond of South Carolina and Fielding L. Wright of Mississippi, Southern Democrats (with dissents from Folsom, Pepper, Kefauver, and a few other liberal insurgents) vowed to reconvene in Birmingham after the Democratic National Convention if that body refused to repudiate Truman's program. The convention called the Southerners' bluff and supported the package. As if playing out a medieval morality play, the Southern dissenters assembled solemnly in Birmingham as promised, formed the States' Rights Democratic Party, and nominated Thurmond and Wright for the offices of president and vice president, respectively. The Dixiecrats, as they were called, overplayed their roles. The South was not yet ready to abandon the Democratic party. The Thurmond-Wright ticket carried only four states—South Carolina, Mississippi, Alabama, and Louisiana—and, not coincidentally, these were the only states that listed the Dixiecrat team under the Democratic party emblem. President Truman was not on the ballot in these states. Virginia Attorney General J. Lindsay Almond explained the Dixiecrat's poor showing as follows: "The only sane and constructive course to follow is to remain in the house of our fathers—even though the roof leaks, and there be bats in the belfry, rats in the pantry, a cockroach waltz in the kitchen and skunks in the parlor."

Though white Southerners were not yet in lock-step with their traditional leaders, the reintroduction of Truman's civil rights package in 1949 fueled the efforts of erstwhile Dixiecrats. In addition, the Cold War began to intrude into Southern politics, an intrusion that served further to stifle debate on race. Red-baiting became second to race-baiting as a campaign tactic in elections after 1948. Though President Truman perceived civil rights as a positive weapon for the United States in the East-West propaganda war, some Southerners alleged that those advocating such a connection had suspect loyalties. Senator James O. Eastland of Mississippi led a probe to root out the "Communist conspiracy" within the SCEF. Though investigators could not document any link, the allegations successfully frightened off contributors and members, crippling the organization by the early 1950s. Even Ralph McGill sought to distance himself from possible contamination by association by suggesting the SCEF was "Communist-infiltrated." Eastland was successful in utilizing the Senate anti-Communist apparatus and the Federal Bureau of Investigation to further his ends to discredit those who sought racial change in the South.

Dorothy Tilly also came under the red fire. She organized the Fellowship of the Concerned in 1949, a group of like-minded churchwomen dedicated to improved race relations. The sanctity of Southern womanhood no longer obtained for a woman who so brazenly violated regional custom. In especially strong language, a Southern journalist in 1949 denounced her as "a parasite who while living upon funds furnished by the Methodist Church had rendered much of her service to the cause of Socialism and Communism." Later on, the harassment of Tilly became so intense that she placed a record player adjacent to her telephone so she could play the Lord's Prayer whenever she received an obscene call.

The tactics of racial and ideological innuendo and allegation were particularly effective in the 1950 election campaign in two states, North Carolina and Florida. The white South was not yet convinced that regional and now national loyalty required them to follow the prescriptions of the old-liners. The Byrd machine was in trouble in Virginia, as young Francis

Pickens Miller captured voters' enthusiasm for a new political era; liberalism remained competitive in Tennessee; "Big Jim" Folsom still reigned in Alabama, along with compatriots Hill and Sparkman; and North Carolina threatened to shed its starchy, slow-witted politics for the dynamic leadership of Frank P. Graham.

In 1949, North Carolina Governor W. Kerr Scott appointed Graham as United States Senator to fill the final year of the unexpired term of J. Melville Broughton, who had died in office. "Dr. Frank" came to the Senate with impeccable liberal credentials and was well respected as one of the nation's leading educators. A former history professor and president of the University of North Carolina, Graham vigorously supported academic freedom and molded the university into one of the major state institutions of higher learning in the South. In the years immediately preceding the appointment, he had provoked some resentment in his home state by serving on the President's Committee on Civil Rights. Despite its progressive reputation, North Carolina harbored strong conservative elements and V. O. Key, in his political analysis of the state, characterized it as the "Rule of an Economic Oligarchy." Yet, Graham's national stature had earned him political support in the state, especially as his numerous alumni began to ascend to power, proud of their resurgent alma mater and cognizant of Graham's role in making it so.

Accordingly, "Dr. Frank" decided to stand for election in 1950 for the Senate seat he occupied, and he entered the Democratic primary. He fell just short of achieving the Democratic nomination (tantamount to victory in November) in the first primary, receiving 49.1 percent of the vote. North Carolina, like most Southern states, required a run-off primary between the top vote-getters if no candidate obtained a majority of the votes cast the first time around. The run-off primary was an electoral device instituted by the Democratic party in the South during the early years of the twentieth century to dilute the effect of bloc voting for minority (race or class) candidates who might be able to muster a plurality in a large field of candidates.

Nevertheless, Graham held a substantial lead over his nearest opponent in the first primary, Willis Smith, a prominent attorney and chairman of the Duke University board of trustees. And, in fact, the lead appeared insurmountable up until the final weeks before the run-off election. At that time, a small group of heretofore obscure campaign workers for Smith, including a young Jesse Helms, launched a massive assault on Graham's alleged racial and ideological loyalties.

Two weeks prior to the run-off, North Carolinians awoke to handbills placed in their newspaper boxes and inside screened doors imploring, "WHITE PEOPLE WAKE UP!" The copy below asserted that "Frank Graham Favors Mingling of the Races," and predicted race warfare if Graham won. Newspaper ads following this opening salvo exposed "Dr. Frank's" secret agenda: "End of Racial Segregation Proposed"; or "The South Under Attack." Additional handbills appeared with a doctored photograph showing Graham's wife dancing with a black man; other material circulated charging that the senator had appointed a black to the United States Military Academy at West Point. When Graham, in response to this latter accusation, brought to a political rally the white teenager whom he had actually appointed to the academy, a reporter sampling crowd response concluded that the sentiment was "Why didn't he bring the nigger he appointed? Who was he trying to fool, showing us that white boy?"

While trumpeting the race issue, Graham's opponents varied the theme by suggesting that the senator's position on race was a result of his Communist sympathies, a charge that followed him for years after the campaign (in 1959, the South Carolina Senate banned him from speaking at a state college campus because of his alleged Communist connections). The media assault was not merely confined to the Grahams, but to their supporters as well. Newspapers reported that some school children who voiced support for the educator were beaten up as "nigger lovers"; women working in the Graham campaign received obscene phone calls; and Graham volunteers confronted stares and verbal abuse as they worked districts throughout the state. Fear and conformity were the inevitable consequences of these tactics: the fear that support for Frank P. Graham was tantamount to transgression from social custom and would result in isolation and ostracism. Since Southerners thrived on vast interconnected friendship networks, especially in towns and in rural areas, such a circumstance would sever the umbilical cord extending from society to the individual. Former supporters dumped Graham literature and scraped off bumper stickers. "My neighbors won't talk to me!" one erstwhile Graham worker complained.

The Graham camp, taken completely by surprise, could muster little resistance during the final days of the campaign. Responding to the charges legitimized them to some degree, and ignoring them appeared as a tacit admission of guilt. Willis Smith cruised to victory in the run-off primary. Though Smith had not resorted to mud slinging himself, neither did he call off his zealous staff, who transformed a losing campaign into a winning one.

A similar scenario was building in Florida, where energetic New Deal liberal Claude Pepper was up for reelection to the United States Senate in 1950. George Smathers, a successful developer and member of the state's economic elite, who were often embarrassed by the boisterous New Dealism of Pepper, confronted the incumbent in the Democratic primary. Although Senator Pepper had been a loyal Rooseveltian, his racial views, at least as reflected in his public utterances and voting record, were closer to the Southern Democratic mainstream than the expressed opinions of Frank Graham. Nevertheless, Smathers mounted a race-baiting campaign against Pepper replete with unsubstantiated quotes, and used the senator's avowed economic liberalism as an opening to imply Communist connections. At his campaign kick-off in Orlando, challenger Smathers spoke of "those in the government who are apologists for Stalin, associates of fellow travelers, and sponsors of Communist-front organizations," without mentioning Pepper by name, though as Ralph McGill noted, "everyone in Florida knew whom he meant." The tactics pushed Pepper into the same defensive stance that Graham had been forced to assume. And, as with the Graham campaign, Pepper's efforts were self-defeating and he lost the primary by a 60,000–vote margin.

The defeat of Graham and Pepper signaled an end to the promising political renaissance that had emerged in the South in 1946. Although the Tennessee trio of Clement, Gore, and Kefauver survived the decade of the 1950s, elsewhere the old-line politicos, the county courthouse cliques, and the economic elites regained or reinforced their hegemony. "Big Jim" Folsom hung on in Alabama, though personal problems and the tenor of the times muted his actions. The springtime of Southern politics, so much in evidence in the immediate postwar years, was now so many dead leaves of late autumn, with winter fast approaching.

Southern blacks watched the deteriorating political promise and listened to the bellicose rhetoric with increasing trepidation. The events of the postwar years—the Truman initiatives, the favorable Supreme Court rulings, and the growing electoral voice—had raised the hopes and expectations of Southern blacks. While the Truman program went nowhere, at the least the civil rights issue was a subject of national debate for the first time in decades; the Court decisions not only brought substantive relief to black plaintiffs, but opened up the political process and portended favorable future judgments on desegregation cases pending in lower courts. Blacks wielded important votes in several Southern cities, which translated into some jobs and a better level of services. But the increasingly hostile racial climate inhibited blacks from building upon these legal and political bases; in fact, they experienced some erosion.

Southern blacks soon discovered, for example, that the regional political system contained several ingenious stratagems perfected over years of hewing to the fine line between legal letter and intent. The more venerable obstacles included the poll tax, a fee required in most Southern states, averaging roughly $1.50 annually, for the privilege of exercising a constitutional right. Since blacks, particularly those in rural areas, found even this seemingly modest charge a burden, they typically exchanged the right to vote for a week's worth of food that they could stretch on that sum. The poll tax operated against poor whites as well, but on frequent occasions enterprising politicians would pay the fee and reap the votes. The existence of the tax reflected the distrust of democracy by the heirs of the Redeemers. As Ralph McGill observed in 1948, the tax "remains largely a defense mechanism for those politicians who are afraid of their own people."

The Supreme Court's decision in *Smith* v. *Allwright* meant that more blacks would be encouraged to participate in the political system. Once they overcame the poll tax hurdle, blacks confronted a range of other devious devices designed to control the voter pool. Literacy tests were common tools of disfranchisement. In Birmingham after the war, registrars were fond of querying blacks, "What is the Constitution made of?" Registrars asked blacks to recite the Preamble of the Constitution from memory. Elsewhere, registrars adopted slow-down tactics, keeping blacks in long lines for many hours, then closing down or sending everyone home because they had depleted their supply of registration cards. In Alabama, registration boards usually required a black registrant to appear with two white men to vouch for identity and integrity.

But even if a black hopeful overcame these subterfuges and secured a place on the voting lists, registrars might suddenly notify him that they had purged his name from the rolls because of an alleged address change or an incomplete application. In 1946, 20,000 black voters in Alabama lost their franchise rights in this manner. That same year, E. C. Boswell, an Alabama state legislator from Geneva County in the Black Belt, sought further assurances against black participation and succeeded in codifying a practice already followed by rural registrars in requiring that an applicant exhibit understanding of a particular section of the state constitution. Though some feared the provision could disqualify white voters from participating in the Democratic primary, appeals to white supremacy overrode such objections and the voters ratified the constitutional amendment. The measure was successful in barring blacks from participation in the primary, but, as one observer in Birmingham commented, "men in overalls and working clothes have been more extensively questioned by the Board than were those whose appearance indicated they were professionals and businessmen."

When these machinations failed to deter blacks, the more direct and traditional deterrent of violence resurfaced. Daniel Guerin, a French journalist touring the South in 1950, remarked that the "most effective means of prevention of the Negro vote remain threats and terror." Soon after he wrote these words, Harry T. Moore, active in voter registration efforts in Florida, was the target of a Christmas Eve bomb that killed him and his wife as they sat in their home. Reports of blacks being beaten or shot at for attempting to register were commonplace by the early 1950s.

Overt force was typically a last resort, however, especially in smaller communities. There were usually other means of persuasion available to whites intent on excluding blacks from voting. Southern politics in these places was a gothic web of interrelationships, with businessmen, professionals, planters, law enforcement personnel, industrialists, editors, and politicians closely connected by interest and in some instances by kin. Though not a monolith on all or even most issues, the power structure invariably closed ranks when a perceived threat surfaced. Labor analyst Robert B. Cooney, for example, explained what confronted a labor organizer in the South during the 1950s: "the activity of union organizers causes a rallying of a town's officials, police, merchants, ministers, teachers and newspaper editors." Black aspirations generated similar if not greater motivation to close ranks. Because of their general dependence, blacks were frequently beholden to a white merchant or planter or social service agency personnel as well as subject to capricious treatment by the police or courts. Community institutions and their personnel could thus be marshalled to discourage black participation in the political process. The withdrawal of credit, the loss of a job, the denial of medical or legal services, and the potential for official harassment weighed heavily on blacks.

Given the range of obstacles, both potential and real, it is perhaps more noteworthy that 20 percent of Southern blacks were eligible to vote by 1954 than that 80 percent were not. Nevertheless, the future prognosis was not encouraging as the retrograde forces seemed to be ascending. As William Andrews, an NAACP field secretary, remarked glumly, "Legal victories are not of themselves open sesame to political suffrage."

The Reaction to *Brown*

Yet, it was a legal victory—*Brown* v. *Board of Education*—in 1954 that inspired new hope among Southern blacks increasingly discouraged by the successful circumscription of their rights by Southern whites. *Brown* was, of course, the culmination of legal precedents dating back to 1938 eroding the concept of segregated education. But because the High Court stated explicitly that segregation itself was inherently unequal, the hope among blacks was widespread that other bastions of racial exclusion would eventually fall. Yet, the thunderclap of *Brown* seemed a distant echo to most Southerners. Those few who had followed Court logic over the previous decade were not surprised, and the rest were aware of the ingenuity with which their white leaders had circumvented potentially damaging decisions, such as *Smith* v. *Allwright*. The Court had spoken before and the South had listened and done contrariwise. Moreover, the Eisenhower administration did not seem especially inclined to enforce the Court's decision. So the alarm was not yet imminent.

In fact, in the months following the *Brown* decision, school districts in various parts of the South moved to comply with the desegregation edict. The Greensboro, North Carolina, school board, on the night after the decision, issued a statement expressing its intention to obey the new law of the land. Several

Southern governors who had weathered the recent storm of reaction against federal initiatives in the late 1940s and early 1950s mostly in silence were quite willing to go on the record promising compliance. Governor Francis Cherry of Arkansas stated simply: "Arkansas will obey the law. It always has." Alabama's "Big Jim" Folsom declared that "When the Supreme Court speaks, that's the law." Few, if any, leaders at the local or state levels of government were openly approving of the decision, to be sure—and given the potential problems of implementation as well as the potential for demagogic appeals, how could they be? Nevertheless, their statements indicated a calm forthrightness that would encourage lawful fulfillment of the Court's ruling.

Indeed, this seemed to be the case as desegregation orders issued forth from a scattering of school boards in Kentucky, Tennessee, Arkansas, and Texas. At the opening of the 1956–1957 academic year, desegregation involving more than 300,000 black children had occurred in 723 school districts throughout the region. Despite isolated outbreaks of violence in Kentucky and Tennessee, the respective governors of those states—A.B. ("Happy") Chandler and Frank Clement—exercised strong leadership with an occasional strategic appearance of the national guard to enforce desegregation edicts. Many other parts of the South did nothing, preferring to adopt a "wait and see" attitude. South Carolina Governor George Bell Timmerman, for example, in his inaugural address in January 1955 in Columbia, only briefly and obliquely alluded to the school controversy.

Timmerman's omission may have been intentional, since most Southerners at that time felt relatively secure and believed, or at least hoped, that as with previous potential outside threats, this one too would dissipate. Writing in 1956, journalist Henry Ashmore noted that, in the South, "The prevailing mood is escapist; actuality is not yet at hand, and most Southerners still hope that somehow it will go away." The relative calm that pervaded the region moved those who had genuinely welcomed the Court's ruling to predict that compliance would be relatively quick and smooth. Ralph McGill termed the sporadic and scattered sniping at the decision as "guerrilla fighting among the ruins of the old segregated society."

But the epitaph for the "old segregated society" was premature. First, while Southern whites hoped that by ignoring *Brown* they could escape its impact, blacks were eager to seize upon the decision and apply it to localities throughout the region. Accordingly, with the assistance of the NAACP Legal Defense Fund, blacks filed hundreds of lawsuits against school boards across the South to push them into compliance with the law. Such aggressive pursuit of school desegregation took many white Southerners aback and reactions to the new realities were swift and strong. Then, too, the *Brown* decision and especially the legal avalanche accompanying it were tailor-made issues for a Southern leadership searching for a cause to reinforce their power, a power vulnerable to apathy, divisions among Southern whites, and outside, especially federal, influence. The race issue had saved their positions in the recent past and would so do again. As one Deep South politician confided to a reporter: "Give me another issue I can run and be sure of winning out in the counties, and I'll drop the nigger question." In the mid-1950s there were no such alternatives for a cynical leadership to employ. For them, the stakes involved in the upset of the racial status quo were too great to go casting about for other issues. James McBride Dabbs explained the thinking of Southern leadership in 1957:

First, being well-placed, they tend to be suspicious of all change. Second, they often profit from racial discrimination. Third . . . the main job of the white community . . . is to keep itself distinguished from the Negro community. Therefore, the main job of these white leaders is to keep unchanged the old distinguishing marks, to stand still racially and see that everybody stands with them.

Of course, a not-so-secondary benefit of race-baiting was that it kept intact the class distinctions within the white community by discouraging challenges to current leadership and enabled that leadership to restrict access to the political process. Besides the obvious damage to Southern blacks, the system victimized the poor whites. As Will Campbell, iconoclastic Baptist preacher, put it, the system "took his head away . . . , he's never really known who the enemy was." Campbell's insight was nothing new; Tom Watson had figured it out during the early glory days of Populism in the 1890s, and it was precisely this analysis that frightened the heirs of the Redeemers most. As Watson explained to the poor of both races: "You are made to hate each other because upon that hatred is rested the keystone of the arch of financial despotism which enslaves you both. You are deceived and blinded that you may not see how this race antagonism perpetuates a money system which beggars you both." The specter of this proto-alliance haunted Southern white leadership for decades thereafter, never quite subsiding, but serving as a strong incentive to quell any changes that could ultimately alter regional institutions.

The attempt to hold off the implications of *Brown* received some assistance from Washington. The first indication of a Washington retreat, or at least a disassociation, from *Brown* actually emanated from the Supreme Court itself. The Justices, in the *Brown* decision of May 1954, had not established a timetable by which school districts were required to comply with the ruling. The implementation ruling came in May 1955. Despite NAACP entreaties to order immediate desegregation, the Justices ordered only that districts make a "prompt and reasonable start toward full compliance," and that desegregation proceed "with all deliberate speed." The Court left the latter phrase ambiguous and, indeed, it remained so for the next decade and a half, until the Court's patience finally wore thin. The lenient implementation decree probably resulted from an agreement that secured unanimity on the first *Brown* decision the previous year. The ambiguity of "all deliberate speed" would encourage extensive circumvention and subterfuge in the South into the 1970s.

And it also soon became apparent to Southerners inclined to ignore the desegregation ruling that the Eisenhower administration was not about to interpret the Court's implementation decision in a manner unfavorable to the South. The president, philosophically wary of federal initiatives in general, greeted the initial *Brown* decision with strong silence, though he later said privately that his appointment of California's Republican governor, Earl Warren, as Chief Justice of the United States Supreme Court was "the biggest damn fool mistake" he ever made. Though no segregationist, Eisenhower sympathized with Southern complaints about unwonted federal intrusion into state matters. He was also aware of the changing nature of the national Democratic party and the possibility of picking up some Southern support in the 1956 presidential election. In his Southern campaign swings that year he stressed the states' rights theme repeatedly and dutifully snapped to attention when the bands played "Dixie."

Loosed from the possibility of forced compliance, yet still threatened by a flurry of NAACP lawsuits and the actions of small groups of black parents, Southerners offered a wide variety of responses after 1955 designed not only to inhibit desegregation efforts, but to snuff them out entirely. This resistance to the *Brown* decision successfully delayed Southern compliance, in many cases for years, and in some instances, seemingly forever.

Southern lawmakers launched a legal assault of their own, enacting nearly 500 bills into law between 1954 and 1957 designed to circumvent or nullify outright the *Brown* decision. In the 1954–1955 legislative session, for example, Georgia passed a contingency plan establishing a "private" segregated school system at state expense if desegregation occurred in the public schools. Mississippi lawmakers authorized counties and school districts to abolish their public schools if the necessity arose. New laws in several states ordered revocation of a teacher's license for instructing integrated classes and ensured that no white child could be forced to attend an integrated school. The NAACP, the organization that led the legal attack against the biracial society, was a particular target of legislation, resulting in measures requiring the publication of membership lists and in turn making such membership grounds for dismissal of public school teachers, and statutes going so far as to prohibit legal challenges to segregation ordinances. Alabama and Virginia lawmakers dredged up John C. Calhoun's ancient and discredited doctrines of nullification and interposition, in effect nullifying the *Brown* decision and interposing state law in its stead.

Southern politicians recognized that most of these statutes were unconstitutional or at least subject to immediate challenge. But that was the point. "As long as we can legislate, we can segregate," reasoned one lawmaker. And if that legislation generated a comparable barrage of litigation, so much the better. The Richmond *News-Leader* explained the strategy in a 1956 editorial: "Litigate? Let us pledge ourselves to litigate this thing for fifty years. If one remedial law is ruled invalid, then let us try another; and if the second is ruled invalid, then let us enact a third."

Perhaps the most common legislative remedy was establishing the mechanism by which school systems could be closed rather than submit to desegregation. W. Scott Wilkinson, a Louisiana segregationist, spoke for the advocates of these measures when he explained that Southern whites "would prefer that our youth grow up in ignorance than permit them to attend integrated schools." Some segregationists even perceived positive attributes to shutting down the public education system. Georgia segregationist R. Carter Pittman looked forward to closing the schools in his state as an opportunity to "get Karl Marx and John Dewey out of our schools."

The school closure movement reached its illogical conclusion in Virginia. Legislators in the Old Dominion passed a contingency law in 1956 requiring the closing of public schools in any district that received a court order to desegregate. The law was part of a studied program of resistance undertaken by the Byrd machine. The machine had undergone a brief resurgence during the Truman administration, but as concern about civil rights waned among white Virginians, Byrd's fortunes receded. Byrd barely survived a challenge in 1953 from

Republican gubernatorial candidate, Ted Dalton, and experienced difficulty holding down younger elements within the Democratic party anxious to see an expansion of state services and an elimination of the burdensome poll tax. The school integration issue appeared as a life preserver, rescuing the machine's sagging fortunes.

When school districts in Norfolk, Charlottesville, and later in Prince Edward County played out their legal options and received court orders to begin desegregation for the 1959 academic year, Senator Harry F. Byrd, Sr., gave word to close the schools. The situation became a national spectacle, with *Life* magazine, among others, doing a feature on "The Lost Class of '59." The photographs depicted white teenagers idling at drug stores, marrying early, and carrying on a few school activities, such as cheerleading, off school grounds. The message was clear that these pupils were as much victims of the biracial society and the maneuvers employed to perpetuate it as the black litigants standing before their padlocked high school. Governor J. Lindsay Almond, Jr., who was embarrassed by the publicity, and the suddenly responsive business communities, especially in Norfolk, which were concerned about the present and potential economic costs of school closures, broke with the Byrd organization and reopened the schools in Norfolk and Charlottesville. Prince Edward County, however, a rural, tobacco-growing area in the conservative Southside portion of the state, held no illusions of economic grandeur and could conveniently place cultural loyalty above the profit motive. County officials refused to raise and collect taxes for the school system, thereby closing them for a period of five years while the inevitable litigation took its tortuous route through the judicial system. During those five years from 1959 to 1964, at which time the United States Supreme Court ordered the reopening of the county's public schools on a desegregated basis, white children grabbed what education they could, frequently attending makeshift private academies of questionable educational quality. Black children, however, possessed only two alternatives—home study or out-migration—and most went without formal schooling for those five years. As North Carolina journalist Jonathan Daniels warned a South Carolina audience contemplating a similar path, "what they propose . . . [is] something beyond secession from the Union. What they urge is secession from civilization."

The Virginia situation underscored an important point about the white South's response to desegregation: the state government played a crucial role in smoothing or inhibiting acceptance. Considering the clubby, inbred, special-interest-seeking characteristics of Southern state government, it is not surprising that responsible leadership at the state level was unusual. State leaders were highly visible models of resistance and those elements so inclined were encouraged to foment their own versions of opposition. "The central theme," wrote former Mississippi Congressman Frank E. Smith, who lost his seat in Congress by urging constituents to comply with the law, "from the day of the long-anticipated decision of the Supreme Court, is the failure of those in positions of responsibility to meet the challenge to secure peaceable, rapid, and orderly compliance with the decision." Smith's concern had been the common lament of W. J. Cash, Howard W. Odum, and other earlier generations of liberal Southerners.

State leaders decried violence, of course, but their actions and rhetoric created an approving atmosphere for such outbursts. The leaders and their white constituents had, over the years, developed a code that did not require explicit instructions as to what activities would be condoned. As James McBride Dabbs observed in 1958: "It is customary for middle- and upper-class whites, when faced with the need for racial adjustments, to say: 'We have no great objection ourselves, but the poorer whites wouldn't stand for it; there'd be violence.' The part about violence is always said publicly . . . so that the lower-class whites know what is expected of them." Indeed there were numerous examples of such rhetorical transparency during the mid- and late 1950s. One leader vowed to a Selma, Alabama, audience in December 1954 that "We intend to maintain segregation and do so without violence." He then added, "But I know the first time a Negro tries to enter Parrish High School at Selma, or any other white school, blood will be spilled on the campus." These combination disclaimer-warnings were not only directed at constituents, but at blacks and outside agencies from district courts to the federal government as well. Intervention, the leaders implied, would precipitate violence.

The failure of state leadership and the veiled invitations to rebellion were exposed particularly in Little Rock, Arkansas, in 1957. The state capital was an unlikely place for what would become a violent and historic confrontation over school desegregation. Since the *Brown* decision, most jurisdictions in the state had announced their willingness to comply, however reluctantly, with the ruling, Little Rock among them. Moreover, a scattering of school districts had already accepted a token integration without incident. And Governor Orval Faubus was not a massive resister who would obstruct compliance. Quite the opposite, Faubus hailed from the Ozarks, an area of the state where the race issue had long been irrelevant. His father, an occasional farmer with a penchant for socialist politics, instilled in young Orval a keen preference for the underdog. The younger Faubus cut his political teeth working for Governor Sid McMath, one of the bright, progressive Southern politicians of the immediate postwar era. When Faubus came to run for governor himself in 1954, he portrayed himself as McMath's philosophical heir, favoring a progressive, modern Arkansas. His campaign was devoid of race-baiting and, more important, once in office he expanded the Democratic State Committee to include six blacks, pushed through a hefty tax increase to upgrade public education, and created a model facility for the mentally retarded, the Children's Colony.

Yet, when Little Rock's Central High School prepared to receive nine black students for the opening of the 1957–1958 school year, Faubus marshalled every device at his command to stop desegregation. What occurred provides an excellent example of the historically close connections between politics and race and how that web of relationships could ensnare a man such as Faubus, a man so seemingly ill-suited for the role he was about to play.

The revelation for Faubus occurred in the 1956 gubernatorial campaign. Arkansas governors serve two-year terms and Faubus stood for reelection, touting his progressive record as the best course for the state's future. Jim Johnson, an acid-tongued former state senator, was the incumbent's major opposition in the Democratic primary, and he offered stiff resistance before succumbing. Johnson had accused Faubus of being "soft" on integration. By the middle of the following year, the governor had decided privately to seek a third term. It was likely that he would face a staunch segregationist, if not Jim Johnson, then another challenger with similar views.

While Faubus was keeping his own political counsel, the citizens of Little Rock were fashioning an integration plan. City leaders, like the governor, looked forward to a new era for their city and state and had attracted a number of industries into the state capital since 1950, eliminated corruption from a once-venal and inefficient local government, and formed a committee to pursue economic development. Their compliance with the *Brown* decision was relatively swift, embodied in the "Blossom Plan," a brainchild of dynamic school superintendent Virgil Blossom, and introduced to a cautiously optimistic, if not entirely approving, city in 1955. The plan devised an integration strategy to be carried out over a six-year period beginning at the high school level in September 1957.

The plan not only revealed the desire of civic leaders to get on with this somewhat distasteful business and continue to recruit and develop, but it also underscored the elitist character of Little Rock and the assumptions of class shared by the dominant Southern whites. The plan proposed the construction of a new high school in a fashionable all-white neighborhood on the west side of Little Rock. Central High, the older institution, would remain the secondary school for working-class whites and would receive black students when the integration program opened its initial phase in the fall of 1957.

The new high school would remain lily white, a circumstance likely to increase the hostility of blue-collar white families, many of whom had moved to the state capital from rural areas after the war.

A few days prior to the opening of the 1957–1958 school year, Governor Faubus had decided to intervene in what was a tense but calm situation. Sensing that the governor was about to alter a lifelong course, Winthrop Rockefeller visited him to urge nonintervention. Rockefeller had arrived in Arkansas after World War II determined to use his family fortune to help change the backward image and reality of Arkansas. He began operating a model farm and joined in the recruitment of outside investment. As Rockefeller recalled the encounter: "I reasoned with him, argued with him, almost pled with him" to stay out of the issue, that it was a local situation and "none of his business." Faubus acknowledged his arguments, but explained, "I'm sorry, but I'm already committed. I'm going to run for a third term, and if I don't do this, Jim Johnson and Bruce Bennett [another segregationist candidate] will tear me to shreds."

The governor played his political hand and, on the day before school opened, he called out the National Guard and ordered them to surround Central High. The following day, the nine black students who comprised the integration were turned away by the soldiers. Faubus's action precipitated a federal showdown, a crisis not relished by President Eisenhower. The governor defended his position by declaring that he acted in the name of public safety to avoid the inevitable violence that would accompany such an assault on Southern traditions. He faced, he told a *New York Times* reporter, "the same fateful decision that confronted Robert E. Lee when he was forced to choose between Virginia and the Union." Thus wrapping himself in the mantle of the Lost Cause, Faubus advanced to do battle with Washington.

A three-ring drama unfolded, with action from the State House, the Oval Office, and the federal district courtroom culminating in a predictable tragedy. The governor met with the president, who urged him to end his obstruction of integration. Federal District Judge Ronald Davies then issued an injunction preventing Faubus and the Guard from interfering with the integration process. The governor complied by removing the troops and replacing them with local police. After a tense weekend, the nine black teenagers entered the school unobtrusively through a side entrance. But when word spread that Central High was integrated, the violence predicted and hence encouraged by Faubus erupted. Whites rampaged through the city for the next two days, finally leading an exasperated Eisenhower to order in the "Screaming Eagles" of the 101st Airborne Division, the first federal troops to invade the region since the Civil War.

For Faubus, thc military maneuvers merely enhanced his status with disaffected whites and, not incidentally, ensured his reelection. Stymied by the show of federal force, he used the federal courts to delay integration. On September 12, 1958, more than one year after Faubus precipitated the initial crisis, the United States Supreme Court in *Cooper* v. *Aaron* ruled that community opposition and the prospect of violence, however likely, were insufficient grounds for postponing integration, and ordered that the integration plan proceed. Faubus shrugged off the adverse ruling and promptly signed legislation closing Little Rock's high schools.

At this point, the heretofore acquiescent business leadership moved quietly to end the crisis and ensure that, integration or no, the schools remained open. As one school board member recalled: "Of course their pride was hurt when the troops came and their pride was hurt when we became sort of a national spectacle, but not very deeply felt. But when you close a school and your number-one son doesn't have a place to go. . . , and all your hopes and dreams have rested on him, it's a very deep hurt." Finally, with the more vocal assistance of parents' groups and an ad hoc organization, the Women's Emergency Committee to Open Our Schools, an integrated Central High opened in September 1959, after two years of disruption and evasion precipitated by a quest for a political main chance.

The Little Rock crisis underscored several elements common to school desegregation across the South in the half-decade following the *Brown* implementation ruling. First, the quality and direction of state leadership was essential to the success of desegregation rulings. The machinations of Faubus in Arkansas and the Byrd machine in Virginia contrasted with the measured calm of South Carolina's Governor Ernest F. Hollings or the drawing back of Georgia's Governor Ernest Vandiver from a campaign pledge to close the schools rather than to desegregate, and, accordingly, South Carolina and Georgia did not offer up material for national news programs and newspapers.

Second, the Little Rock experience indicated the importance of using the federal court system and the law in general to delay desegregation: in effect, to use the law to sustain lawlessness. The irony was that black strategy also relied heavily on litigation. But without the support of other government institutions, segregation could be maintained for a time by the very system that had outlawed it in the first place. The conscious absence of leadership at the state level, the delays that accompanied litigation in the federal courts, and the unwillingness of the Eisenhower administration to fill the leadership vacuum deferred the desegregation process. Official defiance, thinly veiled by legalisms, encouraged citizen defiance of an often extralegal nature.

The cosmopolitan business community of Little Rock might have provided an effective counter to the failure of responsible leadership at the state and federal levels. But here and in such cities as New Orleans and Augusta, only spectacle or chaos moved the economic elite to action. However much they looked to the future, their attitudes were rooted in regional culture, and blood will tell, especially in the South.

There were exceptions to the abdication of leadership—in Charlotte and, most notably, in Atlanta. In the self-styled "city too busy to hate," image gained precedence over culture and the desegregation plan proceeded smoothly in the fall of 1961. Atlanta possessed several positive attributes that ensured an uneventful implementation. Mayor William B. Hartsfield had long held and practiced racial moderation, and the atmosphere in the city between the races was most often accommodating rather than confrontational. Also, Governor Vandiver blustered but never delivered and crossed the Rubicon a year prior to desegregation in Atlanta by reluctantly allowing the University of Georgia to integrate without interference. Moving further along the road to accommodation, he signed an "open schools" package several months later that ensured local autonomy in school desegregation decisions, thus paving the way for Atlanta's program to operate without fear of obstruction. Finally, Atlantans had the benefit of hindsight. Atlanta had approached desegregation at an uncharacteristically leisurely pace. September 1961 was the target date, and by then the civic elite had witnessed the adverse publicity descending on recalcitrant jurisdictions, especially Little Rock and, more recently, New Orleans. The Atlanta *Constitution* made direct reference to this in an editorial expressing the desire "that the schools . . . be preserved and the children spared such experiences as we've witnessed in New Orleans."

Preparation was a vital element in Atlanta's successful compliance. From the Chamber of Commerce to parents and religious leaders, the city's leading citizens bombarded residents with seminars, brochures, television programs, and newspaper stories, constantly reminded people that "the world was watching," and held prayer services at churches and synagogues. Thus covering all bases, the leadership overwhelmed the vocal minority white resistance led by restaurateur Lester Maddox's group, Georgians Unwilling to Surrender (GUTS).

The media assault and education campaign proved effective when on August 31, 1961, seven years after *Brown*, nine black children peacefully desegregated four high schools in Atlanta. "It was the silence heard around the world," one leader boasted. President Kennedy sent a congratulatory telegram and

Newsweek published a feature story on "the city too busy to hate."

But seven years for nine children—at that rate it would take the South several hundred years to desegregate its public schools, a pace imparting a new definition to the phrase, "with all deliberate speed." And, in fact, there was a distinct deceleration in the rate of desegregation by the time Atlanta complied with the Court's ruling. After an initial flurry of desegregation during the twelve months following the 1954 decision progress slowed and, after 1957, virtually came to a standstill. By that time and thereafter, Little Rock symbolized not so much the costs of violence, but that violent confrontation, ironically, sped desegregation. Quiet noncompliance, on the other hand, held out the possibility of stretching out, perhaps infinitely, but at least through the next election, the desegregation movement.

Civic leaders in Greensboro, North Carolina, became especially proficient at evasion, avoiding significant school desegregation until the late 1960s, nearly fifteen years after its school board became the first such body in the region to vow compliance with *Brown*. In fact, the rhetoric emerging from this attractive community was almost always conciliatory and accommodating, a tactic guaranteed to deflect outside attention. The black community soon caught on to the circumspection and filed suit. The specific litigation concerned an attempt by some black students to enroll in an all-white elementary school, and in 1959 the students obtained a favorable court ruling. The school board, nonplussed, promptly merged the white school with a black school, transferred all white students from the school, and altered district lines so that the combined school became an all-black school. The board successfully explained to the court that the issue was moot since, physically, the black students were now enrolled in the school to which they had applied.

Eventually, the school board opened Greensboro's white public schools to six black children. Greensboro and most other Southern cities were able to maintain this tokenism through careful and rigorous review of transfer applications, provisions enabling whites to transfer from schools where blacks were enrolling, and the general intimidating aspect of submitting blacks to probing personal interviews and lengthy application procedures. Greensboro's leaders justified such tactics by lamenting that they were necessary to avoid an uprising of lower-class whites and a regression in race progress. Privately, of course, Greensboro's elite were considerably less concerned about the impact of retribution on blacks than upon themselves. By controlling, if not eliminating desegregation, the leaders were demonstrating their worthiness, indeed their indispensability, as leaders.

The Civil War disrupted Southern institutions and resulted in the subservience and humiliation of the South. Segregation, as the major institution guiding race relations (and therefore the order and safety of society) was under attack and Southerners, remembering their past, were in no mood to surrender again.

Massive Resistance and the Mind of the South

The phrase "massive resistance" that writers have employed to characterize Southerners' defense of the homeland connotes a widespread mobilization of forces in the region to block racial change. Pat Watters of the Southern Regional Council recalled that at this time "It was a frightening thing to go into a small city and to realize that not merely the semi-literate poor white gas station attendant, but also the bankers, the mayor, the editor, even some of the preachers, all those who are personages in such a place supported it [resistance] fervently." Even in Washington, Southern congressmen and senators heretofore embarrassed by the demagoguery of a few of their regional colleagues assumed the pose of massive resistance, some moved by conviction, but more by the intense pressure to conform, or become social and political outcasts.

Southern lawmakers led by Virginia Senator Harry F. Byrd and Richard B. Russell of Georgia issued a "Declaration of

Constitutional Principles" on March 12, 1956. The entire congressional delegations of Alabama, Arkansas, Georgia, Mississippi, Louisiana, South Carolina, and Virginia signed the document with only three Southern senators and twenty-four congressmen refusing to sign. The "Declaration" was a well-reasoned if somewhat exaggerated legal argument in the tradition of John C. Calhoun. The 101 signees insisted that, according to the Court's own precedent, the *Brown* ruling was "contrary to the Constitution," and that the Justices had "substituted their personal political and social ideas for the established law of the land." The legislators claimed that as a result of the Court's precipitant decision "outside agitators are threatening immediate and revolutionary changes in our public school systems," and they concluded with the hope that these "meddlers" would not provoke the Southern people to lawless acts. Historians point to this "Southern Manifesto," as the document came to be known more popularly, as the official opening salvo of massive resistance. Actually, the lawmakers' colleagues back home had already mobilized resistance against *Brown* and any subsequent movements toward racial accommodation.

The White Citizens' Council was the primary apparatus for rallying and disciplining Southern whites to the cause. The group originated in Mississippi under the leadership of Robert Patterson, a veteran of World War II and a prosperous farmer. The idea behind the council was to gather the leading citizens of a community and utilize their expertise, financial clout, and prestige to maintain the racial status quo. The group eschewed violence and took great pains to distance itself from the Ku Klux Klan, though membership lists overlapped frequently, and some referred to the council as "the uptown Klan." When the organization first surfaced late in 1954, in fact, several Southern journalists alleged this connection. Though admitting that violence was not a part of council repertoire, these observers felt that the economic pressure members exercised on blacks as well as upon dissenting whites was just as insidious. As the Montgomery *Advertiser* put it bluntly, "The manicured Kluxism of these White Citizens' Councils is rash, indecent, and vicious. . . . The night-riding and lash of the 1920s have become an abomination in the eyes of public opinion. So the bigots have resorted to a more decorous, tidy and less conspicuous method—economic thuggery."

By the following year—1955—the councils were no longer easy targets. From a small membership base in Mississippi they had grown to hundreds of chapters throughout the region. Fourteen months after the *Advertiser*'s biting editorial, the councils held a large rally attended by 15,000 people in a Montgomery arena. Preachers, politicians, and regional council officers exhorted the crowd to unity and action. Reporter John Bartlow Martin wrote that "It was a political convention and an old fashioned revival all mixed in one big pot." That the pot frequently boiled over was evidenced by the frenzied shouts and applause that greeted every avowal of resistance to integration. Just as the crowd peaked to a fever pitch, a highway patrol car screeched to a halt and disgorged the guest of honor, Mississippi Senator James O. Eastland, a sight that touched off a series of rebel yells and near pandemonium. A local reporter captured the scene: "The flags, the intoxicating popcorn odors and an atmosphere of march music and 'Dixie' renditions did something to this cheering, enthusiastic crowd." The *Advertiser* editorials fell silent and never again printed an adverse word about the council.

In fact, the entire South fell silent as the council and similar groups of community leaders effectively stifled dissent. "Big Jim" Folsom, Alabama's fearless beacon of hope, retreated and promised with uncharacteristic obtuseness, "We ain't going to force our fine colored folks to go to school with white people." Newspapers that had once expressed support for compliance now assumed an obstructionist stance or said nothing at all. Even Ralph McGill, the editorial conscience of the region, back-pedaled and seemed more comfortable discussing the soybean revolution than commenting on civil rights. "I don't know anybody that's demanding integration," he explained defensively in 1957, adding that "a person would be a fool to demand integration now in the Deep South."

To speak out, to resist the inexorable conformity, was to invite an excommunication from the cultural clan; and, if isolation were not sufficient punishment, loss of job or business, or maybe even life, were always possibilities as the whirlwind raged. Willie Morris recounted the formation of a White Citizens' Council in his hometown of Yazoo City, Mississippi. The general sentiment at the meeting was to fire blacks who were in any way involved in school desegregation or NAACP activities. If these blacks rented homes, white landlords would evict them; white grocers would refuse to sell food to them; and black grocers would be denied privileges from wholesalers. Morris recalled that, at that point, a gentleman in the back of the audience stood up and stated that "I agree with everything that's been said and with everything we're trying to do . . . but, gentlemen, . . . all this is unconstitutional." The crowd promptly shouted him down and prevented him from continuing his comments. Morris admitted that "For a brief moment I was tempted to stand up and support my neighbor, but I lacked the elemental courage to go against that mob. For it *was* a mob."

And the dangers from that mob went considerably beyond abridging the right of free speech. There was the case of Reverend Robert B. McNeill of Columbus, Georgia. In May 1957, the Alabama-born Presbyterian minister published an article in *Look* magazine advocating interracial dialogue as a means of restoring racial harmony in the region and discharging Christian duty. Further, while he disavowed sexual and social mixing of the races, he urged whites to share the administration of community affairs with blacks. The suggestions were hardly revolutionary—some form of organized interracial dialogue had occurred in the region since at least 1919, and blacks held political power, however modest, in places as diverse as Montgomery and Atlanta. At the time the article appeared, however, moderation had fled the region. As Georgia segregationist Roy V. Harris explained, "Moderation means gradualism, and gradualism means race mixing." For Harris there was to be no "fence-straddling." He declared that "If you're a white man, then it's time to stand up with us, or black your face and get on the other side." The Jackson (Mississippi) *Daily News* was more specific as to the offenses of moderation and warned readers not to listen to "the twaddle being talked by wishy-washy people who prate about 'academic freedom,' and 'freedom of thought and of speech,' and similar nonsense. Puny parsons who prattle imbecilic propaganda in pulpits about obedience to the Supreme Court segregation decision being a 'manifestation of the Christian spirit' ought to have their pulpits kicked from under them and their tongues silenced. . . . In this fight you are either for us or against us. There is no middle ground."

Reverend McNeill had undoubtedly trod the "middle ground," and for his outspokenness his parishioners were going to follow the *Daily News*' advice. As he was losing his pulpit, Rev. McNeill suffered a heart attack, leaving some of the more adamant opponents in his former congregation to remark that the Lord finally had "taken care of him." They vowed to "find a preacher with the right kind of religion." As the minister analyzed his fate, he expressed with considerable sadness and some bewilderment what religion had become behind parts of the "cotton curtain" in the late 1950s: "It had never occurred to me that for so many people the church was the building, the meeting with old friends, . . . and that Christ meant little, if anything."

For those Southern whites inclined to sense the wrongness of the situation, the pressure to remain silent was less dramatic, but as thoroughly effective. Yale psychiatrist Robert Coles told the story of a doctor in a small Virginia town in 1959 who contemplated the prospect of joining a human relations council to engage in the type of dialogue Rev. McNeill promoted in his magazine essay. Though he was merely thinking about such action, his patients somehow discovered this and threatened to leave him. As the doctor's son recalled, "Several patients said that if my father was called an integrationist, they would deny ever having known him." The doctor did not join the council, and, indeed, he resigned from the town board of health and generally withdrew from political life in the community. Fear had become the currency of the South and the leaders accumulated considerable capital. "The white people of the South are afraid of everyone," a student at Chapel Hill explained, "the Negro, outsiders, the government in Washington, the Klan, students, . . . but most of all, one another. They're constantly trying to figure out what the people next door think—and they're afraid to find out what they themselves think."

Race was consuming the white South. Basic American freedoms were no longer theirs. The steel cage had snapped shut on the white Southern mind. There were now indeed enemies everywhere—from without and from within, others and even oneself. The only solution was to plunge to the depths, maintain the prison of the mind and the blindness of the heart, ignore the beauty of their religion and the humanity of each other, black and white. It was a dark, cold, and empty existence punctuated by war whoops and the occasional rumblings of conscience. But redemption was soon at hand. As Aeschylus wrote, "Against our will and in our own despite, wisdom comes to us by the awful grace of God." And so it would.

CHAPTER THREE

Passive Resistance and Direct Action: The Road from Montgomery, 1955–1965

Montgomery was as likely a place as any for the start of racial redemption, though, in truth, that movement began in slavery times with the first runaway, the first fired tobacco barn, the first lesson to the master that, contrary to his belief, the oppressed wanted desperately to join the society of free men, regardless of the hardships that entailed. Southerners read their Bibles—perhaps that was all they read—and understood that the children of Israel were relatively comfortable in their Egyptian captivity, and that they surrendered that certainty for a hazardous journey whose conclusion knew no time frame or boundaries of distance, guided only by faith and leaders who held doubts as well. White Southerners would make the connection and it would be painful, the only difference being that the pilgrimage would be metaphorical and would include both oppressed and oppressor, and would end where it began, for this was the promised land.

Montgomery was an attractive Southern city, the former capital of the Confederacy, that now served a more modest role as Alabama's administrative center, a place with the requisite amount of Greek revival without being overbearing. The city was a bit frayed at its edges, especially the edges where blacks resided. Yet, as with most Southern cities, the trees, the smell of jasmine and honeysuckle, and the fulfilling spiritual life for both blacks and whites covered up the unpleasantness, at least for the time being. It was not a sleepy town—the machinery of state government whirred and coughed and spun, creating sufficient noise to impart a semblance of activity to the capital. In the summer, when everything hung in a humid haze, the city's pace was more like suspension than sleep, because sleep implies a state of placid and comfortable rest, and summers in Montgomery, with their violent thunderstorms and melting heat, were hardly placid and comfortable. But nature provided the only show in July and August, the legislature being the local spectacle most of the rest of the time, except when "Big Jim," the philandering governor, wandered out of his office.

The setting was attractive and remote enough for a young doctoral student from Boston University's Divinity School to accept the pastorate of the Dexter Avenue Baptist Church, which stood directly across from the Capitol, where the Confederate flag luffed lazily in the occasional breeze atop the domed structure. The rhythms of Montgomery life might have seemed excruciatingly slow for the urbane minister, who grew up in Atlanta and attended schools in Philadelphia and Boston, but this was precisely the situation he sought; a nice quiet place in which to gain some experience and complete his doctoral dissertation. When he arrived in Montgomery in the summer of 1954, there was every indication that the place would be a good, if uneventful, staging area for a prominent career in the ministry, following his father's example. But that would change.

The Montgomery Bus Boycott

It was understandable if the readers of the Montgomery *Advertiser* on the morning of December 2, 1955, skipped or merely shrugged over a headline buried on a back page: "Negro Jailed Here for 'Overlooking' Bus Segregation." It was not the first time a frustrated black Montgomerian had "overlooked" the etiquette of the biracial society, nor was it likely to be the last. Perhaps the *Brown* decision had given black citizens some strange notions, but like locusts, these ideas would flutter, make noise, and then go away for awhile. But this time was different.

The Negro in the headline was a forty-two-year-old seamstress at a downtown department store, Rosa Parks. Mrs. Parks's occupation belied her educational background and reflected the limited opportunities for talented blacks in the postwar South. She had attended the laboratory school of Alabama State College in Montgomery and became one of the city's few black high school graduates. Perhaps because of the frustrating gap between her intellectual abilities and her employment, and perhaps because of the hope emerging from World War II, she joined the NAACP in 1945 and in the ensuing decade became an active and valuable member of that organization. In the summer before the bus incident, the local leadership of the NAACP selected her to attend the Highlander Folk School in east Tennessee to experience a unique experiment in interracial living. The school was a revelation for Parks, who, like most blacks in Montgomery, had only cursory contacts with whites and always within the framework of segregation. Now she saw the possibilities of an integrated society, the shared culture of black and white Southerners, and she returned to segregated Montgomery renewed and anxious to do something.

The situation on the city's privately owned bus system provided that opportunity. The code of segregation relegated blacks to the back of the bus, but the line dividing black from white passengers was rarely stable. That is, if the white section filled up, boarding whites could then displace blacks until, if necessary, whites occupied every seat in the bus and blacks stood. The bus driver controlled the arrangement, and he frequently carried out this duty bluntly and even insultingly. In addition, blacks who paid their fares at the front of the bus sometimes were ordered to debark and reenter from the rear door. On occasion, the black, so ordered, would arrive at the rear door only to have the driver pull away from the curb, having pocketed the erstwhile passenger's fare. The system was capricious, confusing, and frequently humiliating.

So on December 1, 1955, Rosa Parks said no. The bus driver, playing his expected role, stopped his bus and called over a policeman who, according to the script, arrested Parks for disobeying the driver's directive and hence violating the city's segregation statute. The matter might have concluded there were it not for Rosa Parks's status within the black community and the determined efforts of a black women's group, the Women's Political Council, headed by Jo Ann Robinson, an instructor at Alabama State College. Robinson and her organization issued a call for a bus boycott beginning on December 5, a call supported by local NAACP leader E. D. Nixon. Thus began an exercise in passive civil disobedience that was to last for 381 days. The objective of the boycotters was merely to clarify the segregation policy on city buses, *not* to eliminate it.

The boycott, to be successful, required an organization to direct it that would encompass all of the disparate elements within the city's black community as well as a leader who commanded the respect and, equally important, had not earned the enmity of major black leaders. Martin Luther King, Jr., the young doctoral student, possessed the political qualifications for this role. Moreover, in his brief time in the city he had earned a reputation as an articulate, intelligent young man, independent of, yet capable of dealing with, the local white power structure. The new organization he led, the Montgomery Improvement Association, assumed responsibility for all boycott strategy and negotiation with white leaders.

In a by-now familiar scenario, the boycott and the racial issues raised by it became enmeshed in local politics. Blacks had enjoyed voting privileges in Montgomery and had utilized the franchise to secure modest gains for the black community. Just prior to the boycott, the city experienced a heated election campaign for a seat on the City Commission in which the role of black political power became a major issue. During the campaign, E. D. Nixon submitted a questionnaire to candidates, seeking their positions on a range of black grievances, including the segregated bus system, discrimination in hiring for municipal employment, the absence of middle-class black residential subdivisions, and inadequate services in black neighborhoods. Two of the three candidates for this one position acknowledged the legitimacy of Nixon's contentions and issued assurances that, if elected, they would consider these matters carefully. One of the candidates, Dave Birmingham, a Folsom protegé, was the incumbent and had, during his term, championed black causes and succeeded in securing the hiring of four black policemen. Another candidate, James Stearns, sought to split the black vote, figuring that most whites would eschew the brashly liberal Birmingham, and thereby secure victory in the primary. The third candidate, Clyde Sellers, took a different tack.

Since World War II, Montgomery and many other Southern cities had received a significant influx of rural whites, many of them poor and unskilled. In 1940, the city was 55 percent white and 45 percent black; by 1955, 63 percent of Montgomery's citizens were white, 37 percent were black. Sellers resided in the well-to-do area of South Montgomery, so he could count on some support from his home base. The rural newcomers resided, primarily, in the eastern part of town, and they had been attracted to Birmingham's populist rhetoric. Sellers, however, saw an opportunity to win this working-class vote away from Birmingham while retaining white support in his district. And if Stearns and Birmingham split the black vote, this would ensure victory for Sellers. The mechanism for effecting this result was race, and Sellers launched a virulent campaign that depicted his two rivals as deferential to blacks and blacks themselves as stopping at nothing short of racial amalgamation. Sellers's strategy was successful; he gained a small plurality in the primary and avoided a run-off when his nearest challenger, Birmingham, was forced to withdraw due to ill health.

Thus, by the time the boycott began, there existed a volatility in race relations that Montgomery had not experienced since the days of the Ku Klux Klan in the 1920s. In this unpromising atmosphere, it would have been impolitic for the moderate mayor and the two other commissioners to grant the modest concessions sought by King and his group. In addition, Sellers used the boycott to inflate his own political reputation as racial tensions heightened. Membership in the White Citizens' Council doubled in February 1956 from 6,000 to 12,000. Included in that number were the mayor and another commissioner besides Sellers. Scattered acts of violence, including a dynamite blast in King's home that narrowly missed injuring his wife and daughter, and legal maneuvers by local officials to ban assemblages, prohibit blacks from congregating on corners to accept rides from car pools, and even outlaw the pools themselves, moved King to file suit challenging the constitutionality of bus segregation, thereby escalating the stakes in the conflict.

Eventually, the Supreme Court determined the outcome of the struggle, as the white community successfully stared down the boycott without conceding anything. In fact, white leaders were in the process of mobilizing the court system to enjoin the boycott and its leaders, which might have occurred had it not been for the Supreme Court's timely announcement, just before Thanksgiving Day, 1956, that segregation of the races on Montgomery's buses violated the Constitution.

The boycott was a learning experience for King, a lesson he would take with him to his newly formed civil rights organization, the Southern Christian Leadership Conference (SCLC). The Montgomery Improvement Association had submitted relatively modest demands to the city's white leadership, which rejected them out of hand. The protesters cited similar accommodations in Mobile and other Southern cities to underscore the conservative nature of their requests, but these examples were, in fact, irrelevant. The political capital gained by rejection of black demands, the ensuing storm of white public opinion against conciliation, and the further encouragement given to official intransigence transformed a relatively mild racial adjustment into a perceived direct assault on segregation and the Southern way of life. The lesson here was that any attempt to improve race relations, even by minor increments within the framework of segregation, was a questionable strategy at best. Ironically, the chances of success increased with an escalation of objectives.

The boycott also belied the Southern white proverb that Southerners, black and white, were capable of adjudicating their differences without recourse to outside authorities. The unwillingness of white leaders to participate in a dialogue, indeed the negative political ramifications of sitting down with blacks, left black leaders with little choice but to seek external relief, which they found in the court system. As the boycott's leading chronicler, J. Mills Thornton III, has noted, "the South did not possess within itself the capacity to save itself."

But the court system involved a long, arduous, and expensive process. After the initial rush of public attention and sporadic violence, the boycott elicited less and less national media coverage. As white Montgomerians eventually came to ignore the boycott, so did most citizens elsewhere. The newsworthiness and video depictions of mostly empty buses lurching through Montgomery streets waned quickly. The drama was gone.

Perhaps the most positive result of the boycott, in the long run, was the opportunity it offered Martin Luther King, Jr., to test his graduate school theories on dealing with injustice. The boycott and the events surrounding it added a leaven of reality to his ideals. For King, the essence of protest was nonviolence, a position he derived not so much from Gandhi, but from Christianity. The words love, compassion, redemption, and grace comprised the vocabulary of King's Christian vision. In this philosophical rhetoric, he separated the sin from the sinner, believing that the former, not the latter, became the target of exorcism, and the means of this expiation was nonviolent protest. And through this individual salvation, the races and the region would attain redemption.

In all of this, King was not only Christian, but also Southern. The white South understood his message, understood when he said suffering was redemptive, and perhaps the violence of their reactions attested to the depths to which King's rhetoric and actions had plunged into the Southern white soul, dredging up guilt and confusion. For here was a Southerner—King—who not only preached the gospel of evangelical Christianity, but acted upon it as well, thus breaching the gap between preachment and behavior, spiritual and temporal.

Above all, the emergence of King and his developing philosophy from a Deep South city, Montgomery, meant that a movement directed and inspired by him would be inherently conservative, appealing to Christian principles familiar to black and white Southerners, precepts that were parts of their daily lives. King's call was a call for restoration, for redemption, not for radical change. He would demonstrate that white supremacy and Southernness were not inextricably linked, that white Southerners could discard their racial perceptions, their interpretation of history, and still remain loyal Southerners. Slavery and then segregation were temptations to which white Southerners had succumbed and from which they required liberation to attain their true Southern kingdom. Frederick Douglass stated the issue succinctly a century before King: "The struggle for freedom is a struggle to save black men's bodies and white men's souls."

Nor was it a coincidence that King, a Baptist minister and a Southerner, assumed the leadership of a heretofore diffuse and sporadic civil rights movement. Black leadership, at least since the death of Booker T. Washington in 1915, was centered in the North—the NAACP in New York, and spokesmen such as W. E. B. DuBois and Marcus Garvey, and cultural leaders such as Claude McKay, Richard Wright, and Ralph Ellison, who resided in the South at one time or another, but who spent their most productive periods in Chicago or New York. King and the SCLC represented the first major black leadership shift southward in nearly half a century. They also reflected the centrality of religion and of the minister to the incipient struggle for racial equality. The black minister was relatively independent of the white community. His educational and oratorical abilities were likely to attract a large following. Moreover, the black church occupied a central role in the black community: an institution sequestered from white domination, where members occupied and played out roles of their own choosing and interpreted life here and in the hereafter as they wished. As a place where blacks came together, the Southern church was a natural catalyst in mobilizing black Southerners for the cause of racial justice, despite the long and dangerous odds. Religion was an excellent recruitment tool.

But white Southerners did not walk chastened to the altar to profess their renewed Christian spirit, at least in the blacks' definition of Christian salvation. The eventual desegregation of Montgomery's bus system, even more than the *Brown* decision, galvanized Southern blacks, for here was a tangible result, not merely rhetoric and good intentions. Accordingly, they stepped up their legal assaults on all aspects of segregated Southern society. Just as this acceleration of purpose caused white leaders to sound the alarm to fellow whites for the necessity of concerted thought and action, so too did it provoke retaliation against blacks. And here the white response was apt to be swift and violent, for whites acted not only out of fear that their world was being threatened with extinction, but also with a sense of betrayal, an attitude of "Et tu Sambo?"

Journalist Dan Wakefield, sampling white opinion during the Montgomery bus boycott, discovered that the action "increased the mistrust and hatred" of blacks by whites, particularly for devaluing, if not destroying, the historical myth of benign race relations and contented blacks. There was an understandable wistfulness in South Carolina segregationist William D. Workman, Jr.'s complaint in 1959 that court orders and government edicts have erected "artificial barriers" between the races in the South, where heretofore existed "intimate . . . person-to-person relationships." Blacks were not, of course, repentant at the sundering of such intimacy. As James McBride Dabbs explained in 1959: "The Negroes . . . don't feel too keenly the ending of a peace that had been forced upon them. And it is being ended mainly because the Negroes don't care any longer to be loved by the whites. This naturally makes the whites angry."

Whites expressed their anger through emotional and economic pressures on movement participants and, ultimately through violence. The Ku Klux Klan, a moribund band of sheeted misfits in the late 1940s, was revived and active a decade later. Lynching, rarely practiced by the early 1950s, became a more common expression of white hostility after 1954. Other expressions of violence were evident: The Rev. George W. Lee of Belzoni, Mississippi, murdered in May 1955 for attempting to register blacks to vote; Lamar Smith, gunned down in broad daylight in Brookhaven, Mississippi, that same year for the same offense; and Emmett Till, a fourteen-year-old black Mississippi boy, beaten to death and dumped into the Tallahatchie River for allegedly whistling at a white woman in a store. And on Labor Day, 1957, six white men abducted Edward Aaron, a thirty-four-year-old black veteran, from a Birmingham, Alabama, suburb, emasculated him with a razor blade, dressed the wound with turpentine, and left him lying on the side of the road, where he bled to death. This was merely the beginning of an orgy of unpunished violence, blunt notices to whites and blacks to stay in their places.

But blacks, at least, pushed on; once embarked on the road to redemption, there was no turning back to an ignominious past. For death was not the worst fate. "If a man hasn't found something he will die for," Martin Luther King observed, "he isn't fit to live." Like the Confederate soldier, blacks willingly entered the valley of death armed with the faith and righteousness of their cause, though hopelessly outnumbered by a cold and calculating enemy. And like the Confederate soldier, they frequently entered the battle with their addresses pinned on their backs. And, like Grant or Sherman, the white South would occasionally express grudging admiration for the tenacity and courage of their hapless foes before they torched their dreams and extinguished their hopes.

The Sit-Ins

For younger Southern blacks, who were more urban, better educated, and less willing to tolerate the frustrations and humiliations of a biracial society than their parents or grandparents, it became apparent by 1960 that the segregationists would not concede a particle of territory, that the so-called white moderate or liberal had gone underground or joined forces with the other side, and that legal maneuvers cut two ways. Such were the conclusions of four black college students sitting in a dormitory room at North Carolina A&T College, an all-black institution in Greensboro, on the night of January 31, 1960. Earlier that day, one of the students, Joseph McNeill, had attempted unsuccessfully to order a meal at the city's segregated bus terminal. McNeill discussed the incident with three of his classmates at A&T, Ezell Blair, Jr., David Richmond, and Franklin McCain. As the night wore on into the early morning hours, they drew courage and frustration from one another and resolved to go downtown and request service at Woolworth's lunch counter. The idea was not a novel one: CORE had utilized the tactic twenty years earlier in Chicago, and sporadic demonstrations had occurred in several Oklahoma cities in 1958 and in Miami in 1959. But these were scarcely publicized, isolated incidents on the South's periphery. The four students, neatly attired, entered the Woolworth store as planned, purchased a few sundries, sat down at the lunch counter, and politely requested service; they received a large portion of history instead.

The time, the location, the self-effacing manner of the students—whatever the catalyst, their simple request touched off an avalanche of similar demonstrations. Within weeks, the sit-ins had spread to fifty-four cities in nine Southern states, and would continue to gather momentum until the segregation and the inferiority implied by it was buried. The movement elicited a sympathetic response from some white university students, who frequently joined blacks in the sit-ins. The students of both races represented a new generation of Southerners anxious to get on with the future and impatient with the preposterous etiquette of segregation that permitted blacks to purchase toothpaste, but not a soft drink. The University of North Carolina's *Daily Tar Heel* expressed support by declaring: "We hope they win. We hope they win *Big*."

The sit-ins exposed the moral nature of the civil rights struggle, and it was to this issue that whites responded so positively. Of course, morality had been there all along, but the boycotts, court orders, and endless litigation obscured the basically religious quality of black aspirations. And, in a deeply religious region, this could not fail to strike the consciences of black and white alike. "Here we have faith," James McBride Dabbs observed about the sit-ins, "that if men are patient God will reward them; if men will suffer for a cause, God will use their sufferings." For Dabbs, the great appeal of the sit-ins was that they accomplished "the fusion of personal faith and social justice, which the South had never been able to make," while demonstrating "a new religious attitude expressed in the best manners of the South." So the sit-ins, with their intensely religious framework and their emphasis on Southern civility, appealed to the very regional culture that spawned the evils from which they now sought release.

While segregation offered comforting stability for Southern whites besieged by a multitude of changes after World War II, it also burdened them by making them restrict emotions, wink at injustice, and numb themselves to the obvious depredations of the institution. Nearly all Southerners, Ralph McGill claimed, save "the most obtuse and insensitive have long carried a private weight of guilt about the inequities of segregation." Indeed, the sit-ins generated an outpouring of relief from white liberals. The editors of the Greensboro *Daily News* wrote, a few days after the initial demonstration, in terms hardly possible just a month or even a week earlier, "There are many white people in the South who recognize the injustice of the lunch counter system. It is based on circumstances which may have made sense one hundred years ago; today it has a touch of medievalism. It smacks of India's 'untouchables' or Hitlerian Germany's Master Race Theories."

The sit-ins released a great moral energy into the region, touching whites, who were after all the targets of this lesson in Judeo-Christian principles, but also energizing blacks, though in different ways. The sit-ins differed from such earlier tactics as boycotts and litigation in that the demonstrators were now taking direct action, forcing whites either to act out their racial fantasies or to acknowledge sin. Demonstrators were engaged, perhaps for the first time in their young lives, in control over their own destinies. Though avowedly nonviolent, the sit-ins were confrontational, by their nature establishing and demanding the equality of black and white, an assertion heretofore confined to courtrooms or in statements to the press. Here was no rhetoric, however; here was action, a language understood by all Southerners. Above all, the sit-ins made blacks visible. No longer could whites ignore them or categorize them or assume their inferiority; some would do so, of course, but the sit-ins would generate a jarring contradiction between belief and reality, a conflict resolved only by acknowledging the reality or by plunging deeper into fantasy. In essence, the sit-ins legitimized the manhood and womanhood of Southern blacks. As Franklin McCain, one of the original quartet in the first Greensboro sit-in, explained his feelings on that crisp February day: "I probably felt better that day than I've ever felt in my life. I felt as though I had gained my manhood, so to speak, and not only gained it, but had developed quite a lot of respect for it." After a year of sit-ins, *Ebony* magazine made the sentiment universal: "Gone is his [the black man's] celebrated patience, his childlike obedience, and his colossal fear. He has waited 98 years. . . . The day he stopped being a good old Negro was the day he became a man."

This called for a major adjustment on the part of Southern whites, an adjustment their leaders had promised they would never have to make. Touching a Christian conscience was uncomfortable enough for a people bathed in the blood, but recasting basic historical premises about blacks involved a wrenching reassessment of assumptions imbibed by white Southerners since birth, and so ingrained as to be akin to reflex. While some white Southerners breathed a collective sigh of relief at the solution proffered by blacks to their internal dilemma, others reacted violently.

But most whites were not quite certain how to react. The regional culture was very specific on the appropriate response to racial transgression, but the nonviolent, almost passive, and always moral behavior of the demonstrators fell into a different category from sullying white womanhood or attempting to cast a ballot. And when blacks responded to the heckling and the physical abuse by not responding at all or by praying or singing, this was a further digression from the regional script. As black novelist Ernest J. Gaines described a confrontation between the sheriff of a small town in Louisiana and black protesters, "He [the sheriff] had already used his only little knowledge he knowed how to deal with black folks—knocking them around. When that didn't change a thing, when people started getting in line to be knocked around, he didn't know what else to do."

Almost forgotten amid the changing roles of blacks and whites in Southern society was the fulfillment of sit-in objectives. The results were mixed. Greensboro succumbed to the pressure in six months and desegregated its lunch counters, but little else; Charlotte reached a broad accommodation for most public places the following year; desegregation of public places in Atlanta occurred piecemeal beginning in 1960; and in cities in Alabama and Mississippi, integration for the most part would not occur until the passage of the 1964 Civil Rights Act. But as with the Montgomery bus boycott, whose immediate results were meager, the long-range benefits of the sit-ins were significant. The sit-ins provided excellent training grounds for a new generation of blacks. The lunch counter was only one target in an array of segregated facilities, and direct action campaigns soon spread to other areas. A new organization emerged to coordinate, organize, and fund this comprehensive assault on the biracial society, the Student Nonviolent Coordinating Committee (SNCC), formed in May 1960 at a meeting convened in Atlanta by former NAACP official Ella Baker, but consisting primarily of students impatient with King's Southern Christian Leadership Conference and the older, Northern-based NAACP and CORE. Marion Berry, a young militant activist from Nashville (and later Mayor of Washington, D.C.) became the group's first chairman.

The new organization, representing a different constituency from the other groups—younger, more militant, and less tied to traditional Southern black institutions such as the church—intensified the competition within the black community for the mass of as-yet unorganized blacks, for foundation support, for media attention, and for developing innovative programs. Initially, such competition was mostly healthy, but ultimately it would fragment the Southern black community and diffuse the civil rights effort.

The Freedom Rides

Flushed with the confidence of manhood and righteousness generated by the sit-ins and goaded by organizational rivalry, Southern blacks accelerated the pace of protest. While the sit-ins were sweeping the region, CORE leadership thought the time was propitious to resurrect a project that had achieved some token success in 1947, but little publicity. That year, CORE sponsored a small interracial group comprised mainly of Northerners to travel on Greyhound buses to twenty-six locations in the upper South, testing the seating arrangements on those vehicles along the way. On journeys to twenty of the cities in Virginia, North Carolina, Tennessee, and Kentucky, the tests went off successfully without incident; at five of the remaining six cities, police quietly arrested the riders and soon released them. At only one stop—in Chapel Hill, North Carolina—did violence erupt, though local authorities quelled the disturbance quickly. Most white passengers shrugged off the demonstration and, in fact, the media generally ignored the riders and their objectives. This Journey of Reconciliation, as CORE leaders termed the protest, accomplished no lasting result except indicating that whites were generally unprepared or indifferent in the upper South in the optimistic year of 1947 to confront a small group of obviously eccentric, misguided Yankees. Besides, segregation on Greyhound buses was just as rigid after the Journey as before.

But the Journey was helpful as a model when CORE dusted off the concept fourteen years later. This time, however, buoyed by the spirit of the sit-ins, black leaders hoped to extend the idea to the entire South and to desegregate not only the buses, but terminal facilities as well. Also, in January 1961, the Supreme Court had ruled in *Boynton* v. *Virginia* that segregation at bus terminals catering to interstate travel was unconstitutional, thus extending the Court's 1946 decision in *Morgan* v. *Virginia* that prohibited segregated seating on interstate buses, a ruling that had prompted the Journey of Reconciliation.

So on May 4, 1961, two interracial groups left Washington, D.C., to begin the Freedom Rides into the South. Though CORE was headquartered in Chicago, its new leader, James Farmer, had roots in the South and had studied for the ministry at Howard University in Washington. During the 1940s, he became acquainted with fellow Christian activists, Aubrey Williams and James Dombrowski, so he was familiar with both the social and religious milieu of the South. The Freedom Rides, like the sit-ins, were to be examples of Christian witness.

The two groups traveled through Virginia and North Carolina, and except for one arrest in Charlotte, there were no incidents. In fact, at most stops in those two states, terminal managers had already removed the "For Colored" and "For Whites" signs from the premises. The first indication of the troubles to come occurred just across the North Carolina line in Rock Hill, South Carolina, when several white youths assaulted black freedom rider John Lewis as he attempted to enter the white waiting room. Police intervened, however, and though they made no arrests for the assault, they escorted the freedom rider into the white waiting room. The buses then traveled through South Carolina and Georgia to Atlanta, integrating facilities along the way unmolested. All things considered, the Freedom Rides were going remarkably smoothly. But Alabama and Mississippi lay ahead.

The tolerance of the Folsom days had long since dissipated in Alabama as political leaders fell over themselves to convince constituents of their purity on the race issue. As rhetoric reached and exceeded the extreme, some Alabama whites were prepared to extend a peculiar hospitality to the invaders. The buses had separated leaving Atlanta, the Greyhound bus heading for Anniston, an industrial city in the Alabama Piedmont, and the Trailways bus destined for Birmingham. In Anniston, as the Greyhound bus arrived, a group of whites attacked the bus with a variety of implements, including clubs and iron bars, though when the police appeared, the bus limped out of town, the passengers shaken but unhurt. About six miles outside of Anniston, however, the bus tires went flat, and trailing whites, like sharks circling a stricken ship, closed in on their defenseless prey. An incendiary bomb crashed through one of the bus windows, and exiting passengers, reeling from smoke and flying glass, were randomly clubbed by the mob and were saved only by the timely arrival of an armed caravan of cars from Birmingham, organized by a foresighted King aide, the Rev. Fred Shuttlesworth. An era of legal parrying and polite demonstration was merging into a more confrontational period when nonviolence was approaching its limit as a tactic of black resistance.

The welcome in Birmingham for the Trailways contingent from Atlanta was equally violent on Mother's Day, 1961. The riders sensed trouble when they noticed approximately forty whites lining the loading platform as the bus turned into its bay. There were no policemen in sight, in fact no one else save a few reporters. The whites attacked the passengers, beating them severely, injuring nine seriously, only two of whom were freedom riders. As if on cue, after twenty minutes of one-sided brutality, the police arrived and simultaneously the white attackers, many with Klan connections, fled unhindered. When a reporter asked Commissioner Eugene "Bull" Connor why he had not deployed his police force earlier, since a confrontation was likely, Connor replied that the officers were visiting their mothers.

In the meantime, Alabama Governor John Patterson announced that he could not guarantee the safety of the "rabble-rousers"—the freedom riders—and suggested that they abort their plan to continue on to Montgomery. The Justice Department, by now alarmed at what was becoming a media event, airlifted the group to New Orleans and relative safety. The Freedom Ride would have been over then and there were it not for the more militant SNCC leadership's persistence in completing the mission. Reassembling in Birmingham on May 20, six days after the Mother's Day debacle and freshened by new recruits from their headquarters in Atlanta, the freedom riders, now under SNCC sponsorship, embarked for Montgomery. They arrived amid the same eerie quiet that initially greeted their entry into Birmingham, and the result was the same. As SNCC leader John Lewis recalled, "We stepped off the bus and . . . people just started pouring out . . . from all over the place," inflicting heavy blows on the riders, and sending Lewis to the hospital with a brain concussion. But the mob had miscalculated. President Kennedy, moved by a rising public aversion to the violence and concerned about the safety of the riders in Montgomery, had dispatched Civil Rights Division attorney John Doar to the Alabama capital, as well as John Seigenthaler from the Justice Department to serve as a liaison between the president and Governor Patterson.

As the riot proceeded in full view of Doar, he grabbed a pay phone and placed a call to the attorney general in Washington, providing a detailed account of what he was witnessing. Meanwhile, Seigenthaler was helping an injured woman, clubbed by one of the mob, into his car to rush her to the hospital. Whites surrounded him and though (or perhaps because) he identified himself as a federal agent, he was beaten to unconsciousness and left lying on the sidewalk for twenty-five minutes before police took him to the hospital.

The orgy in Montgomery and the earlier violence in Birmingham made national headlines and were lead stories on television newscasts. The nation was repulsed and President Kennedy acted, ordering National Guardsmen to protect the remnants of the riders as they made the final leg of their journey to Jackson, Mississippi. The Freedom Ride concluded uneventfully in Jackson with the arrest of the riders, an arrangement Senator Eastland insisted upon in exchange for a guarantee of no violence. Finally, on September 22, the Interstate Commerce Commission ordered an end to racial discrimination in all interstate facilities and a total removal of signs to that effect. The freedom riders had achieved their objective.

Though the Freedom Rides were logical extensions of the sit-in demonstrations begun a few months earlier (and, in fact, were eventually completed under SNCC auspices), they differed significantly from the lunch counter demonstrations both in the degree of violence generated and in the fulfillment of initial goals. Physical attacks against the sit-in students were sporadic and seldom brutal; desegregation of eating facilities was also sporadic and rarely occurred immediately. Typically, a series of demonstrations over weeks, sometimes months, was required to achieve desegregation. In some cases, managers discontinued food service entirely, rendering the sit-ins moot. The students did not obtain total victory until the passage of the 1964 Civil Rights Act, a measure that owed relatively little to pressure from the lunch counter movement.

The Freedom Rides, however, provided graphic illustrations of the passions that lay beneath the biracial society: the indifference, even complicity, of Southern leaders, the helplessness of the riders, and the armed brutality of white mobs. Alabama became a bloody arena, and an astonished nation looked on in dismay. The sad scenario would likely have been repeated in Mississippi were it not for the belated action of the Kennedy administration, an action that sealed the fate of segregated interstate facilities. The ability of the riders to provoke violence shocked the nation and prodded the federal government into fulfilling objectives that the riders had little hope of achieving by themselves. As James Farmer recalled the philosophy behind the Freedom Rides: "We were counting on the bigots in the South to do our work for us." It was a prescient calculation and a lesson to be repeated in Alabama too many times over the next four years.

Birmingham

Birmingham was never a gentle, soft Southern town, never a place of crinolines, moonlight, and magnolias. Hewed out of the north Alabama woods after the Civil War, it developed into a brawny, brash, big-shouldered city epitomized by Vulcan, a cast-iron deity ruling over the place from atop Red Mountain. Those boys from Bessemer and Ensley and the other steel suburbs were a rowdy bunch, south Alabama farm boys turned stokers or puddlers with prodigious thirsts to quench the fires that burned within and without.

Birmingham's greeting of the freedom riders was within character, that city having established itself during the postwar decade as a particularly unsafe place for blacks and their white friends. Bombings, lynchings, and beatings occurred at frequent intervals. It worked because Birmingham was the most rigidly segregated city in the United States, an American Johannesburg. An NAACP official commented in 1956 that "Birmingham is the worst city for race relations in the South." It was a motto white citizens wore proudly and conscientiously sought to live up to.

The city seemed an unlikely choice for a major civil rights campaign. Its selection however, was an act of calculation. The civil rights movement had become diffuse after the Freedom Rides and characterized by a fragmentation of leadership. Moreover, victories, if they came at all, occurred at an excruciatingly slow pace. School desegregation had progressed little beyond tokenism by 1963, and the integration of public facilities was spotty across the South, rarely yielding to voluntary action.

The situation was especially critical for Dr. King and the SCLC. King had not been in the forefront of the sit-ins or the dramatic Freedom Rides. In addition, he and his organization had suffered a severe setback in Albany, Georgia, in November 1961, that proved a costly loss in terms of credibility and status within the black community. The Albany debacle underscored the limits of King's nonviolent philosophy in its application to the American South.

The Albany police chief, Laurie Pritchett, prepared for King's campaign to integrate the city's public accommodations and register blacks to vote by studying King's philosophy. His tactic simply was to meet nonviolence with nonviolence. He ordered his men not to use force on the demonstrators, merely to arrest them and carry them off to jail. To ensure that the demonstrators would not overflow the county jail and thereby burden the community, Pritchett secured agreements from all counties within a 100–mile radius of Albany to house prisoners. Also, by refusing to accept property bonds, Pritchett assured that the protesters' stay in jail would either be long or expensive.

The strategy worked. Though King and the SCLC probed Albany and rained demonstrations on the city for more than a year, whites maintained their calm and lived and worked around the protests to effect a minimum of disruption. Pritchett arrested thousands of demonstrators and eventually dispirit settled into King's ranks. Because of the lack of violence and the minimal media attention, the Kennedy administration did not feel compelled to intervene as it had during the Freedom Rides. The protest simply fizzled out.

King regrouped at the end of 1962, desperately seeking a way to reestablish the momentum as well as his leadership. It was evident that nonviolence would only be effective if it provoked violence, and the more brutal the force, the more favorable the outcome. As Wyatt Tee Walker advised his SCLC colleagues, "We've got to have a crisis to bargain with." So in January 1963, King and his shaken followers devised "Project C"—"C" for Confrontation—and chose Birmingham as the target city, a place guaranteed to furnish sufficient confrontation for the project. Not only was the city ever spoiling for a fight, but voters had just installed a new governor in Montgomery, George C. Wallace, who functioned as a lightning rod for segregationists. Wallace had vowed in his January inaugural address, "In the name of the greatest people that have ever trod the earth, I draw the line in the dust and toss the gauntlet before the feet of tyranny, and I say: 'Segregation now—segregation tomorrow—segregation forever.'" On April 3, 1963, King went into the lion's den and began his marches.

Compared with its reputation, the reaction of Birmingham was relatively restrained. Perhaps they had learned the lesson of Albany, that the best way to defend segregation was to appear not to defend it. In fact, the most notable event of the campaign's early days occurred not in the streets, but in a Birmingham prison cell occupied by King over the Easter weekend for violating a court injunction. A group of the city's leading Protestant, Catholic, and Jewish clergy had written an open letter to King chiding him for his nonviolent philosophy, asserting that it provoked violence and retarded racial progress. They expressed concern that King might be pushing his program too far, too fast, and accordingly handing white extremists an issue with which not only to suppress blacks but to quell the white moderate sentiment that the clergy represented. Finally, the ministers complained that the movement was attracting a mélange of forces from outside the region that would serve to strengthen Southern white resolve against racial change. These were familiar arguments; King had heard them ever since he set down his doctoral dissertation and took up the struggle for his people, and he had patiently answered them for that long. Now, sitting in his cell on Good Friday with time to think about the meaning of his work since Montgomery and to contemplate the uncertain future ahead of him and his movement, he obtained some scrap paper and a stubby pencil and responded to Birmingham's concerned clergy.

King acknowledged he was an "outsider," an Atlantan in a fiercely provincial city, and so were many of his compatriots. But, he countered, "Injustice anywhere is a threat to justice everywhere." Grounding his response in the same Judeo-

Christian principles that moved him and his organization, he informed the clergy that "Just as the prophets of the eighth century B.C. left their villages and carried their 'thus saith the Lord' far beyond the boundaries of their home towns . . . , so am I compelled to carry the gospel of freedom beyond my own home town."

As for the tactics he chose and the pressure he applied, King noted that, "Lamentably, it is an historical fact that privileged groups seldom give up their privileges voluntarily." It was evident that this argument had worn thin on King, especially since critics usually coupled this reproach with concerns that King should wait and not press his demands in such a volatile climate. "For years now," he retorted, "I have heard the word 'Wait!' . . . This 'Wait' has almost always meant 'Never.' . . . We have waited for more than 340 years for our constitutional and God-given rights." But for King and his followers, it was not only the interminable time to redress an archaic and sinful relationship. The daily humiliation of that relationship itself seared most deeply, as he argued with pointed eloquence to Birmingham's clergy:

Perhaps it is easy for those who have never felt the stinging darts of segregation to say, 'Wait.' But when you have seen vicious mobs lynch your mothers and fathers at will and drown your sisters and brothers at whim; when you have seen hate-filled policemen curse, kick, and even kill your black brothers and sisters; when you see the vast majority of your twenty million Negro brothers smothering in an airtight cage of poverty in the midst of an affluent society; when you suddenly find your tongue twisted and your speech stammering as you seek to explain to your six-year-old daughter why she can't go to the public amusement park . . . ; when you are humiliated day in and day out by nagging signs reading 'white' and 'colored'; when your first name becomes 'nigger,' your middle name becomes 'boy' . . . and your last name becomes 'John,' and your wife and mother are never given the respected title 'Mrs.'; when you are forever fighting a degenerating sense of 'nobodiness'—then you will understand why we find it difficult to wait.

King believed his movement and his letter were, at the least, instruments in education to enable the white man not only to see the black man's problems, but to see the black man himself. King also hoped to demonstrate the link between his protests and the South's religious tradition. When the ministers scolded him for precipitating violence, yet holding fast to the cloak of nonviolence, King replied, "Isn't this like condemning Jesus because his unique God-consciousness and never-ceasing devotion to God's will precipitated the evil act of crucifixion?" And, to the clergy's charge that King's provocative tactics classified him as an extremist, he reminded the ministers that there were indeed bitter and hateful forces within the black community watching, even eager to see him fail, and that he stood between them and the larger community. But he did not renounce the appellation "extremist" completely. Rather he noted that "Jesus Christ was an extremist for love, truth, and goodness."

The "Letter from a Birmingham Jail" passed into the annals of American literature, but when King emerged from his cell on Easter Monday, downtown was still a bastion of segregation. He remembered Albany and he saw his dream wavering in this Southern nightmare city. So he resolved to play out his last strategy by enlisting school children, some only six years old, to continue the protest marches in downtown Birmingham. The children's crusade was fraught with tactical dangers. The public and his followers could consider it callous, cynical, or worse, and there could be severe injuries, perhaps even death. Nevertheless, the fear of failure, of letting down the hundreds of thousands who had marched for all these years with him and for him, propelled him to this decision. And on May 2, 1963, the children, a thousand of them, exited from the Sixteenth Street Baptist Church and marched. It was a gay, colorfully dressed throng, and the television cameras ground away. "Bull" Connor's police, clearly uncertain as to how to proceed, gingerly waded in and arrested the singing and praying children who went willingly, almost joyously to the waiting patrol wagons.

The march was successful in capturing national attention,

but King and his SCLC command understood that daily marches and daily arrests, children or no, would eventually lose their media novelty and the public's attention would move on to something else. There was little choice but to repeat the scenario the following day, and another thousand or so children crowded into the church. The previous day's events had caught the police off guard. From the events that followed, it was clear that Connor had concocted a more direct response to King's employment of young marchers. As the marchers prepared to leave the church, Connor ordered his men to bar the church exits. The police pursued those youngsters who had managed to escape to adjacent Kelly Ingram Park and randomly clubbed demonstrators and onlookers. They turned police dogs loose on the children, and when some adult bystanders sought to distract police from the children by throwing bricks and bottles at them, Connor ordered waiting firemen to turn on their high-pressure hoses. Adult blacks splattered to the wet pavement, and the force of the water propelled children down the street, ripping the clothes off their backs and rending their flesh. Here was the spectacle that would finally horrify the nation. It was time for President Kennedy to intervene, and he succeeded in pressuring Birmingham's white leaders to sit down and negotiate with King. The discussions went nowhere as the businessmen, despite suffering losses, refused to accede to any of King's demands to integrate downtown facilities. King and his children returned to the streets.

When the demonstrations resumed on May 6, it seemed as if Connor had repented his conduct of May 3, as his officers arrested the students without incident. As wave after wave of children submitted to arrest, Connor's patience snapped and a repeat of the earlier melee followed. King decided to maintain the pressure, to break the city's intransigence, and to push a reluctant Kennedy administration, which depended on Southern congressmen to support the president's legislative program, to act. A larger, more militant group of youngsters appeared en masse downtown at high noon of the following day. Some sat down and prayed, others picketed, a group sang here or paraded there, now taunting the embattled Connor, now praising the Lord. Employing a tank, Connor corraled roughly 4,000 blacks in Kelly Ingram Park and ordered fire hoses opened up at close range on the dense crowd, and a by-now grimly familiar scene repeated itself. Birmingham's business community finally had had enough and quickly reached an agreement with King. Birmingham had fallen.

The aftershocks of events in Birmingham reverberated throughout the South. The success of the SCLC in that previously impenetrable city encouraged blacks across the South to accelerate their demands and their demonstrations. The era of gradual pressure for token gain was over. Historian Harvard Sitkoff counted 800 boycotts, marches, and sit-ins in 200 Southern cities within three months after the Birmingham victory, and many were successful in duplicating King's accord. As Sitkoff noted, "More racial change came in these few months than had occurred in three-quarters of a century."

In this heady atmosphere, King prepared for an August march on Washington to dramatize nationwide, interracial support for his Birmingham objectives, and more specifically to lobby for a bill that President Kennedy had forwarded to Congress, a bill that eventually became the 1964 Civil Rights Act. King's fifteen-minute address to the 200,000 people assembled in front of the Lincoln Memorial overshadowed the immediate purpose of the demonstration. The speech was a rhetorical Birmingham. It was not a catalogue of despair or a threat to white society; it was an extended metaphor of the American dream to which blacks aspired, looking forward to "that day when all God's children, black men and white men, Jews and Gentiles, Protestants and Catholics, will be able to join hands and sing in the words of the old Negro spiritual: 'Free at last. Free at last. Thank God Almighty, we are free at last.'" By reiterating basic American values and placing the civil rights movement squarely within this tradition as a conservative force, King's speech "made the black revolt acceptable to white America," as Harvard Sitkoff has noted.

But Kennedy's bill languished in Congress for nearly a year, stymied by a marathon filibuster engineered by Mississippi's James Eastland and South Carolina's Strom Thurmond. It was the Old South's last legislative stand, however. The Kennedy assassination brought a master of Congressional coaxing and dealing to the White House—Lyndon B. Johnson—who convinced some longtime Republican colleagues in the Senate, such as minority leader Everett M. Dirksen of Illinois, to support northern Democrats in a historic Senate vote cutting off the filibuster and clearing the way for the Senate's lopsided passage of the bill on June 10, 1964. The act codified many of the objectives of civil rights demonstrations to that point. It required local voting registrars to treat black and white applicants similarly, prohibited racial discrimination in public accommodations, including hotels, restaurants, and amusement parks, and extended the same prohibition to public facilities, such as parks and pools. This was the beginning of the Johnson administration's commitment to eradicating racial and economic injustice in this country.

The South accepted the legislation surprisingly well. True, George Wallace mourned the passing of "individual freedom and liberty" as a result of the act. Some, perhaps a majority of white Southerners, would have nodded in assent. And even some blacks shared the skepticism of Mississippi's Charles Evers, who was less impressed by the bill's passage than by the implementation that would follow. But by 1964 the mood in the white South was more of resignation, even of relief, rather than of open defiance. The incongruence between the white Southerner's faith and his practice, between his awareness that most of the modern world did not follow such overt racial distinctions and his observance of an etiquette that erected barriers between men, had become onerous. By 1964, many whites were simply exhausted. They had tired of the violence and the exposure in the media. Business leaders, many of whom had sulked on the sidelines, were tired of the disruptions, the adverse publicity, and the potential loss of future investments. In fact, in some quarters there seemed to be a collective sigh of relief. Andrew Young recalled returning to a St. Augustine, Florida, motel after the passage of the 1964 act, where only a week earlier waitresses had poured hot coffee on his party and the manager had laced the swimming pool with hydrochloric acid just as some blacks were preparing to wade in. On the return trip, Young recounted, the personnel were apologetic: "We were just afraid of losing our business. We didn't want to be the only ones to be integrated. But if everybody's got to do it, we've been ready for it a long time. We're so glad the president signed this law and now we can be through these troubles."

And also, by 1964, the white Southerner was witnessing living proof that an end to segregation did not signal an end to his Southernness, and, in fact, could be construed as an affirmation of his regional identity. Southern theologian James Sellers, speaking about the adjustments whites would necessarily make to an integrated society, explained that "The required transformation will not make the Southerner into a warmed-over Yankee, nor deprive him of those special, concrete, personal ways of life that mark Southern society. Instead, it will let the Southerner use his style of life to be *with* other men instead of apart from them."

Cynics would say that although Southerners went through the motions of complying with federal legislation, their attitudes toward blacks remained impervious to the written law. There is a good deal of truth in this charge, but it is also largely irrelevant. When women cast their first ballots more than a generation earlier, there were men who remained convinced that this was unwise and inappropriate, yet who nevertheless complied with the law. By the 1960s, the sight of women voting was hardly a novelty anymore, and most men not only took it for granted but would have thought it odd for anyone to express an adverse view. The legislation aimed to end discrimination, not to alter attitude; but by changing behavior, the new mode eventually becomes habitual and commonplace and attitudes typically follow. When, in 1966, a *Newsweek* reporter had lunch in Atlanta with black essayist Albert Murray, the reporter commented that if he interviewed the young white waitress who had just taken their orders, he would probably find a negative attitude on integration. Murray replied: "But is what she says when interviewed on desegregation as a specific issue really more significant than the way she is acting with me sitting right here?"

Most Southern blacks remained unable to test Murray's theory, for economic reasons, for their rural locations, or for the persistence of fear. Indeed, even as King talked about dreams of freedom in Washington, the reality was that blacks were dying in Mississippi for attempting to exercise the basic right of American democracy, the right to vote.

Voting Rights

The Magnolia State is a study in contrasts: the starkly flat, rich Delta region stretching the course of the mighty river that gave its name to the state on into Memphis; the rolling, green hills and forests along the Natchez Trace, a scenic wonderland; the piney woods region where poor farmers and sawmill workers eked out a meager living; and the Gulf Coast, with its gentle breezes and white homes, where legends of Jefferson Davis, the payroll of the United States Navy, and gumbo provided a strange mixture of sights and smells. But for all its geographic diversity, Mississippi was singleminded in its fealty to the regional culture, particularly white supremacy. Ranking last in virtually every index of modern civilization, Mississippi led the nation in racism. And white Mississippians were intent on preserving this distinction even, and especially, as the rest of the region shed its racial burdens.

In April 1962, the four major civil rights organizations—SNCC, CORE, SCLC, and NAACP—collaborated to form the Council of Federated Organizations (COFO) for the ostensible purpose of launching a voter registration drive in the predominantly black Delta region of Mississippi, the seat of the former Deep South cotton empire. Only 6.7 percent of the state's eligible blacks were registered to vote, and the proportion was around 2 percent in the Delta. Over the years a combination of economic and physical intimidation, as well as evasive techniques practiced by local registrars, kept the registration rolls relatively free of blacks. Perhaps the greatest problem was education in this rural, isolated, and impoverished region. As one farm laborer confided to a COFO worker in 1963, "I had never heard until 1962 that black people could register to vote. . . . I didn't know we had that right."

But in an area where white residents considered anyone from beyond the Delta an "outsider," and where they perceived control of the majority black population as the essential sine qua non of their lives, COFO's entrance was bound to generate a strong reaction. Black leaders recognized this, of course, and they sought to use the Delta for precisely the same reason that King had targeted Birmingham: if they could crack Mississippi, black voting rights in the rest of the South would inevitably follow, just as integration proceeded rapidly after the children's crusade. Further, if violence occurred, and that was a given under the circumstances, the Delta campaign would capture similar headlines and this would accelerate the voting rights victory.

The scenario misfired. The Delta contained a dispersed, rural population; Birmingham was an urban focal point, a convenient stage for massing the media. The rhythms of the rural economy and low population densities inhibited mass marches and demonstrations and, consequently, the collective brutal retaliation of the local police forces. The scene of a few blacks trudging to a dusty, obscure county courthouse and being turned away lacked the drama of the Birmingham events. Delta whites generally reserved punishment for a less public occasion, preferably at night, and in the numerous thickets and creeks that dotted the Delta, far from the limelight of publicity. Rumors began to filter out of the region of beatings and murders of blacks connected with the campaign, but how could these assertions be verified? A black disappearing in Mississippi was hardly newsworthy.

If violence or its threat was insufficient to deter potential black recruits, Delta whites resorted to other intimidating tactics. Since they controlled the Delta economic and political institutions, cutting off welfare funds was an effective ploy to discourage black participation in the campaign. In fact, COFO soon evolved from a voting rights organization to the region's major provider of welfare, a role that effectively undermined its resources and energies in pursuit of the ballot. The Delta Campaign, in short, was a dismal failure, though COFO workers would benefit in the long run from the experience.

Perhaps the only glimmer of hope was the so-called Freedom Election COFO held throughout the state during the 1963 gubernatorial campaign. Since blacks could not vote in the regular election, they nominated their own ticket headed by NAACP leader Aaron Henry. The "election" drew a remarkably high 80,000 ballots, indicating the vast potential for black voting in the state. But it was only potential, and it seemed by early 1964 that the obstacles to black voting rights in Mississippi were insurmountable.

COFO leaders Bob Moses and David Dennis had arrived at the same point that Martin Luther King reached in Birmingham when King made the fateful decision to launch his children's crusade. Something equally dramatic was necessary in order for Mississippi to penetrate the national consciousness. Moses and Dennis planned a new campaign, the Summer Project, for the coming summer. Unlike the Delta effort, this was to be a statewide campaign. The most dramatic wrinkle, however, was in COFO's decision to invite white Northern college students into the state to assist in the voter registration drive. As Dennis explained the strategy: "We knew that if we had brought in a thousand blacks, the country would have watched them slaughtered without doing anything about it. Bring a thousand whites and the country is going to react to that." By his own count, more than sixty blacks had perished during earlier voter registration efforts in the state with nary a murmur from the American public. Now, their sons and daughters were entering a war zone and there would be casualties.

More than 1,100 whites came to Mississippi, a state novelist and native Walker Percy described in 1964 as "insane." The "Freedom Summer" had barely begun in June when three COFO workers disappeared from Philadelphia, Mississippi, shortly after Neshoba County Deputy Sheriff Cecil Price, had released them from jail. The three—Andrew Goodman, a twenty-one-year-old white college student from New York, Michael Schwerner, twenty-four years old and a white New York social worker, and James Chaney, a black from Meridian, Mississippi—touched off an extensive search in the area, eventually including the FBI. Six weeks after their disappearance, federal agents discovered the remains of the three voting rights workers in an earthen dam on a farm outside Philadelphia. The discovery generated the national furor that COFO had predicted. The FBI quickly rounded up twenty-one suspects, including the sheriff and deputy sheriff, and announced that the murders were perpetrated by the Klan. Three years later, seven whites were brought to trial and a federal jury of white Mississippians pronounced them guilty. The judge, Kennedy appointee Harold Cox, perhaps the leading segregationist jurist in the South, meted out prison terms, the most severe being ten years.

The expected federal response was not forthcoming. It was an election year and the Republican candidate, Barry Goldwater, was already sufficiently strong in the South to concern incumbent, Lyndon B. Johnson. The president had already expended considerable political capital during the lengthy battle to pass the 1964 Civil Rights Act, and neither he nor Congress were eager to engage in another marathon debate so soon after the disruptive and acrimonious discussions over the 1964 Act. In addition, the public concern about voting rights in Mississippi soon became buried in the exhilaration of a presidential campaign. The FBI seemed to be handling the situation well and would bring the murderers to justice. The type of sustained brutality evident in Birmingham had not occurred in Mississippi and consequently had not sustained public opinion. For all its trouble, COFO had succeeded in registering only 1,200 blacks. Mississippi remained bloodied, but un-bowed.

The civil rights movement, exemplified by the collaboration in Mississippi, now seemed in danger of floundering. The debates over tactics, the role of whites, and the location of future projects were sapping the energies and direction of the leadership. Doggedly, the organizations continued their voting rights drives, especially in Alabama and Mississippi. Except for a few sporadic incidents, these efforts went generally unnoticed. It was evident that in this theater of the absurd that had become the South, a dramatic spectacle was crucial. Without an audience, the play would close.

Occasionally, in the waning months of 1964 and early in the new year, news filtered out of the Alabama Black Belt, where King and the SCLC were conducting a voter registration drive. King had focused his activities in Dallas County, where only 2 percent of the eligible black voters were registered. Seeking either amelioration or confrontation, King persisted in marching blacks to the county courthouse at Selma in futile attempts to register. The sheriff, Jim Clark, a notorious figure to black residents, dutifully arrested the protesters, so that by February, 2,000 blacks were imprisoned. But on February 18, in the town of Marion in neighboring Perry County, a black teenager participating in a registration drive was fatally shot as he attempted to rescue his mother, who was being clubbed by a policeman. The murder provided King with a strategy to capture national attention and secure, once and for all, the voting privileges for blacks guaranteed by the Constitution. He planned a great march to protest the murder and the continuing suffrage violations in the Alabama Black Belt, from Marion to the state capital at Montgomery. King altered the embarkation point to Selma as the route from Marion was considerably longer.

Thus, Selma rather fortuitously became the new, and as it turned out, the last, major civil rights focal point. Selma was Southern Everytown, or at least the way Everytown hoped to be. The Edmund Pettus Bridge, dedicated to the name of a

Confederate brigadier general, arched high above the Alabama River, coming down gently at the foot of Broad Street, framed by a leafy arcade leading the pedestrian into the well-tended business district. Before the downtown broke through the arbor way, Jeff Davis Avenue crossed Broad and a right turn led to wooden shacks, misplaced refugees from some sharecropper's farm it seemed. Then came some olive-drab low-rise public housing that middle-class folks would call garden apartments, but not here, where diesel soot streaked the facades and the Louisville and Nashville railroad cars rumbled and squealed nearby. But downtown was a world away, crowned by the elaborate Albert Hotel, a replica of the doge's palace in Venice, with a history that dated back before the Civil War. Beyond were neat leafy white neighborhoods, undisturbed by anything that had gone before and determined to keep the wires cut forever more. This was the White Citizens' Council's flagship town in Alabama, and like the Rotary or the Lions, it was something you joined and paid your dues.

So, in this placid, bitter town, Martin Luther King called for a march that would journey across the Alabama River to Montgomery to secure voting rights. The day was Sunday, March 7, a bright, breezy day, and Selma's white neighborhoods were in a festive mood, with brisk sales in Confederate flags and firecrackers. Hosea Williams, a King aide and leader of the march, gathered his flock at Brown's Chapel AME Church on Sylvan Street. Williams, a civil rights veteran, had no illusions as to the probable outcome this day as he addressed the faithful from the pulpit: "I believe in the resurrection, but if you read your Bible carefully, you will notice that resurrection comes *after* crucifixion . . . injustice must become the thud of club upon flesh, and this will echo around the world." Williams was not only steeling the marchers for violence, but asking them to pray for it: "We must pray that we are attacked, for if the sheriff does nothing to stop us, if the state troopers help us accomplish our long walk, if the governor meets us on the steps of the Capitol. . . , then we have lost." But, if the marchers were attacked—and Williams stressed this point in particular, *"we must not fight back!"*

Out into Selma they marched, down Sylvan over to Water Avenue and, finally onto Broad, and steadily they proceeded up to Edmund Pettus Bridge. Sheriff Jim Clark's posse lined both sides of the bridge, but did not bar access to it, and the marchers walked past these men, singing and praying, evoking no reaction. On the opposite side of the bridge, dressed in black uniforms, black helmets, and glass goggles with tin-can snouts of gas masks attached, blocking the road to Montgomery, were 100 Alabama state troopers mounted on horseback, called to the scene by Governor Wallace to prevent the march and ensure public safety. They accomplished one of their missions.

Major John Cloud, wearing mirror sunglasses and no gas mask, stepped forward and ordered the marchers to disperse and return to their neighborhoods within three minutes. The marchers halted their wary progress on the bridge and kneeled down over the Alabama River to pray. Less than a minute had elapsed when Major Cloud gave the order, "Troopers forward!" And they charged, accompanied by ear-piercing rebel yells and hurling tear gas. At that very moment, Sheriff Clark's men converged on the marchers from the side and pursued the fleeing protesters back into Selma, back toward Brown's Chapel, pummeling them as they went with chains, cattle prods, twirling lassos of rubber tubing wrapped with barbed wire, and nightsticks. The national audience had returned.

From Atlanta, Martin Luther King vowed he would come to Selma on March 9 to lead another attempt to march to Montgomery and avenge "Bloody Sunday." At this point, the Johnson administration, fearing an even more violent confrontation with the presence of King, intervened and hammered out a compromise with King and local and state authorities. The troopers and the posse would resume the positions they held on Sunday, but they would not interfere with the marchers. King and his group would be allowed to come onto Pettus Bridge to pray; then Major Cloud would order the

marchers to retreat, and they would return to Selma unmolested. The theater of the absurd had attained a new level of
absurdity.

The scenario went as planned until the 3,000 marchers
completed their prayer over the Alabama River. Then Major
Cloud, instead of issuing the order to disperse, stepped aside
with his troopers and the road to Montgomery lay open to the
marchers. The divergence from the script was an attempt to
embarrass and discredit King, who had given his word to the
president's emissary, former Governor LeRoy Collins of Florida, that he would not proceed to Montgomery. The marchers
knew nothing of this agreement, hence the embarrassment and
confusion when King ordered the marchers to return to Selma.
Members of SNCC in the group openly castigated King for the
retreat and for acceding to what they perceived to be a one-
sided compromise.

But King was in his usual precarious position—attempting
to mollify an administration walking on political eggshells, and
seeking to lead a people and a region out from the bondage
of history. A major reason for King's restraint became apparent
the following Monday, March 15, when President Johnson
announced to the nation that he was about to submit a voting
rights bill to Congress. The president then conferred with Federal Judge Frank M. Johnson, a Montgomery native, an Eisenhower appointee to the federal bench, and a jurist who had
generally been sympathetic to the civil rights cause. The outcome was a lifting of the injunction Governor Wallace had
secured to block the march to Montgomery. The president also
warned Wallace not to interfere with the marchers.

The president's message had come none too soon. Dissension was growing within the civil rights ranks, and the tensions were increasing in Selma's white community. The presence of black and white outsiders, waiting for the order to
march, provoked sporadic violence during the week after King's
retreat. Already a fatality had occurred—a Unitarian minister
from Boston, the Rev. James E. Reeb, had been beaten to death
by a group of white youths. But, finally, on March 21, 3,000

black and white marchers gathered in front of Brown's Chapel to begin their trek to Montgomery. As the marchers prepared to take the by-now familiar walk down Sylvan, over to Water, and onto Broad, King addressed them: "Those of us who are Negroes don't have much. . . . But thank God we have our bodies, our feet and our souls. Walk together, children . . . and it will lead us to the Promised Land."

CHAPTER FOUR

Sunlight and Shadow: New South and Old Realities, 1965–1975

Montgomery to Montgomery: not very far in time and nothing at all in geography, but light-years and leagues from the assumptions held by a region and its people. It was fitting that the drama concluded where it began because Southerners need not have gone far for the answers to their regional dilemma, even if they required the frequently unsolicited and unwanted assistance of others to show the way. So there was a symmetry to the play, and the protagonists were beneficiaries of a happy ending: the whites salvaged their souls and maintained their regional culture, while the blacks attained their dignity and manhood in a typically Southern way, by fighting for them.

The sunlight of reconciliation burned away the fog of pride and prejudice, revealing a renewed South. In 1972, Florida's progressive governor, Reubin Askew, saw a "maturing South . . . a humanistic South, which has always been there, just below the surface of racism and despair, struggling for a chance to emerge." And Askew believed that day had arrived, that the South would not only rejoin the Union, but would have "the opportunity . . . to lead it." Journalist H. Brandt Ayers echoed these sentiments that same year by suggesting that the South may be entering "a postracial era in which the nation can find hope and an example." Though Southerners had roundly condemned the missionary zeal of Northerners, the time was propitious for some proselytizing in the other direction; only this time the reality would match the rhetoric.

The sanguine projections of leading Southerners were understandable considering the contrast between what was now and what was yesterday, a contrast the Southerners' regional historical perceptions had not heretofore permitted. Race had nearly consumed the region; now, just as suddenly, it seemed, like a violent tempest giving way to a blue sky, to have disappeared. The marches, the ugly confrontations, the mighty displays on the television, the challenge to conscience and faith were gone. Blacks were voting, eating lunch at the downtown restaurants, attending schools of their choice, and in general participating in regional life as if they had been doing so for generations. Joel Williamson has contended that with the passage of the Voting Rights Act of 1965, the white South hit the nadir in its self-esteem, besieged by a barrage of federal legislation, the props of segregation and racial exclusion suddenly kicked out from under their world view, and the subject of moral judgment from Walter Cronkite to New England schoolteachers. But if this was a general feeling, it soon dissipated into a self-congratulatory frame of mind. As Florence King observed, "Southerners have a genius for psychological alchemy. . . . If something intolerable simply cannot be changed, driven away, or shot, they will not only tolerate it, but take pride in it as well."

The "psychological alchemy," though, had some genuine elements precipitating the regional era of good feelings. Not only were the public spectacles over and attention wrested away from race, but Southerners were discovering that the South's chronically subservient niche in the national economy was changing as well. The new era of racial progress seemed to dovetail nicely into a new era of unparalleled economic prosperity—not of the chamber-of-commerce-hyperbole variety—but the reality of actual development that promised to touch everyone. As Rupert Vance, hardly a booster type, proclaimed in the *Virginia Quarterly Review,* "Like the children of Israel, the people of the South have undertaken a Journey. The South is on the way to a Promised Land. . . . The pillar we follow is a vision of economic parity with the nation." He concluded that the South would soon be "a land of milk and honey."

All of this marked a significant change in perspective for Southerners. Heretofore, the Promised Land metaphor was distinctly an otherworldly goal, a reward for and respite from the hardships of the here and now. "O come, and join our pilgrim band," went one old hymn, "Our toils and triumphs share;/We shall soon reach the promised land,/And rest forever there." In the new vocabulary, born of the recent racial accommodation and advancing prosperity, the Promised Land implied less eternal peace than an optimistic dynamism with flashing steel and gilded glass; and if the angels were singing they were doing so in the new brick church downtown that had more outbuildings than a plantation.

Economists often use the concept of "take-off" to denote the period of time when a sudden spurt of growth transforms an economy. In the modern era, the decade after 1965 probably qualifies as the South's "take-off" decade. Median family income in the region rose by 50 percent during that time, compared with a national increase of 33 percent over the same period. By 1975, the South was approaching parity in per capita income for the first time since the Civil War. Several factors were converging on the region, some of them fortuitous, to account for this growth at this particular time. The best part was that both the nature of this growth and the results of it required little alteration in regional culture.

The South Rediscovered: Lifestyle, Literature, and Lyrics

The South was simply a nice place to live. Southerners, of course, had known that all along, but now others were discovering regional charms or, more properly, were reordering their priorities to the South's favor. The racial accommodation implied by the series of measures culminating in the Voting Rights Act of 1965 were, not surprisingly, a major factor in enhancing the South's national image. Beginning with the Watts riot that same year, cities outside the South experienced a series of racial disturbances that ultimately paled the South's skirmishes by comparison. The few disruptions of racial tranquility in the South occurring after 1965 framed the region in relative racial bliss as far as the rest of the nation was concerned. The adverse racial publicity now emanated not from Selma, but Detroit; not from Birmingham, but Newark.

More important was a change in lifestyle preferences. With the rapid construction of a national interstate highway network, an increase in disposable income, a lengthening of vacation time, and a decrease in the average retirement age, people were on the move—either on vacations or to establish new homes in more salubrious climates. New Orleans, Savannah, Charleston, and especially Williamsburg scored high on national tourist itineraries. During the 1960s, Southern cities translated the region's perennial interest in the past into a pioneering historic preservation movement complemented by federal legislation in 1966 providing financial incentives for preservation. Though preservation efforts in Charleston and New Orleans dated from at least the 1920s, they operated relatively unnoticed until postwar suburban society began to look to the South for a measure of what was disappearing everyplace else. The South accommodated this craving for popular history by offering some tasteful (and occasionally garish) renditions of the past that had never really become the past in any case.

The Charlestonians' motto was "go away and let me sleep," and they had done so, adopting a perverse pleasure in derogating newness and praising the historic. The city became a major tourist attraction as a result, reaping millions of dollars from doing essentially nothing. With the benefit of historic-district zoning, also part of the 1966 legislative package, cities could now protect blocks of buildings rather than single structures. Though preservation became a national phenomenon, it was most effective in the South because that region had lost less of its building heritage, not always from conscious decision making, but more from the fact that growth pressures that gobbled up real estate elsewhere had been less evident in the South.

It was not only old buildings that Americans sought in the South, but a lost lifestyle. The cities in this urban nation had become shabby and dangerous places where tempers and budgets were chronically coming up short. The exile to suburbia had provided some respite and, after the passage of the Interstate Highway Act in 1956, access was easier. But the traffic had become greater, the pace more frantic and pointless, and the taxes more onerous. In most Southern cities, any place was within twenty minutes' driving distance of any other place, and if the suburban siren proved irresistible, well, Southern cities were suburbs in their own right, grown up with the automobile, sprawled out on the landscape, low density, lending themselves to the convenience and privacy of the car and the single-family home.

And just as they did not look like traditional cities, or at least the ones with which Yankees were familiar, they felt different as well. The South became an urban region in 1960 (some forty years later than the rest of the nation), but the pace was, as Rosemary Daniell noted, "Somewhere between Guatemala and New York." Although one would not readily associate Columbia, South Carolina, with pastoral splendor, John Egerton was impressed by his visit there in the early 1970s and depicted a city much like other Southern cities of similar size at that time: "The charm of it is enhanced by the shady live oaks and the prodigious banks of azaleas that bloom in such profusion every spring." And, while some downtowns in other parts of the country resembled blasted war zones, "Columbia's center is an attractive and inviting place, convenient and accessible, and it is easy to imagine working and living there comfortably."

More subtle regional elements operated on the American consciousness to enhance the Southern image. When Americans read, they often read Southerners. Thomas Wolfe, William Faulkner, Robert Penn Warren, and Eudora Welty were on reading lists everywhere by the 1960s. Their themes varied, of course, but the intrusion of the modern world into insular societies and the moral dilemmas confronting individuals, black and white, who are both victims and beneficiaries of this conflict were common threads. Most Americans outside the South had passed through the gates to whatever characterized late twentieth-century life, and it was edifying to discover a civilization, even in fiction, where the choices were not inevitable and irrevocable, where it was still possible to dangle each foot in a different era without the straddle becoming painful because past and present, as these Southern writers demonstrated, were one and the same.

Some literary critics, most notably Walter Sullivan, have observed a decline in the quality of Southern literature in the 1960s. The resolution of the racial conflict and the emergence of the Sunbelt have led to a contented region, and satisfaction rarely generates memorable literature, they argue. The great artists of the earlier era often felt out of joint with what the South was becoming or might become. William Faulkner, in his trilogy, *The Hamlet* (1940), *The Town* (1957), and *The Mansion* (1959), told the story of the rise of the Snopes clan, a greedy, amoral bunch of interlopers who were no match for the enervated innocents of Yoknapatawpha County. Thomas Wolfe perceived himself as a perpetual wanderer exiled from home, a stranger everywhere else. Robert Penn Warren in *All the King's Men* warned against misusing and misunderstanding the past, and in *Flood* (1964) he depicted the environmental destruction perpetrated by modern technology.

Though Faulkner and Wolfe are gone and Warren and Welty are in their twilight years, a new generation of Southern writers has appeared since the 1960s. The themes of their works indicate that race, the land, and the past remain unresolved issues in the Southern literary mind. William Styron, the dean of the newcomers, deals with race and the uses of the past (much like Warren) in *Sophie's Choice* (1977). Race is also the focus of contemporary Southern black writers. In Ernest P. Gaines's *A Gathering of Old Men* (1982), the scene is rural Louisiana and the story concerns the interplay of race and agriculture—the modern worlds of integration and mechanized farming—and the ambivalent attitudes of whites and blacks toward both. The most noted Southern black author today is Alice Walker. Her trio of novels—*The Third Life of Grange Copeland* (1970), *Meridian* (1976), and *The Color Purple* (1982)—represent her personal accommodation to race and region. Her novels travel from consuming hate in *Copeland* to resignation in *Meridian,* and, finally, to a joyous proclamation of life and faith in *The Color Purple,* as Walker and her characters no longer define themselves by their relations to whites, but by their connections to each other and to the land and faith of their ancestors. The themes of history and family are particularly evident in Alex Haley's *Roots* (1977), which carried the Southern penchant for genealogy in new literary directions.

The good stories told by contemporary Southern writers often translated well into television and theatrical film adaptations. *Roots,* of course, became one of the most-watched television series of all time. Movies with Southern themes were hardly new in the 1960s—*Gone With the Wind* and *Jezebel* had captured national audiences a generation earlier. But the number, quality, and themes of the scripts increased until by the 1970s the "Southern" was as distinctive a film genre as the Western. *In the Heat of the Night* (1967), starring Sidney Poitier as a Philadelphia police detective and Rod Steiger as the prototypical Mississippi sheriff, initiated Hollywood's new version of the modern South, as Steiger warms to his black colleague by picture's end. Indeed, by the early 1970s, the dreaded, big-gutted Southern sheriff had become almost impish in media portrayal: Chrysler Corporation employed a down-home sheriff type to sell Dodge automobiles; his closing words were, "Y'all be careful, now, heah!" Also in the early 1970s, Earl Hamner, Jr.'s novel *Spencer's Mountain* (1961) became "The Waltons" on CBS-TV. And Southern blacks evolved from being victims or Sambos to become heroes (which threatened to become another stereotype) in *Sounder* (1972) and in the television adaptation of "The Autobiography of Miss Jane Pittman" (1974). Finally, the South became the repository of the macho, law-and-order, good-guy type in a nation anxiously seeking out straightforward heroes. *Walking Tall* (1972), the biographical portrayal of Tennessee sheriff Buford Pusser, and the Burt Reynolds vehicle *White Lightning* (1973) provided action and happy endings for all.

If the South emerged as the region of the heart for American literary and film preferences, Southern music generated a loyal following for much the same reasons. The forms of Southern music—jazz, blues, bluegrass, and country—reflected the harshness of life in a poverty-stricken, race-divided, rural, and often violent region. But there were also songs of faith, family, and pride in the land. These forms became virtually synonymous with American music and reflected an amalgam of black and white, of Africa and the British Isles; they are audible proof of the common heritage of black and white Southerners.

When the railroads penetrated the Southern highlands in the late nineteenth century, Appalachian whites met black section hands, who introduced the guitar and hard-driving rhythms to the mountain ballads. The mixture emerged from the hollows and creek beds to regional prominence with A. P. Carter and his family in the 1920s. They made the first popular country music recordings. The National Barn Dance out of WLS radio station in Chicago, and the Grand Ole Opry broadcast by WSM in Nashville and featuring mainly farmers who picked, fiddled, and sang for a hobby, introduced the mountain music to a wider audience.

Although Jimmie Rodgers was the first major country music personality, it was Hank Williams who revolutionized the budding industry with his candid lyrics, borrowing from the diverse cultural heritages of the South, especially black, and with his star-crossed lifestyle. He was also a forerunner of the postwar national permeation of Southern music. Born in poverty in Georgianna, Alabama, in 1923, Williams went on the road with his string band, the Drifting Cowboys, at age thirteen. Like the South at that time, he spent the remainder of his tragically short life moving on, never quite finding his niche in a world he could not accept or handle. Though Williams was not a major national musical luminary, he helped gain regional and eventually American acceptance of the peculiarly Southern fusion of white and black music. Williams's nasal twang and string accompaniments were in the Scotch-Irish traditions of his ancestors, but his subjects were black and blue—music up from slavery, known as the blues. His song titles—"Low Down Blues," "Lovesick Blues," "Long Gone Lonesome Blues," and "The Blues Come Around," reflected his debt to that black musical form, which also provided a base for jazz.

Like his Southern literary contemporaries, Hank Williams wrote and sang about the sense of drift and alienation in a changing society. He longed to "scat right back to my pappy's farm," because "this city life has really got me down." Yet, as did Thomas Wolfe, he realized he could not go home again for there was nothing (and everything) there for him, caught up as he was, however involuntarily, in the whirlpool of a new life; and, like Wolfe, this knowledge proved self-destructive.

Country music was the people's music, and the lyrics reflected the deep attachment to place, especially for those working on railroads, on chain gangs, or "up North." The themes stressed the wanderlust, yet rootedness, of everyday Southern life, of love lost and won, of families held together through faith and fortitude and torn apart by infidelity, death, or leaving. Country music emerged as a black-and-white art form, with emotions depicted in primary colors, and the musical accompaniment simple. The music told of a life that was hard, yet fulfilling in its own way, with always a promise of reward in "the better world in the sky." The lyrics told stories because, after all, the tradition of the plain folk was oral, and storytelling was an important means of communicating and passing time. Sometimes a William Faulkner would immortalize these tales;

other times they would be set to music, such as the "Wreck of Ol' 97." The national popularity of country music in the troubled 1960s and 1970s, as with the fondness of other things Southern, owed to the passage of these oral traditions from an electronic America, as well as to the simplicity and forthrightness of the lyrics and melodies in a time of ambiguity and uncertainty. By the 1960s, country music had a national audience, and instead of one major personality, an array of popular entertainers, such as Patsy Cline, Loretta Lynn, George Jones, Merle Haggard, and Waylon Jennings—all with rural roots and lives of personal hardships—commanded the airwaves. In 1971, New York City surrendered as radio station WHN shifted to a country format and the Lone Star Cafe became the habitat of the button-down crowd.

Even while the nation became accustomed to and even entranced by the distinctive siren of the steel guitar or the invigorating riffs of a banjo or mandolin, teenagers had discovered another form of Southern music that did not drift down from the mountains, but rather cut through the swamps, canebreaks, and piney woods of the Deep South—another black-white mixture that rumbled from the depths of the regional soul. Growing up in Lubbock, Texas, Charles Hardin ("Buddy") Holly, listened to "race" music—the recordings of black rhythm-and-blues artists that filtered into white Lubbock neighborhoods like Radio Free Europe. The subjects of "race" music influenced Holly as they had impressed Hank Williams. But Holly was also taken with the hard, driving beat and creative instrumentation that was lacking in most country music at the time. Bob Wills and his Western Swing style shared the country spotlight with Williams in Holly's Lubbock, and Wills's mode was more polite and even than Williams's plaintive wails. So Holly combined the themes of Williams's songs with black rhythms and instrumentation to create a white rhythm and blues, eventually dubbed "rock and roll." In fact, Holly's sound was so black that booking agents for Harlem's Apollo Theater invited Holly to appear on the stage of the famous black music emporium. When Holly and his band materialized in the theater offices prior to their performance, a combination of embarrassment and panic greeted them because the assumption was that Holly was black. The show went on, however, and Buddy Holly and the Crickets became the first and last white act to perform at the Apollo.

Holly was hardly the first white Southern musician to owe a debt to black musical forms; in fact, the interconnectedness of white and black music goes back to the colonial era in the South and is difficult to unravel. But Southern music, an amalgam of white and black, became a national phenomenon by the 1950s, at the same time that Southerners themselves were grappling with a racial accommodation of a different sort. The amelioration of race, in broad outlines at least, ran concurrently with the growing national acceptance of the new music. And just as the South had become the focus of American literature, so it became the wellspring of an unparalleled mass musical movement. It was a movement tinged with tragedy, in typical Southern melodrama—the early deaths of Holly and Williams, and later Hendrix, Joplin, and Presley, not to mention the carnage in country music's Grand Ole Opry ranks in the 1960s—Hawkshaw Hawkins, Patsy Cline, Jim Reeves, and Johnny Horton, among others.

So the South was "in" as far as the national consciousness was concerned, long before Jimmy Carter sent Yankees running to their dictionaries or to the foreign food sections of their supermarkets to locate grits. America has always loved the ideal of the South, even as it hated the region, from the dime novels of the 1830s to Al Jolson, the cantor's son, singing about his heartstrings tied around "Alabammy," to the box office success of *Gone With the Wind.* Like an errant though beloved child, the South's periodic tantrums evoked national reproach; but after 1965, when Southerners had seemingly adjusted to new race relationships, and racial harmony and peace prevailed where everywhere else there existed only turmoil, the South could be taken to the nation's heart again, not only for its music and literature, but for its lifestyle and its economic promise. The style of living had been there all along of course, but always with the rough edge of frontier primitivism sticking up, a gap-toothed poverty of mind and body, a kudzu-covered rusty Chevrolet. But now the South was clean and shiny, with glass and steel, indoor plumbing, and air conditioning to remove the more threatening aspects of the region's potentially volatile human and natural conditions. The South was now the repository of the "Good Life," up from the nation's "Number One Economic Problem" to the Promised Land in a generation. At a time when the American pursuit of happiness was coming a-cropper in the ghettos of Northern cities, in the rice paddies of Vietnam, and on the college campuses, a time when everyone, it seemed, was angry about something, the South appeared to be a happy place. As Walker Percy observed in his 1966 novel, *The Last Gentleman,*

The happiness of the South was very formidable. It was an almost invincible happiness. . . . Everyone was in fact happy. The women were beautiful and charming. The men were healthy and successful and funny; . . . They had everything the North had and more. They had a history, they had a place redolent with memories, they had good conversation, they believed in God and defended the Constitution, and they were getting rich in the bargain. They had the best of victory and defeat.

And as the nation had trekked to the American West with high hopes and a glimmer in their eyes a century earlier, so now Americans heeded the call of "Southward this star of empire." The region's population increased by more than 7 million during the 1960s, the largest advance in the nation, and by the early 1970s, the South had become the country's most populous region, holding more than one-third of America's people. During the 1960s, for the first time in 100 years, more people moved into the South than out of it. Roughly 50 percent of the region's growth in the 1960s and early 1970s occurred from in-migration. Moreover, unlike some of the immigration growth in the North in earlier decades of the twentieth century, the "quality" of the South's newcomers was higher in terms of education, income, and skill levels.

A Transforming Economy

A major result of the population shift away from the Northeast and Midwest (the two most common regions of origin for in-migration) was the rapid development of the service and wholesale-retail trade activities responding to a burgeoning consumer demand. During the early 1970s, wholesale and retail employment in the region was advancing at three times the rate of similar job creation in the North, while growth in service employment experienced a twofold advance over the North. The federal bureaucracy increased by 5.4 percent during this time (1970–1975), while the North suffered a 3 percent loss.

The employment figures reflected a transformation of the Southern economy in the decade after 1965. During those years, the regional employment base grew by 22.1 percent compared with a national average of 11.6 percent. Services and government employed nearly one-half of Southern jobholders, with manufacturing a distant third at 15.7 percent. The proportion of Southerners engaged in the first two activities was higher than the national average, slightly below in manufacturing employment. The South was moving rapidly into a so-called post-industrial economy with scarcely a backward glance toward its industrial heritage—for good reason: its manufacturing base was oriented to rural sites and labor, an adjunct to an agri-cultural-commercial economy. The South, in effect, bypassed the industrial era and leaped directly into a service economy, avoiding the burdens of a cumbersome and expensive indus-trial infrastructure, especially in its cities. The transformation of the Southern economy further encouraged quality in-mi-gration, as service-oriented activities from banking to insur-ance to corporate and government administration required well-educated, skilled individuals. This influx, in turn, spurred consumer demand and increased the service sector to an even greater extent. The South, at last, was experiencing the type of self-reinforcing development enjoyed by the North until the 1960s.

Though Northerners assumed that the South accomplished at least some of this economic development with the equivalent of mirrors, luring Northern-based entrepreneurs to pick up lock, stock, and loom in the dead of night to steal southward, industrial relocation represented only a fraction of the region's growth. A group of Northern congressmen went so far in 1973 to form the Northeast Congressional Caucus to monitor alleged Southern pirating activities. By 1976, three other conglomerations of Northeastern and Midwestern officialdom had emerged to stem the alleged Southern economic invasion and prevent "the entire industrialized Northeast and Midwest [from becoming] the sophisticated Appalachia of the Nation."

Part of the Northern concern was the supposed lopsided extent of federal disbursements to the South, particularly in defense spending during the Vietnam era. But even here, federal expenditures were remarkably evenhanded, favoring no particular region. In terms of defense dollars, the South actually received less than the per capita national average on primary contracts and considerably less on subcontracts. The presence of armed camps, such as Charleston and the Hampton Roads region, skewed perceptions about Southern military prowess.

Southern economic development and its attractions rested upon more solid structural foundations than footloose industries and federal funding whims. The changing nature of the national economy away from certain types of heavy industry, alteration in lifestyle values, and the increasingly positive image of the South in the national consciousness were more important factors. The South, as had the West of yore, presented a fresh, untried, unspoiled image as a place of possibility, of the future.

Perhaps most impressive about the Southern economic advance was its diversity. It was as if the region had absorbed the lessons of the declining rust belt not to mortgage its future on the promise of one industry. The service economy, by its very nature, provided for a variety of activities to make the whole less susceptible to collapse in a national economic downturn. This was especially so for the high-technology research and development field. On the surface, at least, the South appeared to be ill-suited for favor in this highly competitive area. Research and development activities were dependent upon a specially trained and educated work force, and the South's educational system had historically lagged behind the rest of the nation's. Further, the salaries at research and development facilities far outdistanced prevailing industrial wages in the region, and powerful textile moguls in particular had a clear stake in discouraging such intrusions into their cheap labor domain. Despite these apparent obstacles, Southern states by the 1960s began to court high-technology industries and think tanks. North Carolina led the way.

The combination of intellect and industry had long been a dream of Howard W. Odum, who believed his Institute for Research in the Social Sciences at Chapel Hill would become a regional prototype for investigation into a variety of Southern issues. But the postwar era was not propitious for scholars seeking answers to controversial regional questions. After Odum's death in 1954, the institute drifted into other locales for its material. Nevertheless, before his death Odum had convinced North Carolina Governor Luther Hodges of the efficacy of a nonprofit, taxpaying corporation devoted to research and development apart from, but at times associated with, the three universities in the capital area—The University of North Carolina, North Carolina State University, and Duke University. Thus the Research Triangle Park was born in 1958 on an expanse of land donated by private sources. By the end of the 1970s nearly thirty research and development firms were located there and another research park was blossoming in Charlotte near the campus of the University of North Carolina at Charlotte.

The Research Triangle Park was a portent of a significant diversification and acceleration in the regional economic base over the ensuing two decades, especially in the half decade between 1970 and 1975, when the South led the nation in the growth of every industry but mining. While low-wage, labor-intensive industries were declining as a percentage of the whole, high-wage industrial employment was advancing to meet and surpass that percentage. Just as the quality of the Southern population was increasing, so was the quality of employment, and the two were interrelated, of course. Once the civil rights movement broke the orthodoxy of white supremacy, the value of intellect and expression rose, and the quality of Southern institutions of higher learning as well.

But even below the university level, once the assault on public education had subsided, funding soared and attendance and graduation statistics reflected a greater emphasis on education. The declining significance of agriculture and the increasing number of employment opportunities that required at least a high school diploma contributed to the lengthening of education among the region's population. The education gap between the South and the rest of the nation began to close in the 1960s, and by 1970 Southerners between the ages of twenty-two and twenty-four, the South's coming generation, had attained the educational level of their cohorts elsewhere in the country. Also, by 1970 most Southern states had established systems of technical schools and community colleges designed to meet the needs of employers in the postindustrial economy; and the educational advances included both blacks and whites. So looking to the 1980s and beyond, there was general optimism that the region's revitalized educational structure and the amelioration of race would secure a prosperous future.

But to many Southerners already basking in the glow of prosperity, deliverance had come already. The Sunbelt had arrived. The Sunbelt was as much, if not more, a creation of Yankee publicity as it was of Southern derivation. The nation was always ready to believe the worst and best about the South, and by the early 1970s, the pendulum was swinging wildly to the good side. Kevin Phillips, a conservative theoretician, was among the first to utilize the term Sunbelt in his book *The Emerging Republican Majority* (1969). To Phillips the Sunbelt encompassed a broad region, including but not limited to the South, that was "undergoing a massive infusion of people and prosperity," transforming traditionally Democratic party strongholds into Republican districts. Whatever the shortcomings of the political analysis, the shift of population and economic base southward was indeed in full swing. By 1976, when a Southerner (a Democrat) was running for the presidency, the word "Sunbelt" had attained widespread currency. National publications rushed to squeeze the latest revelation out of this new regional phenomenon, frequently employing "South" and "Sunbelt" interchangeably. The liberal *Saturday Review*, which had skewered the South during the early 1960s, now proclaimed "The South as the New America." *Time* magazine portrayed an almost idyllic region, bursting with progress, yet still a largely rural land of spectacular beauty and prolific resources for recreation and sentient delight," where "life seems to move more slowly . . . because southerners take more time to enjoy it." Perhaps former Houston Mayor Fred Hofheinz, quoted approvingly by the *New York Times* in 1976, expressed the regional feeling best when he asserted: "People have been saying for years that the South and Southwest are frontiers of the new industrial America, where people can still reach the American dream. This is the new Detroit, the new New York. This is where the action is."

Marshall Frady, a few years later, called the South, "this peculiar dream-province of the Republic," and the nation was off on a bender of dreamspinning, intoxicated by the South's numerous wiles, both real and imagined. The inevitable hangover would come at a later time, when some sobering facts about the Sunbelt prosperity began to emerge from the region, but in the meantime Southerners enjoyed this newfound adulation and publicity, all the more because so little of it was deserved. To be sure, the South experienced a significant leap in its gross regional product, but the economic "take-off" was uneven. The South of the mid-1970s was a crazy quilt of patches of prosperity zigzagging between traditional areas of poverty, further bisected by pockets of growth and snippets of new decay.

The Dark Side of the Sunbelt: Farms and Factories

The rural South reflected one aspect of the region's uneven economic development. The farm had been, in the recent past, the standard economic unit of Southern society, the cultural and behavioral fount from which sprung distinctive regional patterns. Since World War II, and especially after the 1960s, Southern agriculture receded in regional significance even as it experienced its period of greatest prosperity, and even as it continued to influence regional mores as sons and daughters of the soil migrated to Sunbelt cities. By 1975, the number of farms in the region had declined to 720,000 units, from 2.1 million units in 1950. At the same time, the average farm size rose from 93 to 216 acres during that period, implying significant alterations in tenure patterns, mechanization, demography, and crop cultivation. By the 1970s, owners or part-owners came to characterize Southern farm tenure as the once-ubiquitous tenants and sharecroppers virtually disappeared, particularly in the Deep South states, where these individuals now comprised less than 8 percent of the farm population. These former croppers and tenants did not usually move into the ownership ranks, but rather left farming altogether; the farm population dropped by 50 percent during the 1960s. By 1970, farmers comprised 6.9 percent of the Southern population, compared with 43.1 percent in 1940.

The new agricultural look presented by Southern farms in the years immediately following World War II had filled out by 1970. In that year better than one-third of the crop land in Virginia, Tennessee, Mississippi, Alabama, and Florida was in pasture, underscoring the growing investments in livestock. Soybeans and poultry were as common as cotton had been a generation earlier. Phrases such as "multiple-unit operations" and "fragmented neoplantation" entered Southern agricultural parlance after 1960, generally referring to the operation of numerous noncontiguous tracts by one individual or corporation who may lease or partially own many of these tracts. The advance of blacktop roads in the rural South facilitated the employment of machinery on these scattered holdings.

The transformation of the massive Delta and Pine Land Company plantation in Scott, Mississippi, epitomized the changes in Southern agriculture by 1970. Prior to World War II, 5,000 tenant farmers cultivated 16,000 acres of cotton. At the end of the 1960s, the company had purchased additional land to comprise 25,000 acres, 7,000 of which had remained in cotton, and the remainder in a variety of crops, including pasture, soybeans, and corn. More than 3,000 head of cattle grazed on the extensive pasture lands and almost all farm operations were mechanized. The total work force stood at 500; they were strictly laborers who lived elsewhere, as no tenants remained. It was agribusiness, no longer agriculture and, as journalist Fred Powledge noted, the difference between the two is "the difference between business and culture."

The confrontation between tractor and cropper, with the inevitable outcome, had gone on since the 1940s, but the battle was over by the 1960s, and whatever the burdens of the share-crop system, and they were many, there existed a culture, a camaraderie among croppers and between croppers and the soil. "Y'all remember how it used to be?" a character in Ernest Gaines's *A Gathering of Old Men* queried his companions about to be made superfluous. "Thirty, forty of us going out in the field," he recalled, "with cane knives, hoes, plows—name it. Sunup to sundown, hard, miserable work, but we managed to get it done. We stick together, shared what little we had, and loved and respected each other." But that culture was fading, if not already gone. "Where the people?" he asked "Where the roses? . . . Where the people used to sing and pray in the church? I'll tell you. Under them trees back there, that's where." And the living were being plowed up by the tractor, removing the traces of their existence as they were reclaiming farm land from the graves. "Like now they trying to get rid of all proof that

black people ever farmed this land with plows and mules—
like if they had nothing from the starten but motor machines."

In fact, the last major uprooting of mostly black sharecroppers occurred during the 1960s, with the civil rights activities providing a last pretense for white landowners to divest
themselves of families who had lived on the land sometimes
for generations, and to do so without the necessary accompaniment of conscience or even of paternalism that had marked
an earlier era. Thus, Mrs. Deborah Calhoun of Panola, Alabama, informed her sharecropper, Charlie White, and his family, one month before Christmas, 1966, that they would have
to vacate the premises by the first of the new year—barely five
weeks away. The Whites had no inkling as to where they would
go or what they would do and live on as winter approached.
As one black farmer in the neighborhood noted, "them white
folks got a lot more interested in machinery after the civil
rights bill was passed." Removal was not only punishment,
but a mechanism for the whites to avoid confronting an integrated society.

The displaced, mainly black, farmers scattered everywhere, continuing a pattern begun a generation earlier, though
fewer made their way to Detroit or Chicago, and more to
Birmingham and Atlanta. Some, however, stayed behind, trapped by age, demoralized by poverty and illiteracy. In the 1960s,
only 1.3 percent of rural black farmers rose above the federal
poverty standard; but only 14.8 percent of white farmers exceeded that standard, underscoring the uneven prosperity of
the rural South. By the mid-1970s, although rural Southerners
comprised slightly more than one-third of the region's population, they accounted for 55 percent of its poor. And the gap
between those left-behinds and the other, more prosperous,
agricultural sector was immense and growing. The prosperous
sector had adopted an urban lifestyle with modern technological conveniences, well traveled, well clothed, and well read
by the standards of the region, living in brick homes and sending their sons and daughters to the best universities. And then
you go down a back road, maybe one not even paved or where

the electricity pole has not come yet, where the houses, or more properly shacks, are distinguished by sagging porches, broken windows covered over by cardboard, and rusted tin roofs, "and you think oh God," as journalist Joel Garreau did, "please don't let there be anybody living in that; please let it be abandoned. But a line of laundry flutters out back."

And the people residing in these places exhibited many of the debilities more closely associated with the last century than with the Sunbelt era. In 1968, a committee comprised of personnel from philanthropic foundations designated 256 predominantly rural "hunger counties" in the United States. Of the total, 220 were located in the eleven former Confederate states, thirty-seven in Mississippi alone. The criteria for selection included an infant mortality rate of twice the national average, and a level of participation in social services such as welfare and food stamp programs of less than 25 percent of the eligible poor. In other words, through discrimination, chicanery, ignorance, or a combination, these rural Southerners were not receiving the benefits their poverty entitled them to receive.

The particularly distressing conditions in rural Mississippi led the Southern Regional Council to send Dr. Raymond Wheeler, a Charlotte physician, to investigate first-hand the faces behind the poverty-related statistics. Dr. Wheeler uncovered shocking instances of malnutrition, premature deaths, and unsanitary living conditions in the course of his tour. Mississippi Senators James O. Eastland and John Stennis belittled the findings and suggested that the doctor had an agenda other than research. Dr. Wheeler replied:

I invite Senator Eastland and Senator Stennis to come with me into the vast farmlands of the Delta and I will show you the children of whom we have spoken. I will show you their bright eyes and innocent faces, their shriveled arms and swollen bellies, their sickness and pain and the fear and misery of their parents.

The senators never accepted the invitation.

Soon, other physicians journeyed into the fields and backways of the region to search out the unlikely phenomena of poverty and hunger in the Sunbelt. Dr. Donald Gatch was a physician in rural Beaufort County, South Carolina, "where breakfast for a shack full of kids is grits and lunch is grits with a bit of fatback added—if there is lunch," and where the shack itself was insulated with the Savannah *Morning News,* with no running water or electricity, standing adjacent to shallow, contaminated wells, where even an outdoor privy was sometimes lacking. Gatch did not need to travel far to confirm the suspicions of the Southern Regional Council that rural Mississippi was not unique in the South of the late 1960s. He reported children dying needlessly of parasites and concluded testimony before the national Citizens' Board of Inquiry into Hunger by noting the obvious: "There's no damn sense in people going hungry in this country."

But South Carolina's leaders, as had their Mississippi colleagues, focused less on the news than on its bearer. The Beaufort *Gazette* reported that the county's fourteen other physicians had agreed that "an objective analysis of the various allegations made reveals no factual substantiation." The denials were not merely racially inspired, for after all a majority of the South's rural poor were white; they were part of that old Southern tradition of circling the wagons against criticism, of protecting the fortress regardless of the rotting foundation. The poor were invisible physically because they were invisible mentally. Everyone was happy, as Walker Percy noted, and Drs. Gatch and Wheeler were party poopers or worse.

South Carolina Senator Ernest F. ("Fritz") Hollings admitted his skepticism when he first heard Dr. Gatch. Well, maybe this thing in Beaufort County was a small isolated patch that could happen in the low country, shut away as it had been for centuries, and now, coming to light, it creates a great deal of furor, as if these people knew something about the twentieth century in any case. "Rustic" and "backward" may be more accurate words than the ones Dr. Gatch was using; and he *is* from Nebraska, where the hogs and other people are all ruddy, round, and well fed. But Hollings, who had always marched to a somewhat different drummer, yet had kept in step often enough to avoid being drummed out of the political fraternity, was touched enough by Gatch's report to embark on an investigative tour of rural South Carolina himself. The result was a book, *The Case Against Hunger* (1970), detailing Hollings's own conversion to the reality of poverty in his state and chronicling that poverty in vivid detail. As a political man, he was particularly scandalized by the indifference of his colleagues to undertaking remedial measures to ameliorate the hunger problems of their constituents, not surprising since they denied the existence of the problem in the first place. "Hunger myopia," Hollings called it, and he pointed out a bitter irony of American political culture. "Within a forty-mile radius of Timmonsville," he wrote, "there are forty farmers who each received last year over $40,000 from the U.S. government—for not working. This doesn't affect the character of the farmer. He's still as red-blooded, capitalistic, free enterprising, and patriotic as ever before. But give the poor, little hungry child a forty-cent breakfast and you've destroyed his character. You've ruined his incentive."

It was little wonder that the President's National Advisory Commission on Rural Poverty concluded: "Most of the rural South is one vast poverty area." It was an exaggeration, of course; the rural South had undergone a remarkable transformation since another presidential commission thirty years earlier had reached a similar conclusion. But it was a helpful warning that while the nation was taking the South to its bosom in all its newness, an older South still prevailed, hidden from the rays of Sunbelt publicity, but present nonetheless. A cartoon in the *New Yorker* depicted a run-down farmhouse at the side of which a woman was hanging out the wash. Her husband, carrying the morning newspaper, related the lead story: "Guess where we've been living all our lives? The Sunbelt."

For those who probed beyond the surface appearances of the region, the revelation implied by the term "Sunbelt" would have seemed equally ironic. The scenery had changed, to be sure, but the players, their roles, and their dialogue maintained a strong continuity with an earlier era, proving again the resilience of Southern culture.

Take industrial recruitment, for example. The Southern lust for outside investment persisted, though with the region's advantages after 1965, the process took on greater sophistication than the sideshow-barker mentality and rhetoric that characterized earlier eras. By 1960, North Carolina Governor Luther Hodges had logged 67,000 miles seeking investments, including tenants for the new Research Triangle Park. His successor, Terry Sanford, at times seemed more a traveling salesman than a governor. On one six-day swing through the Ohio Valley in 1961, Sanford began his itinerary in Pittsburgh on Sunday night, where he received a briefing. On Monday he launched into his recruitment pitch for several industrialists over an eight-hour period, culminating in a reception-dinner at his hotel with the prospects. He rose before dawn the next morning in order to be in Columbus for another full day of discussions and dining. Sanford repeated this program at a different city every day for the rest of the week. Historian James C. Cobb, who chronicled Sanford's movements, claimed that this exhaustive schedule was by no means unique for the 1960s. In fact, Cobb related a not-so-far-fetched dialogue making the rounds of corporate board rooms in Northern cities:

Secretary: There's a salesman here to see you.
Manager: Does he have an appointment?
Secretary: No.
Manager: What's he selling?
Secretary: A state.
Manager: A what? Who is he?
Secretary: He claims he's the governor.

While Hodges and Sanford received deserved credit for attracting the high-tech industries to North Carolina, they were careful to frame their appeals to suit their listeners. The region's education system, though improving, had not yet produced a significant number of high-skilled workers to hold employment in high-tech industry. In fact, such firms locating in the South typically brought managers and some skilled personnel with them or recruited them from outside the region. Lower-skilled, lower-wage industries actually generated more indigenous employment in the South's industrial sector. Though high-wage employment grew fastest in the region during the decade of 1965–1975, by the end of that period, more than two out of every five industrial workers in the South labored in low-wage occupations, compared with a national average of one in ten. So, as Cobb noted, the South's sales pitch "was a curious blend of the old and the new." Officials touted old causes such as cheap nonunion labor and low taxes, while for upscale industries they promised state-funded technical training and research assistance.

The vestiges of old recruiting traditions dating back to the 1880s were particularly apparent with regard to labor. After World War II, the CIO launched "Operation Dixie," designed to bring the Southern workforce into the union fold. It was a dismal failure, encountering hostile receptions from employer and worker alike. On the other hand, organized labor had signal success in attracting Northern workers, especially in the 1960s, when unions began opening membership to blacks. Southern union membership remained static from the mid-1960s to the mid-1970s. While Northern employers, operating on declining profit margins, found themselves evermore encumbered with union contracts, right-to-work statutes blanketed the South. In so-called closed shops, every worker must join the union in order to work; in right-to-work states, the employee has the right to choose membership, the result being to divide the work force and decrease, if not eliminate, union influence even in those industries where unions had gained a foothold. The obstinacy of both labor and management to unions was likely to persist in the South, a right-to-work region. Southern recruiters touted this labor advantage, now more evident by contrast with the North, as they had in the past. In 1976, the Columbia, South Carolina, Chamber of Commerce produced a twenty-page promotional brochure that boasted at least three times that unions claimed only 4 percent of the metropolitan area's work force. By that year, one out of seven Southern workers was unionized, compared with a national average of better than one in four.

Low wages tended to accompany nonunion status. But this did not embarrass recruiters operating in the context of Sunbelt publicity; on the contrary, they continued to trumpet their low-wage work force. In 1976, the Rock Hill, South Carolina, Chamber of Commerce announced with pride that three-quarters of the town's work force earned less than $5,000 per year, about 50 percent of workers' earnings outside the region. It was hardly an anomaly that in 1980 North Carolina was the South's most industrialized state, yet it ranked dead last nationally both in union membership (7 percent) and in hourly wage paid (74 percent of the national average). More than this, in the midst of state- and region-wide prosperity in the 1970s, the average hourly manufacturing wage dropped from $1.05 below the national average to $1.90 under the standard.

The South's industrial base never would catch up with its service sector, and in fact the two general activities operated on distinct planes, with different work forces, and in different locations. Industry remained a rural or small-city enterprise. Georgia, for example, in 1975 counted 56 percent of its manufacturing labor in rural counties. In the South as a whole, more rural nonfarm dwellers worked at manufacturing jobs than did urban residents. The willingness to commute long distances—greater than thirty miles each way—continued to reinforce the pattern of a rural-based work force and hold those workers outside the more lucrative, urban-centered service activities. Also, it was likely that educational opportunities were inferior in rural jurisdictions: they usually could not afford to supplement state educational appropriations, as the more affluent urban counties were able to do. So a two-tiered employment structure solidified during these years, further setting off urban from rural and factory worker from service employee. And as certain industrial opportunities vanished due to mechanization, foreign competition, or changes in fashion, these rural districts were decimated. Rural eastern North Carolina, for example, produced the highest percentage of volunteers for the army in 1972, a reflection of declining fortunes in that area.

Region-wide statistics also masked differentials among states. Though Southern per capita income approached the national average by the mid-1970s, much of this parity resulted from the boom economies in three states—Florida, Texas, and Virginia. Several other states—such as Georgia and South Carolina—lagged fifteen or more percentage points behind the national average (invariably, Mississippi straggled in at 71.6 percent of the national per capita income). These states were still predominantly rural and small-town, and relied inordinately on low-wage industries based in those locations.

Traditional intrastate divisions prevailed as well. If the nineteenth century represented the high tide of the Tidewater, with its commercial and agricultural activities, then the twentieth century belonged to the Piedmont. Though the trend of intraregional geographical-economic shift had been apparent since the 1880s, the gap widened after World War II. Traveling through both districts in the mid-1960s, Walker Percy's protagonist in *The Last Gentleman* observed that "Along the Tidewater, everything was pickled. . . . Backcountry everything was being torn down and built anew." And in the string of medium-sized cities (with the exception of bulging Atlanta) extending in a southwesterly crescent from Richmond to Birmingham, growth was relatively evenly distributed. Greenville County, South Carolina, in the heart of this district, presented a typical pattern of growth for the Piedmont, tripling its number of service-related jobs between 1960 and 1976, adding $650 million in new industrial investment during that period in such industries as chemicals, electrical equipment, and aerospace, while shrinking its traditional textile base from one-half of the total value of manufactured production in 1960 to less than one-third in 1975.

But even within the generally prosperous Piedmont there existed vestiges of the *ancien régime* as late as the mid-1970s, most prominently the domination of the smaller communities

in the subregion by one labor-intensive industry. Philip Morris
hoped to locate a major cigarette plant in Concord, North
Carolina, county seat for rural Cabarrus County, during the
mid-1970s. Cannon Mills dominated the employment base of
the town and county (and the politics as well). As one Cannon
employee noted, "Mr. Charlie [Cannon] don't want nobody
coming in here and running up wages," and the Philip Morris
facility presented the double threat of a unionized work force
laboring at $1.00 per hour more than the prevailing industrial
wage in the county. Cabarrus County also happened to be, not
coincidentally, the least unionized county in the United States.
Philip Morris eventually succeeded in locating its facility outside Concord, but within the county. An official "Welcome to
Cabarrus County" greeting from the Chamber of Commerce
ended in a tie vote. The cigarette manufacturer apparently had
experienced a rough odyssey through the Piedmont, since it
sought Greenville, South Carolina, as an alternate site only to
run into the sentiment expressed by a local construction company executive, "Let's run those bastards off." As Robert Penn
Warren put it in his 1964 novel, *Flood,* these were "the Cap-
tains of Second Class Industry and First Class Extortion."

On occasion, these obstructionist tactics were evident even
in some of the Piedmont's larger urban centers. In 1974, the
Raleigh Chamber of Commerce attempted to block the Xerox
Corporation from locating a unionized facility near the city.
The company's wage scale was twice as great as the state average. At the same time, the chamber was promoting a ref-
erendum to approve industrial development bonds so that
North Carolina would be able "to compete with neighboring
states for blue-chip, high-wage industry." A few years later,
the chamber flexed its muscles again, running out the Miller
Brewing Company, a firm that similarly carried high wages
and union labor. Marshall Frady claimed that "the devout
acquisition of factories became a kind of second religion" in
the South. But in some places there was strict adherence to
denominational lines.

In addition to urban-rural, geographic, and subregional

differentials, the two-tiered Sunbelt economy functioned side-by-side in the urban South. According to urban historian Arnold R. Hirsch, roughly one-half of New Orleans's labor force has been underemployed since the late 1960s. In fact, jobs were a major source of poverty in Southern cities, with Memphis, Birmingham, Miami, Fort Worth, Houston, and Atlanta experiencing an underemployment rate only slightly less severe than the Crescent City. An estimated 70.3 percent of these workers subsisted below the poverty line.

The emphasis of the postindustrial economy on higher skill levels implies increased foreclosure of employment opportunities for those urban residents unable to attain appropriate educational levels. Further, the general prosperity accompanying postindustrial economic growth has had an inflationary impact on urban housing prices and services, depressing the condition of the underemployed.

There was even some question as to whether the statistical shift of economic base and population southward had in fact terminated or seriously modified Northeastern hegemony in the national economy. Aside from the tobacco manufacturers in North Carolina and Coca-Cola in Atlanta, the South possessed relatively few indigenous industries. Major branches of the Fortune 500 firms were located in the region, to be sure, but these subsidiaries, however beneficial to local economies, siphoned capital away from the region. Officials seemed more intent on luring Northern and foreign companies than in assisting the development of local enterprises. Since the region lacked sufficient investment capital—and in the mid-1970s the South remained a net importer of capital—the prospect for major new firms springing from Southern soil was limited.

The Sunbelt, whatever its media rendition, had a distinctive Yankee component, not only in capital, but in labor and entrepreneurial expertise as well. In the 1970s, the South's high-tech work force came from outside the region. In the Research Triangle Park there were scarcely enough Southerners in skilled positions, especially at the executive level, to claim even a token representation. "Yankee" was spoken in shopping malls, and supermarkets carried bagels, ricotta cheese, and other ethnic exotica. For a region that had long resisted such intrusions and that had, in any case, provided few opportunities for the talented, there was a refreshing quality to the Yankee invasion, especially since it did little to jar regional culture other than to reorder a few supermarket shelves. But it also underscored the shortcomings of the regional educational and vocational training systems. In 1974, Edward D. Smith, chairman of the First National Bank of Atlanta, asserted: "You can go to any gathering of businessmen in Atlanta, and I'll bet you five dollars to a ginger cake that at least fifty percent of them will not be natives."

The potential problem, aside from the educational and capital shortcomings revealed by the origins of workers and managers, is that these newcomers may perceive themselves as temporary sojourners in the region, especially at the executive level, where periodic mobility is not uncommon, and where promotion to the corporate headquarters (usually located outside the South) is viewed as a major career objective. Their adherence or even awareness of regional culture depends on self, rather than regional, interest. In 1971, Mississippi businessman Stewart Gammill III, observing the proliferation of "foreign"- (i.e., Northern- and overseas-) owned corporations in the South, wondered aloud whether they would indeed be positive agents for change in the things that required changing, and preservation in those aspects that deserved preserving:

many of these 'foreign'-owned companies have, through the years, had little if any concern for the natural resources, the level of education, or the quality of life in the South. On the contrary, it has been in their interest to maintain a low level of achievement and limited political awareness among both blacks and whites. To have it otherwise would directly threaten long-term profits and growth potential.

Local recruiters knew about the difficulties of building a regional economy with outside resources, even as they did everything within their power to attract Northern and overseas investment. They also understood that they were playing "catch-up" and there was nearly a century of poverty and its associated debilities to overcome. Gene Patterson, who in the mid-1970s was with the *Atlanta Constitution*, and was a frequent critic of the frantic scrambling after industry regardless of its quality, reminded himself that, whatever the drawbacks of such a scattergun approach, "It beats the hell out of pellagra." And, in the recent past, many Southerners knew firsthand about such indigenous diseases and the lifestyle accompanying them.

The rise of the urban South reflected a new Southern lifestyle (and the decline of pellagra) perhaps better than most indicators of a new economic era in the 1960s and 1970s. For the first time in the region's history, the Southern city was the locus of the regional future. "The 'New South'," economist Thomas H. Naylor predicted in 1971, "will be an urban South." And the cities in the 1970s became a regional economic microcosm, with all the good, the bad, and the in-between mixed in a volatile, disparate mélange. Here the complexities of regional economic development were evident, if not understood very well.

The Urban South as a Regional Microcosm

The demographic transformation from 1920, when one out of four Southerners resided in cities, to 1970, when two out of three claimed urban residences, was unprecedented in this country. Much of this growth occurred since World War II. Houston, Dallas-Fort Worth, Tampa, Miami, and Atlanta increased fourfold in population during the generation after 1945. As journalist H. Brandt Ayers noted in 1971, "All roads in the South now lead to the city." Ayers and others were cognizant of the disarray experienced by Northern cities at that time and understood that the South's urban lag was not, in itself, a guarantee against falling into the social, economic, and structural quagmire threatening cities elsewhere. Ayers hoped that the South's rural heritage would act as a check on the excesses indulged in by the great cities of the North, and that it would be possible to transfer the amenities of the small Southern town—the characteristic urban settlement of the region for decades—to the large city. Anyway, it was unlikely that the South would develop the giant urban settlements of the North. As Ayers wrote, 80 percent of urban Southerners lived in cities of between 50,000 and 1,000,000 inhabitants; in the Northeast, 65 percent of the urban population resided in cities greater than 1 million in population. The types of industrial activities requiring immense work forces, the extent of European immigration, and the vast migrations from the farms were trends of an earlier era unlikely to be repeated in the post-World War II South. Finally, aside from the most rapidly growing cities, and they were few, growth occurred at a steady pace after 1945, avoiding a boom-and-bust cycle that upsets planning and incurs heavy social and financial costs.

Actually, what occurred after World War II in Southern cities paralleled developments in the regional economy. Just as the South leapfrogged the industrial revolution, so it bypassed America's urban age. The region traveled almost directly from the countryside to suburbia. Southern cities by the 1970s were immense consumers of space. Dallas grew from 42 square miles in 1942 to 266 square miles thirty years later, assisted by a liberal annexation law that was characteristic of most Southern states. In 1945, Houston comprised a modest 73 square miles, but had burgeoned to 556 square miles by 1975, with an option on annexing an additional 2,000 square miles. In fact, much of the spectacular urban population accessions cited earlier resulted from the voracious territorial appetites of Southern cities. Were it not for annexation, Southern cities collectively would have lost population during the 1960s.

These suburban cities—for the average density levels were almost 50 percent of the national urban average—were growing so large in area that, like giant underground platelets, they were beginning to mass together by the 1970s to form conurbations. A conurbation is simply a formless urban-like mass, and if a picture of oozing settlement comes to mind, that is an accurate depiction. A comparable but different settlement pattern would be the Boston-Washington, D.C., corridor, or "megalopolis." Cities along a 200-mile corridor of Interstate 85 from Raleigh to Greenville, South Carolina, are slowly growing together to form a giant conurbated chain, eventually to link up with Richmond on the northern end of the Interstate and with Atlanta at its southern tip. The interstate highway forms a vital transportation bond, and several of the cities within this Piedmont conurbation have regional airports further blurring urban boundaries. A newer conurbation is emerging along the Gulf Coast, expanding from Pensacola, Florida, to New Orleans, and encompassing federal installations and growing port facilities as well as a rapidly developing tourist industry.

The Tidewater Virginia area encompasses a more specific conurbation, the origins of which are almost as bizarre as the spatial form. As an alterative to being "pickled," (to use Walker Percy's term) by stagnant and racially diverse Norfolk, surrounding counties merged with the small cities in the area to form Virginia Beach, an amorphous 300-square-mile semi-urban sprawl. A group of adjacent jurisdictions then formed the city of Chesapeake, an even larger geographical entity than Virginia Beach, with agriculture as the urban economic base. Finally, the town of Suffolk merged with its county, comprising a larger area than either Virginia Beach or Chesapeake. Agriculture was the primary activity of this "city" as well. The confluence of rural and urban had always been a characteristic of Southern urban settlements, but these entities seemed bent upon taking this tradition to its illogical conclusion. Nevertheless, the consolidation movement in Tidewater Virginia in the 1960s was an effective means of preventing the territorial imperialism of larger cities in the area, pooling services in a region of uneven densities, and capturing the population and economic base of a growing and affluent resort area.

Similar smaller conurbations existed in other parts of the South, such as along southern Florida's Atlantic coast from Dade County (the location of Miami) up to Palm Beach County. Though of greater density than its Tidewater counterpart, the southern Florida sprawl exhibited similar spatial characteristics. Journalist Tad Szulc described his meanderings through the area in 1974 as follows: "Driving along the coastal highway in Florida say from South Miami to Palm Beach, I never had the sensation of advancing from one place to another, though I crossed three counties. It was one continuous, homogenized, semi-urban landscape."

These new types of urban settlements sprouting along the Southern landscape confounded urbanists more accustomed to Northern models of city growth. Brian J. L. Berry, a geographer, termed the pattern "urbanization without cities," and Pat Watters of the Southern Regional Council declared that the South "had no real cities," even referring to Atlanta as "an overgrown county seat." But if Southern cities did not conform to traditional perspectives on urbanization, they may have heralded a new era in American urbanization. In other words, rather than being urban mutations, these sprawling low- and medium-density entities may be the forerunners of a new urban America—more dependent on the automobile, with a dispersed population and economic base, in proximity to the countryside and recreational amenities, and with predominantly low-rise residential and commercial structures. It was a more private, less confrontational, and more relaxed way of living than the older pattern of urbanization implied. It was Southern.

But the new urban form did not imply immunity from old urban problems. While Southern metropolitan areas grew at national pacesetting rates, almost all of the growth occurred outside the central city. Those cities unable to annex adjacent territory because of incorporation of these suburban districts or legal obstacles experienced demographic and economic losses. During the 1960s and early 1970s, Atlanta and New Orleans, for example, were losing populations at rates comparable to Newark and Detroit, two troubled Northern cities. The population loss generated economic flight. Between 1960 and 1975, Atlanta's share of the metropolitan employment base declined from 20 percent to 12 percent, reflecting an absolute loss of 2,000 jobs. Office and industrial parks were scattered across the metropolitan horizon, hugging interstates and exchanges far from the snarls and high land prices of downtown Atlanta. In 1960, 90 percent of the metropolitan area office space was situated in Atlanta. By 1980, the city's share had declined significantly to 42 percent.

Highways have become the major determinants of growth in the metropolitan South, and they invariably attract a variety of economic activities once reserved for the central city. Aside from their location, the great commonality of these strips of concrete and kitsch was their commonality, their complete divorce from any relationship to the regional milieu save the chronic entrepreneurial grasping after the tin ring of Yankee-style growth. "Coming into Greenville [Mississippi]," Joel Garreau related in the late 1970s, "on the inevitable strip-development highway, one sees, just after the Country Club Estates, the intriguingly named Mainstream Mall. Bright, shiny, and utterly interchangeable with any shopping center in North America."

While business boomed along the suburban strips, Southern downtowns, large and small, began to take on aspects familiar to observers of Northern cities: vacant stores, a derelict and despairing population, and a decline in the quality and quantity of services. Actually, preliminary indications of downtown decline had surfaced in the urban South as far back as the late 1940s and early 1950s. Part of the problem was self-inflicted. Southern urban leaders were either unprepared for the extent of peripheral growth that would occur or adopted policies that inadvertently enhanced the centrifugal trends. When noted planner Clarence Stein proposed growth controls and preservation of open spaces to Miami leaders in 1945, they ridiculed him. The South had scarcely advanced beyond the frontier mentality of the nineteenth century and, on occasion, with good reason: any growth, no matter how haphazard and chaotic, would be preferable to the stagnation and misery of the previous decades.

Some cities operated without any growth controls whatsoever. Zoning was foreign to Houston, both as a policy and

an ideology. Planning meant some sort of centralized control
and an incursion on the inviolable right of private property.
So Houston burgeoned willy-nilly, and even though other cities, such as Dallas, possess zoning ordinances, they bear a
striking resemblance to the pattern of development in Houston. By the late 1970s, Houston was spending $0.32 per person
for city planning, compared with $2.79 for Baltimore or $7.24
for Kansas City.

For other cities, it was not a question of too little planning,
but of the wrong kind. For the rapidly growing, freely annexing
cities the chaos of growth was not particularly alarming, since
it all eventually would come under the purview of the central
metropolis. But for those central cities experiencing slower
growth or the development of hostile incorporated suburbs,
policies were necessary to reverse the trend, or at least to halt
urban decline.

Urban renewal became a common redevelopment strategy
in the South during the 1950s and 1960s. The federal government, in a postwar effort to maintain an active economy and
provide housing for returning GIs and their families, passed
the 1949 Housing Act, which amounted to a substantial federal
subsidy to builders of large numbers of homes. Such a scale
of construction was possible only in the relatively inexpensive
and empty suburban areas. Coupled with the federal Interstate
Highway Act of 1956, the housing legislation funneled billions
of public and private investment dollars into suburban home
and infrastructure development and diverted the same from
urban neighborhoods. This is not to say that federal housing
policy ignored central cities. Since the policy emphasized new
construction, the translation to the urban environment meant
slum clearance and erection of new housing on the cleared site.
Land assembly in other parts of the city was simply too expensive to serve as alternative locations. The result was two-
fold: first, new public housing tended to perpetuate the patterns
of segregation—invariably, concentrations of blacks and designations of slum areas coincided; second, the number of new
units rarely matched the number of units destroyed by the

clearance process, resulting in displacement, overcrowding in adjacent areas, and the flight of those who could afford to move to the attractive housing market in the suburbs.

This was not a particularly Southern phenomenon but, rather, a national pattern. In the urban South, however, five units were demolished for every new unit built compared with a national average ratio of three to one; that is, displaced residents in the South were less likely to find housing in their old neighborhoods than residents elsewhere. An extreme but by no means atypical case occurred in Charlotte in the early 1960s, when the city destroyed Brooklyn, a viable black neighborhood near downtown. The homes in Brooklyn were of marginal quality and doubtless most deserved their fate. The city, however, chose not to erect housing on the site, creating instead an early 1960s version of what today would be called an urban enterprise zone. Unfortunately, renewal funds and the economy in general began to sputter at this time, and the land remains partially vacant to this day, adorned only by a hotel, a park, and a few office buildings. The displaced blacks filtered into other black neighborhoods, depressing housing conditions there and solidifying residential racial segregation. A similar situation occurred in Atlanta during the late 1960s when a black neighborhood on the eastern edge of downtown became the site of highway construction, office buildings, a stadium, and a civic center. By that time, in fact, Atlanta officials had evolved a policy that expressly prohibited the utilization of renewal land for public housing.

Part of the private rationale for gutting the downtown area of residential units was to secure the area for shoppers, conventioneers, and tourists. If affluent residents were going to live elsewhere in the metropolitan area and more than likely patronize the ubiquitous suburban shopping malls, downtown, in order to survive, had to become more than a retail center and had to cater to a clientele other than the locals. Again, this was a national phenomenon, but in terms of glitter and exaggeration, the South easily led the field, displaying its historical self-consciousness, bursting into the party with the most outlandish sport coat and the loudest voice.

It was as if urban Southerners had read so far in Genesis and no further: "Go to, let us build us a city and a tower . . . lest we be scattered abroad upon the face of the whole earth" (Genesis 11:4). And they did, of course build the towers, but as in the Book, they were indeed "scattered abroad upon the face of the" metropolitan area. John Portman, Atlanta's skyscraper prophet, enamored of Copenhagen's Tivoli Gardens, where everyone smiled, sought to create the architecture of entertainment north of Five Points, the city's old downtown. The result was the Peachtree Center complex, which catapulted Atlanta into becoming a major convention city and prompted an orgy of hotel and office construction in the city's new downtown area. But most of the smiles were seen inside these structures on the faces of conventioneers with expense accounts and bug-eyed tourists, spinning happily in revolving bars or shooting up rocket-style elevators. Outside, the streetscape is a wasteland of concrete and parking lots that becomes an insecure no-man's-land at night between the island fortresses looming above. Atlanta was not alone, of course, merely the most publicized, thanks in part to such glitzy campaigns as Forward Atlanta, devised by Mayor Ivan Allen, Jr., in the late 1960s, essentially a building and industrial recruitment program that lifted Atlanta into the class of a national, if not international, city by the mid-1970s. Downtown was saved, but for whom?

So Southern metropolitan areas, the gem in the Sunbelt crown, took on a disparate aspect, much like the rest of the region. The endless suburbs look like Southern California with a bad case of kudzu choking the natural environment, and the new downtowns look like New York with sunglasses, mirrored towers reflecting each other, but not much else.

It appeared that as the South rode off into the Sunbelt, it was losing itself; that the price for national parity and acceptance would be its regional soul. As a young Atlantan who was poised to leave the Emerald City of the Piedmont for the

refuge of a small town outside the irresistible ooze of the metropolitan area blurted to Marshall Frady, "Hell, you talk about
Gone with the Wind, Sherman and the Civil War were only
an illusion, for all the smoke and roar. This time, without
anybody even noticing it, it's really happening. The South is
vanishing quietly as a passing of summer light—and this time,
for good."

But numerous others before this soon-to-be erstwhile Atlantan had written or spoken an epitaph for Dixie. There was
something so Southern about Pasadena-amid-the-kudzu or New
York-on-the-Chattahoochie. It was a capital-poor region attempting to build a transcontinental railroad before the Civil
War; an impoverished people striving to create an industrial
empire afterward; the board of trade boosters erecting skyscrapers on dreams of the future in the 1920s; and every striving and hoping since then. Things had gone easier for the
North; there was no need to try so hard, no need for feeling
inferior or defensive, aware that when they played "The Star-
Spangled Banner" it was your song because you had fought
and bled and died living its meaning. When you start from
behind with severe emotional and physical handicaps, the alternative to giving up is to try harder. But now, in the mid-
1970s, that things were becoming easier for the South, it was
difficult to slough off old habits, regardless of Yankee prattle
to the contrary. Perhaps deep in their Calvinist souls, Southerners believed this new prosperity was another chimera; it
could not last. Perhaps some of them realized that the Sunbelt
was part or maybe mostly figment; that hunger and poverty
stalked the region, that some places, try as they might, could
not catch the rays of light.

But there was another perspective that Frady and his dis-
illusioned young Atlantan should have considered as well.
There was at least another urban community available for
retreat, where the values of past and place lingered and flourished. The Sunbelt not only implied a crazy-quilt pattern of
rich and poor and in-between, but cultural shades as well.
Those small towns and cities under 50,000 inhabitants, still

the characteristic urban South, where front porches have not yet surrendered to air conditioning and the radio tower is the extent of the skyline—in these places, as Fred Powledge noted in his travels through the region in the mid-1970s, "many of the good and interesting qualities of the region have been least diluted; where the individualism and good humor of the place most easily show through."

Whether covert in the minarets or malls of the metropolis, or more overt in the smaller places that retained their perspective, sometimes against their will, the South persisted. The overlay was there, but it had not penetrated much. It had been the Promised Land all along anyway; the land was there, only the promise remained to be fulfilled. And for some Southerners that promise was coming to fruition; for others, it remained in hymns or dreams with a vast Red Sea before them.

CHAPTER FIVE

After Civil Rights: Consolidation and Struggle, 1965–1975

Martin Luther King lingered awhile in Montgomery, as if to savor the moment, to frame it within time and lock it away with his other historical mementos from a decade of struggle. But the news jarred the reminiscence: a white Detroit house-wife, Viola Liuzzo, ferrying marchers back to Selma from Montgomery after the demonstration, was ambushed by Klansmen, shot and killed. The triumphs, it seemed, were always bittersweet, a mixture of joy and sorrow: the success of the sit-ins and the brutality of the Freedom Rides; the victory in Birmingham and the church bombing; and now this, equally senseless, but invariably part of the regional drama in which the players, no matter how small their roles, never seemed quite willing or able to bid farewell.

But the violence abated, emerging fitfully and sporadically over the next decade or so like a beast occasionally awakened from a prolonged hibernation. The South went on to other preoccupations, mostly making money, and the civil rights movement was over, forgotten. Warren Fortson, a sympathetic white attorney from Americus, Georgia, toured the Deep South in 1967 and observed that "the Movement . . . just doesn't exist anymore. I've been all over Mississippi and all that's left of it here is a few scattered seedy students who never went back up North. . . . As for the Negroes . . . [t]hey've quit the field."

The epitaph for the civil rights movement was as premature, however, as the eulogy for the South would be. Much of the activity after 1965 occurred in low profile, individually, consolidating the gains of the previous decade; and most of the resistance, what remained of it, was more subtle, less violent. But Fortson was accurate in noticing the dispirit, because the civil rights crusade was more akin to a family, a community, than to a mass movement; the emphasis was greater on relationships than on ideology. It was, after all, a Southern movement. As in all families, there were internal disagreements, but in times of crisis, there was an instinctive pulling together. Now that the crisis seemed to be passing, the urgency leaving, the family began to disintegrate.

Divided Voices: Dissolution of the Movement Coalition

It was not that the work was finished; there just was no clear consensus on what that work should be. Unfinished agendas abounded: desegregation of schools was moving slowly, if at all; blacks, especially in rural areas, were not taking advantage of the new Voting Rights Act in appreciable numbers; and there were pressing economic issues relating to employment, housing, and services. Each of these objectives, in turn, appealed to different segments of the black community. Through 1965, the civil rights movement maintained essentially middle-class objectives. The victories obtained by the movement enabled blacks to eat in restaurants, sleep at hotels, and cast ballots, among other rights. Middle-class blacks, especially in urban areas, were most able both geographically and financially to take advantage of these gains. The movement leadership represented the traditional black middle-class protagonists, especially the preachers. The economic issues, while of concern for all blacks, were most pertinent for those who had least. Many middle-class leaders relied on an exclusively black clientele in any case—the ministers, barbers, realtors, physicians, and attorneys—so job discrimination and the absence of decent public housing were less central to their program.

The variety of potential issues also implied numerous choices in tactics. There was a growing restlessness, especially among younger, poorer blacks, with King's nonviolent philosophy. The physical and psychological toll they felt was too great a sacrifice for the sometimes modest achievements. Also, if whites kept their tempers, the effectiveness of nonviolence was limited. Militant black leader Floyd McKissick declared succinctly after the Watts uprising in August 1965 that nonviolence had "outlived its usefulness." But there existed no general agreement on alternatives.

There was also no guarantee that an agreement on tactics and objectives would counter the centrifugal forces propelling the various civil rights groups away from each other. There were egos involved, foundation money, membership, and media coverage. In addition, generational and class differences were likely to evoke different perspectives. Finally, some leaders understood Southern peculiarities better than others and were willing to use the language of religion, past, and place rather than to adopt rhetoric more suited to Northern conditions. All of these divisive factors were evident in the final cooperative effort attempted by the diverse organizations, an effort that began as a quixotic endeavor by one man to conquer the fear of and in Mississippi.

James Meredith was a slight man who had, by 1966, already undertaken the large task of integrating the University of Mississippi four years earlier, an event that left two dead and scores injured. He had entered the maelstrom and survived. Understandably, he lived with fear; it gnawed at him, alternately weakening and strengthening his determination, but always there, like Banquo's ghost, to remind him, if such reminders were necessary, of the dark evil that encircled him for his ambition. Yet, Meredith proclaimed to all who would hear him: "I am a Mississippian in all respects—even the bad ones." To claim his birthright and to dissolve the fear within, he proposed to walk through Mississippi. His objective was not only personal; he also hoped to give courage and resolve to black Mississippians gripped by that same fear, too paralyzed to cast a ballot, claim a job, and demand decent housing and services.

So on a dewy spring morning in April 1966, James Meredith began his march against fear. As he left the town of Hernando in the Delta, some twenty-eight miles into his walk, a shot crackled through the warming air and he fell, wounded. Meredith's wounds were not life-threatening, and state troopers accompanying him rushed him to a Memphis hospital for immediate treatment. The shot was like an alarm to the disparate civil rights organizations, and their leaders converged on Memphis, seizing upon the incident as the dramatic *deus ex machina* to set again in motion the process of racial change. King was on hand, but his charisma and reputation no longer dominated the proceedings. His erstwhile partners in the movement, SNCC and CORE, had changed leadership and tone. Their field workers were chanting "Too much love/too much love/Nothing kills a nigger like/Too much love," mocking King as much as warning whites. CORE's Floyd McKissick had openly dismissed the nonviolent philosophy, and Stokely Carmichael, SNCC's new director, charted an even more militant course, renouncing the interracial objectives of the movement and running off the organization's white membership. The three black leaders resolved to take up Meredith's march through Mississippi to the state capital at Jackson.

From the outset, Carmichael attempted to assert his leadership style over the demonstration. In the early stages of the march, Carmichael and his lieutenant, Willie Ricks, agitated the demonstrators by repeatedly using the phrase, "Black Power," much to King's discomfort. "Black Power" was not a new slogan, though it had not yet burst on white consciousness. Novelist Richard Wright and Harlem religious and political leader Adam Clayton Powell had employed the phrase in the 1940s. The growing belligerency of the march alarmed white Mississippians, as well as some blacks who would still have to live among the whites once the marchers passed on by. But a year and a spate of federal laws had made a significant difference. The state's new leaders now had to contend with, or at least acknowledge, a black political presence. Also, other priorities, especially economic development, were preempting race. Accordingly, the law enforcement authorities, so prominent in earlier violent responses to black protest, now functioned as reluctant protectors. Whatever violence occurred would necessarily be random, individual forays under cover of darkness, and even these nocturnal missions were becoming futile. Carmichael could, therefore, stretch his rhetoric and push his program.

The opportunity occurred on June 16 when the caravan entered Greenwood, Mississippi, and Carmichael and several of his companions bivouacked on the grounds of the town's black high school, contrary to the order of the state troopers. The troopers arrested them quietly and detained the group for about six hours before releasing them. Though hardly an incident of major import, Carmichael seized the moment of his release to take command of the march and, by extension, of the civil rights movement, from a faltering King, who was no longer able to stir a new generation of Southern blacks. Vaulting onto a flatbed truck with a clenched fist thrust defiantly into the air, he hurled a vow to his supporters: "This is the twenty-seventh time I have been arrested—and I ain't going to jail no more!" The crowd roared its approval. He continued: "The only way we gonna stop them white men from whippin' us is to take over. We been saying freedom for six years and we ain't got nothin.' " The crowd again roared "Amens." Carmichael concluded, slowing his cadence and shouting each syllable: "What we gonna start saying now is Black Power!" And Willie Ricks in the crowd picked up the chant: "We want Black Power!" And the crowd echoed. "That's right," Carmichael implored, "that's what we want. . . . What do you want?" In unison: "Black Power!"

Ten days later, the protesters, now swelled to a mostly black throng of 15,000, marched into Jackson chanting "Black Power! Black Power!" Floyd McKissick declared at the end of the rally, "1966 shall be remembered as the year we left our imposed status as Negroes and became *Black Men* . . . 1966 is the year of the concept of Black Power." Five years earlier, *Ebony* magazine had issued a similar declaration, citing the sit-ins as the turning point in the self-elevation to manhood; now a new definition appeared, more strident, yet more ambiguous. It was not quite clear how blacks, especially Southern blacks, would live up to its standard.

By 1966, even King began a perceptible shift in his rhetoric. His nonviolent philosophy was never immutable in any case; it evolved gradually since the Montgomery boycott and took on a more confrontational aspect during the Birmingham crisis. The change was not so much away from the philosophy of nonviolence as it was in the tone and scope of his program. He was at once more pessimistic about the operative abilities of love and more certain that broad, fundamental alterations of society were necessary to dissipate the sin of racial subjugation. "For years," he noted early in 1967, "I labored with the idea of reforming the existing institutions of the society, a little change here, a little change there. Now I feel quite differently, I think you've got to have a reconstruction of the entire society, a revolution of values." Though he stated it quietly, without the menacing fanfare of a Carmichael, it was a statement with which the SNCC leader could agree.

King continued to play the role of troubleshooter, an ambassador of compromise. He moved from one place to another, lending his name and bargaining abilities to resolve racial deadlocks before one side or the other lost patience and resorted to violence. Memphis was one such place, a grubby, down-at-the-heels city sitting above the Mississippi River, living in memories. The famed Beale Street was now home to winos and their fellow travelers, and the sweet sounds of jazz no longer wafted into the still night air. Cotton Row on Front Street, a brick and mortar monument to the days when the wharves groaned under the weight of the white gold from the rich Delta lands below the city, was now quiet. The once-proud Peabody Hotel, which had welcomed cotton merchants, and planters, and drummers from everywhere, still had those ducks that startled first-time visitors by marching briskly out of the elevator onto a red carpet and into a fountain, but they paraded now for a lesser audience.

This city on the river, which once rivaled New Orleans as both jazz mecca and cotton port, now concerned itself with garbage. As with most other points of public contention in Memphis in the decade or so before January 1968, the garbage question related closely to race. Specifically, when it rained in the city, officials sent black sanitation workers home with two hours' pay while retaining white workers on a full day's payroll. When this occurred on January 31, 1968, black trash collectors voted to strike.

White political and economic leaders were not in a conciliatory mood. It was more than money; it was principle. The feeling in Memphis was that the civil disturbances in Northern cities over the previous three years were inevitable results of Northern urban leaders' generous social programs, which only stimulated further demands in a deadly round-robin of political blackmail. A hard, firm line was necessary to douse militancy before it flared into something worse.

As the strike dragged on through March, the strikers' plight began to receive the attention of black leaders throughout the country. On March 14, NAACP officials Roy Wilkins and Bayard Rustin traveled to Memphis to pick up sagging morale and stimulate national support for the black trash collectors. Four days later, Martin Luther King visited the city, interrupting his planning for a poverty march on Washington. King urged a general strike and a mass protest march through the downtown. At this point, the resistance of Mayor William Loeb and his colleagues stiffened further and the mayor cut off food stamps to the strikers. Local newspapers accused King of inciting blacks as tension and animosity heightened. On March 28, negotiations, fitful as they were, broke off, and King led his march through the city.

But times had changed since he walked at the head of an orderly interracial and mostly adult column on the road from Selma to Montgomery. Whites were considerably less evident now and younger blacks more prevalent. There was no federal legislation this time that could cure the injustice. What was the cure for unemployment, for job discrimination, low wages, and low skills? Neither King nor the marchers had ready answers, the economic equivalent of the Voting Rights Act. So the frustration boiled over and scalded King's reputation another time. The violence at the fringes of the march ended with the death of a black teenager who was caught looting a store. The mayor sought and obtained an injunction against further marches and King left the city disappointed and troubled, but vowing to return.

He came back on April 3, determined to maintain the pressure, injunction or no, on the intransigent city and, not incidentally, to reaffirm the viability of nonviolence in those violent times. King met his faithful, 2,000 of them, at the Mason Temple Church of God in Christ. Many of them were migrants from the dying sharecrop agriculture of Mississippi who were clinging to the hope shared by so many immigrants to our land of something better, even if the journey from plantation to city was not very long and what they witnessed when they arrived was not much different from the Delta. It was a familiar audience in a familiar setting.

But the speech was different. Memphis was not on King's mind that night. The speech was reflective, almost a reminiscence, a past-tense summation of an era and of himself. He related how fortunate he felt to have lived in that time and recalled his greatest struggle and triumph in Birmingham. And then he talked about his own mortality, a subject which had intruded increasingly into his thought and private conversations and public utterances. He recalled a day ten years earlier in New York, where he was holding an autograph party for his first book, when a black woman stepped up and stabbed him in the chest, missing his aorta, the body's main artery, by centimeters; the wound's location was so precarious that if he had sneezed he would have died. He used the story as a way to express his gratitude to the Lord for allowing him to live through a great time—the sit-ins, the freedom rides, Birmingham, and Selma, and now Memphis, as if this were somehow the last stop on a grand odyssey of fulfillment. And then he spoke about recent threats against his life, as recent as that day; but somehow, he allowed, "it doesn't matter with me now." "Why?"

Because I've been to the mountaintop. And I don't mind. Like anybody, I would like to live a long life. Longevity has its place. But I'm not concerned about that now. I just want to do God's will. And He's allowed me to go up to the mountain. And I've looked over. And I've seen the promised land. I may not get there with you. But I want you to know tonight, that we, as a people, will get to the promised land. And I'm happy tonight. I'm not worried about anything. I'm not fearing any man. Mine eyes have seen the glory of the coming of the Lord.

It was a farewell address, a valedictory, a plea to pursue the dream after he was gone. Like Moses, he would never see the promised land, a South cleansed of its biracial sins. Twenty-four hours later he lay dying, a victim of an assassin's bullet; James Earl Ray completed the scenario that King seemed to know all along.

Part of King's mastery was to assume the lofty ground, to frame his objectives in the basic religious principles of his region, in order to sustain the difficult, dirty, and dangerous work down below in the streets, at the courthouses, and in the shops. With King gone, the connection between the ethereal world of faith, of dreams, and the work remaining unfulfilled was severed. Perhaps the new agendas did not lend themselves to the ministrations of the clergy in any case, but the righteousness of the cause touched friend and enemy alike until the barrier was breached and they were joined together, metaphorically, in a new understanding. The dream persisted, to be sure, but there emerged no successor to articulate it so well, to impart a collective purpose to the individual hopes of black Southerners. So the triumphs in the ensuing years would be small and come tediously, with the framework of the dream frequently obscured or forgotten entirely. The dream lived on in the black Southerner, but struggled for survival in the South.

The Voice of Hope: Black Ballots

Despite the uncertainties of direction and resolve, there was the clarity of the 1965 Voting Rights Act. The act, specifically aimed at Southern states below Virginia, ensured the rights of blacks to register and vote and provided for federal intervention if Southern officials inhibited those rights. In addition, in order to prevent legislative sleight-of-hand, such as altering the election process to disadvantage blacks, the act provided for the preclearance and approval by the Justice Department of all electoral changes after 1965. Though the department has rejected only a tiny fraction of electoral changes in the affected jurisdictions, the process itself has limited circumvention of the act's intent, since differences between Justice and the locality have usually been resolved before the objection reaches the litigation stage; and to avoid a protracted (and expensive) negotiation, localities take more care to frame their procedural changes within the framework of the act.

These safeguards translated into votes, and the votes in turn translated into a political revolution. Within a week of President Johnson's signing of the act, the federal examiner in Selma registered more blacks than had enrolled since the beginning of the century. In Leflore County, Mississippi, where dogged efforts by SNCC had resulted in 300 black registrants, federal personnel enrolled 5,000 blacks in a few weeks. Within a year of passage, the Voting Rights Act had doubled black registration in the five most difficult Deep South states (South Carolina, Georgia, Alabama, Mississippi, and Louisiana) to 46 percent of eligible black voters; within four years, the figure had risen to 60.7 percent, only slightly below the regional average of 64.8 percent.

If the civil rights movement had rendered Southern blacks visible, then the Voting Rights Act turned visibility into influence. White politicians in most of the affected jurisdictions now confronted a black political force. Among the results were enhanced electoral fortunes of beleaguered white progressives and a political climate conducive to the emergence of new leaders no longer burdened by the race issue that had monopolized Southern politics. The change was especially noticeable in governors' mansions throughout the South. The Democratic gubernatorial class of 1970, like the group that ascended to short-lived power in 1946, reflected a new regional agenda. Unlike the progressives of that earlier era, however, the new state leaders' power rested on a broader electorate which, because of its nature, would be less sensitive to overt racial appeals. Dale Bumpers, emerging from the rural Arkansas foothills, handily defeated venerable segregationist Orval Faubus in 1970, waging a campaign that emphasized the commonalty of all lower-income people, regardless of race. Reubin Askew, from Florida's conservative panhandle, won a similar campaign for governor, also in 1970. Askew had risen from an impoverished rural Oklahoma childhood to the Sunshine State's highest office, stressing such populist issues as tax reform and education. Bucking the rising tide of sentiment in his state against busing to achieve school desegregation, Askew remarked in 1971 that "We cannot achieve equal opportunity in education by passing laws ... against busing—they could deny us what I believe is the highest destiny of the American people. That destiny, of course, is to achieve a society in which all races, all creeds, and all religions have learned not only to live with their differences—but to *thrive* upon them."

In Georgia in 1970, Jimmy Carter, a peanut farmer and engineer from conservative south Georgia, became governor after running a campaign that was ambiguous on the race issue. But he did not equivocate in his inaugural address: "I say to you quite frankly that the time for racial discrimination is over"; and he proceeded to act on those words during his administration. Republican Linwood Holton, newly elected governor of Virginia, the birthplace of massive resistance, expressed similar sentiments in his 1970 inaugural speech: "it is clear that problem-solving, and not philosophical principles, has become the focal point of politics. ... No more must the slogan of states' rights sound a recalcitrant and defensive note for the people of the South. For the era of defiance is behind us."

Indeed, state leaders could now move to new agendas, not the least of which was promoting the economic development that was moving southward. The rabid racial rhetoric that characterized successful political campaigning in the South was waning, soon to be an anachronism, except for a few diehards who cared more for principle than office. Political scientist Earl Black quantified the change by noting that "During the period 1966-1973, for the first time in the twentieth century, there were more nonsegregationists than militant segregationists among major candidates." Even the "militant segregationists" were moving away from their obstreperous rhetoric and policies, in some cases becoming indistinguishable from the upstart white progressive candidates. As early as 1966, Herman Talmadge of the Georgia dynasty that ascended to statewide power on the white supremacy issue began to openly court black votes. That same year in Alabama, the Democratic party, under the leadership of segregation's high priest, George Wallace, removed the state party's motto—"White Supremacy— For the Right" from the ballot. Alabama Congressman Walter Flowers, whose district underwent reapportionment to include the highest percentage of black population in the state—38 percent—improved his support rating for civil rights legislation from 0 to 44 percent. As the press secretary to Mississippi Governor John Bell Williams remarked, "If blacks hadn't registered things wouldn't have changed one iota."

The new political realities produced some interesting scenes across the South by the early 1970s. There was Eugene "Bull" Connor in a black Birmingham church singing "We Shall

Overcome," seeking votes (he lost); George Wallace crowning a black homecoming queen at the University of Alabama, not far from his stand in the schoolhouse door a decade earlier, and planting a kiss on her cheek; Jimmy Carter hanging a portrait of Martin Luther King in a prominent location in the state capitol building, a spot that Lieutenant Governor Lester Maddox, erstwhile ax-handle wielder and rabble rouser, would have to pass by daily; and in 1972 in Jackson, Mississippi, capital of a state that itself had been a powerful symbol in the 1960s, a black gubernatorial candidate was emoting from the capitol steps, as well as in every dusty county courthouse town in the state, and living to read about it in the next morning's newspaper.

More than symbols, these scenes were also reflections of power. Blacks were not only lending their votes to preferred white candidates, but electing members of their own race as well for the first time since the Reconstruction era. Though black elected officials comprised only 2 percent of Southern officialdom in 1975, the figure represented a 2,000 percent increase over the situation a decade earlier. Most of these 1,400 black officeholders held positions in small towns and counties of heavy black concentration, and even here the offices were relatively minor—such as school board member and justice of the peace. But it was a beginning. More encouraging was the fact that some of these black elected officials obtained their offices with modest white support. In 1972 Andrew Young became the first black congressman in this century from the Deep South by garnering 26 percent of the white vote (and 98 percent of the black vote) in his Atlanta jurisdiction. Young's district included a majority white population (62 percent) and he received a good cross section of middle- and upper-income white support in the affluent northside neighborhoods.

While the mere presence of a black on the city council, in the state legislature, or in the mayor's office generated significant psychic benefits in the black community, it remained to be seen whether or not blacks and their white allies could reorient state and local policies to their specific benefit. Services and jobs were of primary concern to the black community. The difficulty, of course, was that the service backlog in black neighborhoods was huge, more than urban revenues could cover, and in the traditionally low-tax South, even talking about raising taxes was risky. Atlanta's mayor Ivan Allen, Jr., ticked off the legacy of neglect in his city's black neighborhoods: "There were no building regulations. There was no code enforcement. . . . There was no effort to provide any form of housing . . . the garbage was not picked up regularly . . . the streets were not paved." Now Allen noted, politicians had to rectify these inequities and that in itself presented urban administrators with a huge task: "Not only are we endeavoring to provide extended and better services for all of the people . . . , but also we are trying to take up the slack of what has [sic] been the slums or the deteriorated areas." And the reason for this sudden blossoming and awareness of black service needs was the black vote.

In the smaller communities, the expanding Great Society programs of the federal government and, subsequently, revenue sharing provided working capital for service projects otherwise beyond the financial capabilities of these localities. So black urban administrators and their white allies learned to court the federal government as much, if not more, than potential industrial recruits. In 1969, voters in Fayette, Mississippi, a struggling town with a 75 percent black population, elected a black mayor, Charles Evers, and five black town councilmen. Prior to the election, the town lacked medical facilities, schools, paved roads, and a water system. Evers secured $400,000 in federal grants and used the money to erect a community center which would house, among other activities, health and job-training facilities. The government paved streets, built sidewalks, and added a police force. The Ford Foundation assisted with a $400,000 economic development loan, which led to the establishment of a chemical plant, and soon thereafter an ITT subsidiary moved into the community. The new economic activity generated 500 jobs in a town of 2,000 inhabitants.

In the region's larger cities, the service issue, while important, was part of a broad array of policies necessary to upgrade black life. When Maynard Jackson became Atlanta's first black mayor in 1973, he set about redistributing a variety of community perquisites, especially city-related employment opportunities. He required minority hiring for companies contracting with the city, named a black commissioner of public safety in order to ensure equal police protection for blacks, and staffed his office with several blacks.

This is all not to say that the Voting Rights Act transformed Southern politics into an interracial paradise. Obstacles remained to the fulfillment of the dream of political equity and equality and to the type of life those objectives implied. Black voters themselves represented an impediment to political equality; how could it be otherwise with political novices, relatively unschooled in democratic practices, thrust suddenly into the political arena? Generally, voter participation by blacks tended to be less than by whites—unfamiliarity with electoral procedures, fear, and changes in polling times and places were among the factors limiting their participation. Blacks also suffered from factionalism. Never a monolithic group on most issues, blacks confronted class divisions, generational conflicts, urban-rural animosities—the same divisions that plagued the white electorate. But since blacks were in the minority in all states and in most jurisdictions within those states, divisions could and did reduce the number of black elected officials, especially since white voter registration increased as well during the decade after initial passage of the Voting Rights Act. The Sunbelt prosperity drew affluent whites to the region who were more likely to vote than poorer blacks. Also, with the removal of such bars as the poll tax and literacy requirements, native white participation increased, motivated, too, by fear of growing black political power.

Black voting power was less than the population figures would seem to indicate. Blacks, especially in the rural counties, were victims of a skewed demography, exacerbated by continued out-migration in the 1960s that left these areas with disproportionately high numbers of elderly and the very young. Panola County, Mississippi, for example, held a majority (51 percent) black population, but only 21 percent of the eligible voters.

White officials, especially in rural districts with higher black concentrations, manipulated the electoral machinery to minimize the impact of the new electorate (another indication of the uneven patterns of change in the South). In areas where blacks did not comprise a majority of eligible voters, switching from district to at-large voting to dilute black voting strength occurred, and some cities, such as Richmond, resorted to annexation to increase the white electorate. Other manipulative devices included gerrymandering—confining the black population to a particular district, conceding representation in that area, or diluting black concentrations by redrawing district lines to distribute smaller portions of the black electorate to majority white districts. Thus, the Delta congressional district in Mississippi, a thin elongated strip stretching several hundred miles north and south with a majority black population, was the subject of a gerrymander, with the area being distributed to five other congressional districts with boundaries drawn across the state horizontally. In Tuskegee, Alabama, white officials greeted the Voting Rights Act by redrawing district lines to isolate that town's sizable black population. The resulting map, according to Marshall Frady, resembled "a Picasso abstract of a chicken."

Other methods designed to limit or eliminate black political influence included changing the venues of registration or balloting; requiring reregistration; making certain local offices appointive rather than elective posts; or eliminating an office altogether. Local leaders could easily accomplish these latter transformations, since they could count on the complicity of county or state officials if their approval was necessary to effect these changes. The Voting Rights Act framers foresaw the likelihood of such electoral chicanery, hence the Section 5 preclearance provision. But the process was slow and, during the Nixon administration, actual litigation to force compliance was less likely. Also, though theoretically all ju-risdictions were required to submit electoral changes to the Justice Department, some did not, forcing local blacks to in-itiate lengthy and expensive litigation.

The Voting Rights Act frightened some Southern whites, especially politicians, more than any other previous civil rights legislation. It was not only the traditional conflict of the "ins" versus the "outs," though that played a role; it also was the fear of new agendas, higher taxes, perhaps even of exclusion—a return of the treatment visited upon blacks by white offi-cialdom. A white citizen of Green County, Alabama, where black voter registration exceeded white figures as the 1966 election approached, worried almost hysterically, "Goddam, nothing could be worse than this, this is *Armageddon.*" For so long blacks had been invisible and subservient; now the power of the ballot and its likely result overturned the white world view to the point where they believed that world was coming to an end. And it was, to some extent, but both blacks and whites tended to overestimate the power of the ballot.

Indeed, with the passage of the Voting Rights Act, some black leaders assumed that the results would reach consider-ably beyond the ballot box. The vote, Martin Luther King believed, would "help to achieve many far-ranging changes during our lifetime." Specifically, "there would be no more oppressive poverty. . . , our children would not be crippled by segregated schools, and the whole community might live to-gether in harmony." In fact, the general optimism of Southern blacks concerning the ballot, even after it became clear voting rights would not produce regional miracles, was one of nu-merous factors distinguishing them from Northern blacks, who had grown cynical over the political system. Ralph McGill flew up to Chicago from Atlanta and engaged a black woman sitting next to him on the plane in a conversation on the relative merits of Chicago and the small town near Atlanta where she taught school. All of her family had migrated from Georgia, yet she had decided to stay in the South because "That's where the big change is taking place. You can be a part of it. You feel you are making a contribution. The South is alive—in motion."

The danger in the cumulative optimism of the late 1960s was that reality could never live up to expectations (not a new problem for Southerners, white or black), at least not just yet. There was indeed plentiful evidence that inequalities remained in parts of Southern society, unperturbed by or beyond the purview of the ballot.

Mixed Grades on the Racial Report Card: Schools and Public Policy

The school situation was a frustrating exercise in delay and disappointment. Until 1969, fifteen years after the *Brown* v. *Board of Education* decision, tokenism characterized school desegregation in the South. More than 80 percent of the region's black children attended all- or mostly black schools. The "freedom-of-choice" plan under which many Southern school boards operated allowed relatively few blacks to filter into white schools but followed a liberal transfer policy for whites who wished to pursue a segregated public education. Further, the Nixon administration was unwilling to press litigation against recalcitrant school districts, and in fact had granted numerous delays to such jurisdictions.

The United States Supreme Court, however, was running thin on patience, its implementation decree being more honored in the breach. The NAACP had recently challenged a ruling by the Department of Health, Education, and Welfare (HEW) that granted thirty-three school districts in Mississippi a one-year delay in carrying out a desegregation plan. The Court upheld the challenge in *Alexander* v. *Holmes County Board of Education* (1969) and ordered the districts (and by implication all others) "to terminate dual school systems at once," thus ending the "all deliberate speed" charade. Within the next eighteen months, the number of blacks attending integrated schools jumped from less than 20 percent to 38 percent, compared with 27 percent in the North. By the mid-

1970s, white Mississippians would be claiming with only a little exaggeration and a great deal of pride that their state was the most integrated state in the Union.

The *Alexander* case directed school boards to prepare desegregation plans immediately. Most did so, but some districts submitted half-hearted or incomplete proposals. In Charlotte, North Carolina, the school board devised a plan to desegregate secondary schools while maintaining segregation in the elementary grades. Judge James McMillan, the federal district court judge in Charlotte, threw out the plan and, under the *Alexander* ruling, hired an expert to prepare a suitable plan that would be binding on the consolidated city-county school system. The proposal included a variety of measures to effect desegregation, from reassignment of faculty and staff according to specific ratios to the pairing of schools (combining the facilities of two schools). Most prominent in Judge McMillan's decision, however, was the order for extensive busing to achieve an equitable racial balance. The defendants appealed to the Supreme Court, and in *Swann* v. *Charlotte-Mecklenburg Board of Education* (1971), the Justices unanimously upheld the lower court, and busing to achieve racial integration became a controversial fixture in Southern education. The Supreme Court, anticipating the public outcry as well as the opposition of the Nixon administration, observed that already "forty-two percent of all American public school students are transported to their schools by buses; an additional 25 percent ride public transportation," although only 3 percent of this bus riding was for the purpose of achieving school desegregation. In Charlotte, prior to Judge McMillan's ruling 23,600 pupils in the system were bused on the average of fifteen miles in each direction or a round trip of one hour in duration. McMillan's plan would not have altered the typical bus trip for a Charlotte student.

The *Alexander* case confronted white parents with the inevitable, but the *Swann* decision set the inevitable in motion. Busing, or "forced busing," as its opponents termed the system, became a convenient target for parents. As a result of these two decisions, by the end of 1972 only 9.2 percent of

Southern blacks attended all-black schools, compared with 68 percent just four years earlier. No longer able to ignore the issue, many white parents fled either the jurisdiction or the public school system.

School desegregation did not precipitate so-called white flight. Whites had been moving outward from Southern central cities since early in the century, and especially since World War II, for a variety of reasons, with race not always the most prominent. But the movement accelerated appreciably after 1970. Of course, increased affluence associated with Sunbelt prosperity and the suburbanization of employment, road systems, and institutions played a role, but some evidence suggests a direct link between white flight and school desegregation. In 1970, the Montgomery, Alabama, school board redrew district boundaries to comply with recent court rulings and included a white neighborhood within the catchment area of an all-black high school. Within months of the plan's publication, the *Montgomery Advertiser* reported "a drastic turnover of housing" in the white neighborhood due to the school situation. Four years later, an adjacent white residential area was added to the black high school's district and precisely the same wave of selling occurred in that neighborhood. These were not affluent areas and families moved at some sacrifice, as one white homeowner told a reporter in December 1970: "This is our home and we love it, but we just can't stay here any more. We can never replace what we had here . . . we can't buy another house as good as this for the price . . . but we are willing to make the sacrifice."

The growth of private schools, "seg academies," was another manifestation of white flight. In Summerton, South Carolina, for example, where the *Briggs* case originated, *all* white parents deserted the public schools for private education. Though few communities replicated such wholesale abandonment of the public school system, private education blossomed suddenly all over the South. Between 1972 and 1974, for example, the number of private schools in Memphis jumped from forty to eighty-five. One result of the academy movement was to inhibit the integration of the public school system by seriously reducing the number of white students. As one Atlanta school official put it: "There just aren't enough white children to go around." So, resegregation loomed in the future as a major problem for public school systems across the South.

In those jurisdictions, especially in such consolidated school districts as Charlotte-Mecklenburg, where white flight implied a move not only out of the city, but outside the county as well, and where local leaders stressed their commitment to public education, integration worked. After three years of desegregation at Wade Hampton High School in Greenville, South Carolina, a white student offered his assessment: "The older integration gets, the better it gets. The ninth graders get along better than the seniors. The generation after ours is gonna have it all together. They may have a lot of other problems, but they're not gonna be hung up on the race thing."

So school desegregation, as with most aspects of an often confusing, sometimes contradictory, and always evolving Southern life, indicated diverse patterns, depending on the size of the local black population; a large (40 percent or more) black proportion invariably countered desegregation efforts. The availability of alternatives, both in education and housing, and the willingness of local leadership to support or neglect public education also determined in great part the success or failure of the school-district plan.

Other elements of race relations secured by federal legislation were also dependent upon local conditions. Urban planning since World War II had not so much ignored black neighborhoods as it had destroyed their fabric. Urban renewal, the siting of road systems, the construction of public housing projects, and the use of zoning all worked against black residential interests. In Atlanta through the 1960s, zoning variances to higher land uses, i.e., commercial or industrial, were considerably more typical in black areas than in white districts. One result of these policies was to increase racial residential segregation. In the early 1970s, however, when blacks achieved political power in Atlanta and in several other cities, adverse

planning policies stopped, but it was difficult to reverse dec-
ades-long patterns of residential disinvestment.

In many areas of urban life, not only residence, integration
remained elusive—in the clubs, in executive positions with
leading firms, and in socializing after school or work hours.
The job market in the postindustrial society was increasingly
segmented and thus reinforced the residential and social exclusion. In some rural areas the pattern of exclusion went considerably beyond the urban version. The skewed demography
among rural blacks—overrepresentation of the very old and
the very young—implied economic handicaps, as a large segment of the black rural population depended on public assistance. Dependency enhanced the opportunities for discrimination, a continuation of the old ways of life. In the early 1970s
there was little prospect in these districts, according to one
observer, "that their [blacks'] needs would be realized in the
near future. . . . Public policy was still more concerned with
neutralizing their aspirations than with helping them realize
them." Although the tactics of neutralization could be various,
the old gnawing fear remained in some places. As Joel Garreau
noted in his visit to Terrell County, Georgia, in the late 1970s,
"black people still make a point of getting off the downtown
streets before sundown."

And even where blacks had obtained some political power,
it was oftentimes difficult to dislodge the patterns of dependency and chronic poverty. And a poor population implied
meager resources and greater service burdens on local government. The number of families below the poverty line in counties with a majority of black votes was twice the regional average in 1975. Greene County, Alabama, residents had elected
blacks to all the most important offices by 1972—the county
was 80 percent black—but its unemployment rate was 40 percent and per capita income an incredibly low $400, while they
owed various creditors a total of $5 million. Under these cir-
cumstances, the fruits of black political power were limited.

Short of a major transformation of the American economic system, many of these chronic debilities, the legacy of

a centuries-old biracial society, were beyond the capabilities of regional politicians. This was especially true of black regional politicians, many of whom were newcomers to public office, represented impoverished constituents, and governed without the cooperation of white economic elites and white county and state officials. To be sure, the Voting Rights Act enabled more white progressives to secure political office, and the changing Southern congressional delegations attested to this fact. Democratic congressmen elected after 1966 tended to have considerably more progressive voting records, especially on civil rights legislation, than their predecessors. When the Senate agreed to extend the Voting Rights Act in 1975 by a 77 to 12 margin, Southern Democrats favored the measure by a 9 to 6 count, a great change from the previous decade, when Southern Democrats led filibusters against passage. Those senators elected after 1966 voted 8 to 1 for the extension; those senators who entered that body prior to 1966 opposed the extension by a 5 to 1 margin.

But the increasing sensitivity of Southern Democrats to civil rights issues was only one part of the transformation of Southern politics wrought by the Voting Rights Act. A new force had emerged in the regional political arena that modified black prospects for racial change through the political system, a force that would keep progressive whites to moderate positions with regard to race, leaving numerous items on the black agenda untouched or only partially addressed. When Alabama Senator John Sparkman was asked in 1974 to name the greatest change in Southern politics during his lifetime, he replied without hesitation, "the elimination of the civil rights question as a political issue." Senator Sparkman might have been influenced by the contrast between the belligerent George Wallace of yesteryear and the conciliatory politician of 1974. But as a general assessment of Southern politics at that time, it was inaccurate, primarily because the new actor in the region pulled race stage front and center.

A Two-Party South: Race and Politics

The Republican Party was not a major force at the local level in Southern politics until the 1980s. But the gradual emergence of Republican strength in national and later in statewide contests helped to direct the political agenda of the 1960s and 1970s. In 1943, a Southern legislator noted that "If the Republican party would come out on the issue of white supremacy, it would sweep the South." Republicans, though, retained an interest, sometimes a strong interest, in civil rights until the early 1960s. Indeed, there was very little to differentiate candidates John F. Kennedy and Richard M. Nixon on the issue of civil rights in the 1960 election. In 1961, however, Arizona Senator Barry Goldwater gave a speech in Atlanta outlining what would later be called a "Southern strategy" for the Republican party.

Goldwater, in that address, acknowledged that the GOP was not likely "to get the [Northern] Negro vote as a bloc in 1964 and 1968, so we ought to go hunting where the ducks are." And the "ducks" were the Southern white electorate. The Arizona Republican believed that the school integration issue could be an opening wedge in the region, urging the party to declare that the school question was "the responsibility of the states." Since, in these years prior to the 1965 Voting Rights Act, the black vote was a relatively minor factor in the South, Goldwater felt a states' rights campaign would secure the region for Republicans. Goldwater never made or advocated racist appeals, nor did he cynically employ the limited government concept as a race surrogate; states' rights was his genuine political philosophy. In the volatile atmosphere of the South during the early 1960s, white Southerners, besieged by federal legislation, hostile courts, and suddenly militant blacks, easily translated "states' rights" into their own language, and when strategist Goldwater became candidate Goldwater in 1964, whites in the Deep South deserted their ancestral political home and voted overwhelmingly for the Arizona senator, enabling him to carry South Carolina, Georgia, Alabama, Mississippi, and Louisiana. In Mississippi, Goldwater received an unprecedented 87 percent mandate. As Walker Percy analyzed the vote: "It would not have mattered if Senator Goldwater had advocated the collectivization of the plantations and open saloons in Jackson; he voted against the Civil Rights Bill and that was that."

But GOP strength was soft. Below the presidential level, Democrats remained solidly ensconced throughout the region. Moreover, the upper South was unswayed by the racial implications of Goldwater's rhetoric, even though the urban and mountain regions of these states had long provided the only Republican glimmer in the South. But these Republicans were of a different ilk than the recent converts in the Deep South. The extremists attracted to the Goldwater campaign worried the business-oriented urban Republicans, and the racial overtones bothered the more moderate mountain wing of the party. In fact, these groups constituted the body and soul of the Southern Republican party. And the candidates they presented during the 1960s and early 1970s tended to reflect this traditional moderate bent. The "Southern strategy" had stirred up the electorate, but had not yet transformed the party or Southern politics.

Indeed, black and white progressives found some Republicans to be welcome respites from the race-oriented, conservative Democrats that characterized that party's Southern wing in the 1960s. Election precinct results indicated that Arkansas Republican Winthrop Rockefeller, for example, received 81 percent of Little Rock's black vote in his successful 1966 gubernatorial bid, and won reelection two years later, receiving 88 percent of the capital's black ballots. In 1969, Virginia mountain Republican Linwood Holton became governor in this former Byrd-Democratic party stronghold, putting together a labor-urban-black coalition. Winfield Dunn in Tennessee and James Holshouser in North Carolina became Republican governors in the early 1970s, elected as moderates against conservative Democratic opponents.

These victories, as with the Goldwater phenomenon in 1964, were not indicative of a major long-term party realignment in the South. Nor were the Republican governors harbingers of a shift in the "Southern strategy." Rather than cultivating these Republicans, national party leaders favored the Goldwater line. Northern blacks had long since committed to the Democrats, they felt, and the time was propitious to take advantage of the disparity between the Northern and Southern wings of that party, as well as picking up some white ethnic support in the urban North in the wake of racial unrest there.

The strategy solidified during the 1968 presidential election campaign, when Richard M. Nixon, who ran as a civil rights proponent in 1960, entered into a bargain with Democrat-turned-Republican Senator Strom Thurmond of South Carolina in order to gain Southern support for his nomination, thereby staving off a late surge by California Governor Ronald Reagan. Nixon promised to take the voting rights "monkey . . . off the backs of the South," and not to press the school desegregation issue to the contrary. Nixon also agreed that if vacancies occurred on the Supreme Court, he would consider nominees who were more congenial to the Southern viewpoint than the present group of Justices. Once elected, Nixon carried out his promises, though with little success. His Supreme Court selections, Clement Haynesworth of Greenville, South Carolina, and Florida Judge G. Harold Carswell, failed Senate confirmation both because of their racial views and, in the case of Carswell, on the issue of competence. Though Nixon sought to undermine the Voting Rights Act enforcement provisions by firing Leon Panetta, director of the Office for Civil Rights, and replacing recalcitrant Secretary of Health, Education, and Welfare Robert Finch with the more amenable Caspar Weinberger, both the Congress and the federal judiciary prevented a major retreat in federal civil rights enforcement. In the South, however, where winning or losing was not as important as how one played the game, Nixon's gestures received wide approbation and helped to enhance Republican respectability in the region.

The president's rising esteem among Southern whites translated into significant victories at the congressional level in the 1972 Republican landslide. Nearly one out of every three Congressmen elected from the South that year ran under the GOP banner. Though they captured only 16 percent of the seats in Southern state legislatures, Republicans were effecting a coalition of whites disgruntled by altered race relations and those basking in the Sunbelt prosperity and wanting more of the same. The combination of fiscal conservatism plus states' rights was in the process of transforming the South into a two-party region.

Republican advances, of course, alarmed Southern Democrats, who had enjoyed an electoral monopoly, more or less, for a century. While the national Democratic party was increasing its commitment to civil rights and the Republicans were retreating on the issue, the Southern Democrats were confronted with the choice of fighting or switching. Although the new party affiliations of such erstwhile Democrats as Strom Thurmond and former Texas Governor John Connelly received widespread publicity, in truth, formal party hopping in the South during the late 1960s and early 1970s was unusual. This was so for several reasons. First, most Southern politicians, especially those in local, county, and state races kept winning as Democrats. Second, when some Republican candidates sought to preempt the right wing of Southern politics they found some Democratic candidates standing there. Third, changing parties could mean loss of seniority and patronage. Finally, Southern Democrats discovered that the alchemy of regional politics permitted them to appeal, albeit modestly, for the black vote while retaining a good portion of the rural white vote, for years the backbone of the party.

This last point was especially interesting because it required successful Democrats to perform a political balancing act with two essentially different, even conflicting, components of the electorate. The tightrope walk brought more progressive Democrats into political prominence, such as Bumpers, Askew, and Carter, who would have greater credibility in the black community, yet whose populist rhetoric and modest background appealed to the traditional element of the party. This was a facile merger of class and race, and it became the standard Southern Democratic strategy of the 1970s. The gubernatorial class of 1970 utilized the tactic to good advantage.

The shift toward class-oriented issues was especially noticeable in Mississippi, where race-baiting had attained the status of an art form. No longer. With blacks accounting for nearly two out of every five voters in the state, the old-style rhetoric would be highly inappropriate. In the 1971 gubernatorial primary, arch-segregationist Jimmy Swan ran poorly and failed to make the run-off. While the two remaining candidates opposed busing, they avoided race completely, an unusual omission from a Mississippi political campaign. Instead, class became the issue as the successful candidate, former Jackson District Attorney William Waller, attacked his opponent, Lieutenant Governor Charles Sullivan, a wealthy Delta planter, as being part of the "Capital Street Gang." His campaign slogan was "Waller Works," and he referred to himself as a "redneck." Waller advocated consumer-protection legislation and an end to the practice of placing state funds in banks without accruing interest. Waller's successor, Charles "Cliff" Finch, adopted the same strategy, employing a lunch pail as his campaign symbol. During the campaign, he worked one day each week at different manual labor occupations, from operating a bulldozer to bagging groceries. By the time Finch ran for office in 1975, Mississippi, according to his predecessor, Bill Waller, had undergone "a sociological as well as an industrial revolution." While Mississippians might have stood for the latter with some equanimity, the very mention of the word "sociological," let alone in conjunction with "revolution," would have, in earlier times, sent them to the barricades. That in itself testified to at least some accuracy in Waller's assessment.

Democratic candidates donned the hair shirts. Lawton Chiles walked 1,000 miles in his 1970 Florida senatorial campaign. Richard Stone, a Jewish candidate for the senate in 1974, cut up like a "good ole boy" with his harmonica in conservative and very Southern North Florida, which led one skeptical journalist to complain, "Stone ran as a redneck in North Florida and in South Florida as a Jew." In the same campaign Stone garnered the black vote and enough of the Gold Coast vote to win. Even George Wallace dropped the racial imagery to effect the long-dreamed-of interracial populist alliance in Alabama. Accordingly, Republican gains were modest, considering the promise of a Southern strategy designed to take advantage of widespread white disaffection in the region. The situation exasperated Republican leaders, who had, in effect, written off the black vote, only to receive a tepid reception from conservative Southern whites, especially in the rural districts. Georgia Republican State Chairman Robert Shaw complained in 1974 that:

You find the conservative rural vote going in voting the straight party ticket, and by the same token you find the urban blacks voting the straight party ticket. And they'd be considered a liberal element, with the South Georgia farmer voting conservative. And yet they're voting hand in hand, and when they do, they're squeezing the lives out of us. And yet there's no tie-in between the two at all. Ideologically they're as far apart as night and day.

The precarious balancing act was apparently going well for the Democratic party, but the future efficacy of the class appeal was in doubt. Newcomers arrived in the region daily, many of them white middle-income professionals unimpressed and perhaps uncomfortable with populist-style appeals. They had fled from redistributionist states and cities and were not about to accede to rising taxes and social programs in their new homes. Republican candidates who, as political scientist William Havard noted in 1972, "are attempting to translate business-issue orientations into public policy" in the manner of "the McKinley era," found a receptive audience out among the chickweed and crepe myrtle.

Also, the solid Democratic phalanx in rural areas was weakening, especially in Black Belt areas bypassed by Sunbelt prosperity, yet threatened by awakened black awareness. The

Democratic party as the party of Redemption might work on older voters, but a newer generation of white Southerners, cast adrift from the past by recent events, now felt the time propitious to make their own political choices rather than having history decide for them. In 1960, 60 percent of the South's voters identified themselves as Democrats, with 20 percent as independents; a decade later, 40 percent of Southerners called themselves Democrats, and 34 percent as independents, this despite the fact that the 1970 figure included blacks, almost all of whom were affiliated with the Democratic party. The most striking example of erosion of Democratic strength occurred in the 1976 presidential election. For the first time since 1848, a candidate from the Deep South, south Georgia no less, ran on a major party ticket. Yet, Jimmy Carter could not muster a majority of the white vote in his own region, doing poorest among the growing white middle class in the towns and cities, and generating only 56 percent of the white lower-income vote in the South, heretofore the most loyal white segment of the party.

Though Southern blacks had played a major role in effecting the transformation of the South into a two-party region, at least at the presidential and congressional levels, the benefits of a two-party system for blacks were unclear. V. O. Key, in his classic 1949 study of Southern politics, predicted that the rise of the Republican party, if and when that occurred, would have an ameliorative effect on the region's Gothic politics. Unforeseen by Key, newly enfranchised blacks flocked to the party of white supremacy, the Democratic party. They did so because the national party had taken a leadership role in securing the civil rights for which Southern blacks had fought and died—to them, the Democratic party was indeed the party of Redemption. Soon, also, the national party would insist on their greater representation in state and local party affairs, and Mississippi, Louisiana, South Carolina, Georgia, and Alabama party organizations sent interracial delegations to the 1968 Democratic National Convention in Chicago.

This is not to say that the Southern Democratic party

reciprocated in kind for black support. Blacks, in effect, had little choice: their enfranchisement coincided with a sharp rightward movement of regional Republicans. Black voters demonstrated, on occasion, that they were prepared to offer their ballots to deserving Republican candidates, but, for the most part, the GOP directed their appeals away from blacks. The situation left blacks less bargaining power. They could withdraw from major party politics and stay home or run their own candidates—usually futile exercises enabling the greater of two evils to triumph in the end. Democrats, including the promising white progressives, recognized this and typically worked harder to retain their insecure white political base than to reassure a bloc upon which they could usually count. Black voters, of course, even though a minority, could make a difference in a hotly contested primary or general election, so Democratic candidates could not spurn their support. This contributed to more liberal Democratic congressional delegations, greater visibility of blacks in local and state appointive positions, improvement in services, and heightened sensitivity to black dignity. But the Democratic officeholder required prudence on race, at least the appearance of not moving beyond public sentiment. And, of course, as a major orchestrator of his state's economic development, a Democratic governor particularly was often preoccupied with other issues. Of the progressive group of Democratic governors in the early 1970s, *New York Times* Southern correspondent Roy Reed noted some disappointments by 1974: "None of the new leaders has made real headway in providing industrial jobs for the multitudes of poor people who still live in the black belts. None has found the answers to newer problems such as urban blight and the growing concentration of economic power in fewer hands." Perhaps this was asking too much considering the political realities and insecurities confronting Southern Democrats, but for some their collective performance had fallen short of even modest expectations.

AFTER CIVIL RIGHTS   193

Assessing Racial Change, 1965–1975

Though blacks were operating with political constraints, at the
least they operated. And from the perspective of Southern history, the alteration in the black situation in the South from
1965 to 1975 was titanic. Blaine Liner of the Southern Growth
Policies Board, a research and statistical clearinghouse in North
Carolina's Research Triangle Park, declared that "1965, the
year by which both the voting rights and civil rights act had
been passed, was for the South what 1945 had been for Germany and Japan." Those two nations, liberated in spite of
themselves from the evil within, proceeded not only to recon-
struct their respective societies, but to prosper as well. The
South's racial armistice, which, unlike the Allied victory, did
not imply total surrender, nevertheless enabled the region to
concentrate on something other than its historic obsession with
race. It was a healing time, those years after 1965, when economic progress replaced race as the most prominent regional
phenomenon. As Pat Derian, a white civil rights advocate from
Jackson, Mississippi, observed in 1976, "Before everybody was
entirely absorbed, socially and intellectually, with the struggle
that was centered around race." But now, she continued, "as
tensions have subsided between people, it's been a kind of like
springtime. People are relaxed enough now to think truly about
the quality of their lives."

Perhaps some of these white testimonials to the decline
of race can be questioned as conscience salving rationales.
Numerous abolitionists, of course, had worried about the slave,
but soon forgot about the freedman. But Southern blacks, despite the obstacles to fulfillment of the dream that emerged
after 1965, were also sanguine about their situation and their
future. In 1969, Charles Evers, black mayor of Fayette, Mississippi, wrote a symbolic letter to his martyred brother, Medgar, concluding with thinly veiled glee, "Remember, Medgar,
what that old Bilbo warned that rabble if they weren't careful
they'd wake up to find those two little nigger boys representing

them? Well, he wasn't far wrong. We are representing them, quite a few of them."

Celebrating the tenth anniversary of the Selma-to-Montgomery march, hundreds of blacks and whites strode across the Edmund Pettus Bridge, the local police at ease and friendly. Reverend Frederick Reese, one of the participants in that historic odyssey, and now one of five blacks on the Selma city council, noted the change that had occurred in one decade: "We've come a long way. Whites who wouldn't tip their hats have learned to do it. People who wouldn't say 'Mister or Miss' to a black have learned to say it mighty fine. We've got black policemen, black secretaries, and we can use the public restrooms. The word 'nigger' is almost out of existence." While some might scoff that these behavioral modifications are merely superficial manifestations, it is important to recall that public behavior and manners play a crucial role in Southern society, designating place for both actor and recipient. A gesture speaks volumes about Southern race relations.

Rev. Reese's remarks also underscored the notion that once Southerners declared a racial cease-fire, the attributes of their region could flourish. This is what Pat Derian implied when she noted the "springtime" in Jackson. Andrew Young, Sr., a New Orleans dentist and father to the civil rights and political leader, observed the contrast between North and South. When he walked into New York's Lord & Taylor, he and his wife were studiously ignored; returning to New Orleans and entering a comparable establishment "they meet you at the door." Young's New York experience may have less to do with race than with the fact that salespeople in the Big Apple frequently do not discriminate; they are just rude to everyone, regardless of color; in New Orleans, the personal attention is merely part of the culture.

There is no gainsaying that problems of race remained, more in some parts of the South than in others, and that politics contained limitations and frustrations, with the Republicans seeking to revive race as the dominant electoral theme. But it is the nature of the struggle for justice that it is never finally won. As theologian James Sellers reminded, "Every advance teaches us how we must yet do still more."

And with every small advance in race relations during this springtime, Southern culture advanced accordingly. The Southern sense of past and place, of faith and fortitude, which had captured a nation's fancy at periodic intervals when that nation seemed insecure, could now more readily operate. And the preservation of this culture would become the civil rights movement of the next generation.

CHAPTER SIX

Promised Land or American Region: The Modern South Since 1976

Economic prosperity and racial amelioration have lifted two historical burdens from the South, leaving Southerners free to indulge in preservation of the most basic sort: their culture. The challenge to the present generation is whether, in the midst of distractions from within and outside the region, they will be able to pass along a distinctive South to their successors. The fate of the environment is crucial to this challenge. However footloose the Southerner has been, the land has represented a rootedness from which other cultural elements—ties to family, religion, place, and people—followed naturally.

The Battle for the Land

Though love of the land and a strong sense of place were traditional elements of regional culture, so was their abuse. Intimacy with the land bred both admiration and contempt—admiration for its beauty and contempt for its richness. Abundance encouraged waste, and the South had too much of everything except wealth, so it sought that wealth from the land. "The greater cultural tradition of the South," Howard W. Odum wrote just after World War II, "has been one of exploitation of the land and its resources. Great pine forests . . . were . . . wasted beyond the measure of the needs of the region. And the erosion of the soil has been so great."

Southerners, as always, seemed anxious to get on with their economic regeneration, and hang the environmental cost. In 1956, the South Carolina legislature expeditiously granted the Bowater Paper Corporation of England an exemption from state water pollution control standards. Another paper mill intruding its stench into the Alabama Black Belt less than a decade later led Governor Wallace to take a deep breath and exclaim: "Yeah, that's the smell of prosperity. Sho' does smell sweet, don't it?" And a survey of South Carolinians in 1972 revealed that 65 percent felt that attracting industry was a higher priority than environmental protection. They obtained their collective wish. During the 1970s, four of the five states that led the nation in attracting polluting industries were located in the South—Texas, South Carolina, North Carolina, and Florida.

The results of this profligacy were evident throughout the South by the 1970s, as rapid and often unimpeded economic development ruined or threatened the region's distinctive habitat. The South's abundant, life-giving and life-preserving water resources became suddenly vulnerable. The Mississippi River, which gave life and prosperity to an entire valley, has become a deadly mixture of sewage, industrial waste, and insecticides below fire-belching and befouled Baton Rouge. The effluent pouring into the Gulf threatens to transform the blue-green body into a Dead Sea. The petrochemical industry along the Gulf generated so many ship collisions, fires, and chemical spills that 25,000 pounds of the highly toxic chemical pentachlorophenol (PCP) had accumulated at the Louisiana outlet to the Gulf by 1980, ruining the oyster beds. Oil rigs encroach upon marshlands and wildlife sanctuaries, polluting the region's high water table in the process. Cajuns, those eighteenth-century refugees from Acadia (now Nova Scotia), forsook their south Louisiana bayous and fishing livelihoods, as well as their culture, to work in the much better-paying oil industry beginning in the late 1960s. By the mid-1980s the depression in oil threw these Cajuns back to the bayous, only to discover their old fishing and trapping grounds dredged, polluted, or off limits.

The prospect from the Atlantic coast was equally disturbing. There, the paper industry had served as a two-fold predator, clear-cutting the abundant pine forests and polluting tributaries and fouling the atmosphere with its distinctive sulfur dioxide aroma. The Union Camp Company, located near Savannah, diversified into recreational community development in the late 1970s, transforming ecologically sensitive islands and marshlands—land which the company purchased at $50 per acre in 1941 and by 1980 sold for $125,000 an acre—into condominiums and golf courses.

In terms of water pollution and real estate free-for-alls, few Southern states can match the destruction of natural Florida, once the nation's most sought-after retirement and recreational haven, but now threatening, literally, to sink in its own slime. Miami possesses the most chemically contaminated drinking water in the country, though other communities in the state are challenging this supremacy. According to one report in 1982, "in many locations, Floridians have, in essence, run a hose from their toilet to the kitchen faucet." The oyster population is almost gone from polluted Tampa Bay. The state leads the nation in the number of hazardous waste sites, with no barrier between these dumps and the ground water. The sprawling development of south Florida threatens the Everglades, already endangered by its use as a water supply source and the disappearing agricultural land and mangrove swamps around it.

Further up the Atlantic coast, the development industry has become a major water polluter. The problem has accelerated with the growing popularity of the Carolinas' coast for resort and recreational properties. Improperly secured septic tanks and run-off from development have hurt the North Carolina fisheries, contaminating 317,000 acres of oyster and clam beds. Perhaps the most notable water pollution disaster in recent years occurred in Hopewell, Virginia, which proudly declares itself the "Chemical Capital of the South." In 1976, Allied Chemical dumped kepone into the James River, closing the waterway to commercial fishing for the next five years and further endangering the environmental status of an already fragile Chesapeake Bay. Pollution in the heavily urbanized corridor from Baltimore south to Washington, Richmond, and the rapidly developing Norfolk-Hampton Roads-Virginia Beach region has reduced fishing in the Bay and tainted the oyster crop. Water for fishing, drinking, and maintaining the regional biological chain, once one of the region's most abundant and reliable resources, may become one of the South's more serious ecological problems in the 1990s.

In *Go Down, Moses* (1942), William Faulkner wrote that "The people who have destroyed it [the woods] will accomplish its revenge." Indeed, the millions of acres laid waste by the ax and the saw are now gaining their retribution in the forms of appalling soil erosion, periodic flooding, and ground water pollution. But for decades the South has had a model for its own ecological trauma tucked away in the folds of the region, long hidden and neglected: Appalachia. Though once primarily an agricultural region, since the early 1900s it has become an industrial and mining area, as poor as in its earlier incarnation, as Northern-based and foreign firms have leached land, profits, and lifestyle from the mountains. This is not a scenario of Yankee greed overtaking mountain innocence, however, because the people of this complex subregion assisted, sometimes unwittingly, oftentimes consciously, in their own debauchment.

If any doubt exists as to who and what runs this region, the sign plastered on the tallest building in Harlan, Kentucky, dispels it: WORK, THINK, BUY COAL. It is a land of slag heaps, slate dumps, and sawdust piles, some still smoldering after years, a coal haze hanging over the little towns, moving into every pore. The mountain carcasses, denuded by strip mining, eroded by rain and snow, loom over a desperate scene of desolation, a moonscape gouged, not carved, by 'dozers, trucks, and trains. At the beginning of the century often-illiterate highlanders, whose conception of property holding resembled that of the Indians—the land belonged to all and to none—signed a broad-form deed transferring mineral rights beneath the land to the company forever for fifty cents an acre, essentially giving the firm the right to knock down buildings and tear up farms and dig up family cemeteries, signing over 94 percent of Kentucky's mineral wealth. The land turned barren and the rivers to acid.

The Tennessee Valley Authority (TVA), once the salvation of a backward part of the South, has become the region's (and the nation's) largest consumer of coal, and, since the 1960s, a major presence in Appalachia. In 1964, TVA equipment began moving into Knott County, Kentucky, on Clear Creek. Journalist Osborn Segerberg described early activity: "When blasting dislodged the chimney stones of another neighbor's house, [one] house caught fire and burned down. Another dynamite explosion broke a gas line and, when a housewife lit a match, the resulting fire burned *that* house down. A third house was buried by tumbling overburden, a mother and her children escaping just in time." A resident assessed additional environmental damage after nearly a decade of such activity: "Mine water as black as my pants came rolling down into our crick. People came here to fish. There used to be big chubs, but that cleared ever'thing out of the holler." The sedimentation from the stripped hillsides degraded water quality, destroying most fish species.

During the past decade, a new intrusion has appeared in various parts of Appalachia; the recreational and resort industries have seized upon the relatively isolated, pristine beauty of the subregion outside the mining territories, and soon condominiums sprouted on the hillsides. Pat Watters of the Southern Regional Council wrote with some surprise in 1969 that "the tourist industry has staked no claims" to these parts. The

situation altered drastically during the next two decades, with
the North Carolina hills threatening to become, as one resident
put it, "a Miami Beach in the mountains." One result has been
skyrocketing property values and consequent higher taxes, reducing farming activity by forcing farm families to sell most
or all of their land. Second-home residents and developers
demand urban services, further increasing tax burdens. "The
way I see it," observed small farmer Cloyd Bolick in 1983,
"about the only thing we cultivate anymore is Floridians." By
that time, outsiders owned 44 percent of the land in Appalachian North Carolina. Land ownership and the lifestyle accompanying it are inextricably connected with the cultural and
kinship patterns of the mountains, as it was in eastern Kentucky a century ago. Development is not only rending the
sociocultural fabric, but threatening to replicate the ecological
waste visited upon other portions of Appalachia.

Since the Reagan administration took office in 1981, oil
and gas companies have been leasing U. S. Forest Service lands
in the area for mineral rights. AMOCO alone has purchased
100 leases on 135,000 acres of land. North Carolina residents
have seen films and have heard lectures on the environmental
destruction in Kentucky and are fearful of similar devastation
in their home counties. The companies, for now, are holding
the lands, paying one dollar per acre per year for the lease,
and they claim that new techniques of extraction and restoration will limit adverse environmental impact.

As Southerners have seen an end to their chronic status
as the nation's underclass, the temptation to reap from their
patrimony becomes greater. But Southerners have been fortunate in the timing of their economic development, even as
the pace and volume of it has placed unprecedented pressures
on their increasingly fragile land. For the 1960s and 1970s were
years of heightened environmental consciousness across the
nation, culminating in the Clean Air Act of 1970 and the establishment of the Environmental Protection Agency (EPA).

As with many other aspects of Southern life since World
War II, federal legislation spurred or forced compliance with

national standards. The legislation also lifted a burden from local and state officials in the South, who were not oblivious to the deteriorating quality of the environment. The fierce rivalry over economic development discouraged measures that limited or added costs to the development process. Journalist Joel Garreau depicted a new scenario after 1970 in this fictive exchange between an Alabama mayor and a developer: "Now, Fred, you know how much I'd like to let you dump your purple widget waste right into the drinking water here. . . . But you know those damn boys in Washington would be all over me." Or the industrialist could no longer come into town and say, "Well, in Arkansas, they told me different."

So Southern states in the 1970s passed legislation to reflect federal environmental standards. The debates accompanying these measures brought ecological issues to the forefront of public awareness, as surprisingly few Southerners were well informed about the threats to their patrimony. And the awareness became a major public interest by the end of the 1970s, challenging the development mentality that had dominated Southern polity and economy. In fact, a growing sense of urgency emerged that unless this generation of Southerners acted, the next would bear the loss. "Take away the environment of the South," Fred Powledge noted, "and you might as well have New Jersey." In some quarters, the environmental question would become the race issue of the 1980s, with one difference, according to Georgia ecologist Eugene Odum: "You can have failures from time to time in human relations and recover from them, but you can't have any failures in the environment. There's just no second chance."

In 1971, Alabama passed tough new environmental standards, the same year the EPA shut down Birmingham's steel mills temporarily because of flagrant violations of the Clean Air Act. A water quality measure assessed violators $10,000 per day and permitted civil actions to recover damages from the fouling of fish and wildlife habitats. The legislation also empowered the state to secure reimbursement for cleanup operations. Other Southern states followed with variations, depending on particular environmental problems. North Carolina, for example, passed its Coastal Management Act in 1974, establishing a Coastal Resources Commission, which holds public meetings every six weeks to announce policy and review permit appeals. The law also required counties to prepare land-use plans and established "areas of environmental concern," requiring permits for any development in these zones.

The enhanced environmental consciousness led to closer cooperation between state development agencies and the new state water and air pollution control agencies created by the legislation of the 1970s. The objective was to screen out potential polluters, or at the least apprise them of the new standards. As for existing industries, several states—Alabama, Georgia, Florida, North Carolina, and Tennessee—offered tax incentives for the installation of pollution abatement equipment. Florida and Georgia went so far as to issue industrial revenue bonds to finance such devices, and the city of Savannah floated $32.5 million in bonds to subsidize the cleanup and emission control operations of American Cyanamid and Union Camp.

But the cooperation between development and environmental interests during the 1970s and 1980s was spotty and conflicts often resolved themselves in industry's favor. In 1979 Louisiana passed, belatedly, one of the strongest environmental protection acts in the nation. But the intimate relations between state government and the petrochemical companies inhibited enforcement. That state's intricate system of bayous and streams continued to succumb to oil rigs, chemicals, and industrial scrap. By the mid-1980s, the petrochemical parishes (counties) in South Louisiana had a cancer rate five times higher than the national average. Though the situation was not as critical in other Southern states, there were similar examples of strong legislation and weak enforcement. Foreign investment boomed in the South from the mid-1970s on, and much of this influx resulted from the export of polluting firms from Germany and Japan. The Japanese consul general in Atlanta explained candidly that "Older industries, like textiles, are being phased out in Japan and exported to other countries. . . . We will put these high-pollution industries where there is space and water enough to handle them . . . like here in the South."

Though some Southern leaders continued to display a Third World approach to economic development—any industry is better than no industry at all—there were enough environmental victories in the late 1970s and 1980s to generate some optimism about the future of the Southern patrimony. North Carolina officials, copying an idea popular in several European countries, launched a Pollution Prevention Pays program in 1982 to assist industries in eliminating wastes before they were emitted into the air, water, or land. In order to ensure participation in the program, the state's Department of Environmental Management has reminded firms that the agency must review all air and water permits every five years. The most celebrated transformation to date occurred with Burlington Industries, a firm that was dumping liquid waste from its furniture-spraying operation into the Lexington, North Carolina, sewage treatment plant, as well as shipping inorganic sludge to a hazardous waste landfill near Sumter, South Carolina. With state assistance, Burlington devised a plan to mix the waste with sawdust and burn it to make steam used in the industrial process. Burlington transformed 2.4 million pounds of waste annually into an energy resource, saving the company $905,000. North Carolina has also pioneered stiff coastal development regulations to combat shoreline erosion and the threat to wetlands, even battling the U.S. Army Corps of Engineers' dredging operations.

In fact, some states have not been averse to challenging the federal government on environmental issues. South Carolina officials have awakened to the knowledge that their state has become a national dumping ground for hazardous waste, especially radioactive waste. Since the 1950s, the state vigorously courted the nuclear weapons and energy industries. By 1980, nearly one-half of the energy generated in this state originated from nuclear facilities, the highest percentage in the nation. At the Savannah River Plant, near Aiken, South Carolina, the Dupont Company has been manufacturing nuclear weapons since the early 1950s, pouring scalding water from its reactors into nearby streams. In recent years, two carcinogenic industrial solvents seeped into the critical Tuscaloosa aquifer running beneath the plant. In 1983, the state sued the U.S. Department of Energy to either close or clean up the facility. South Carolina Attorney General Travis Medlock explained: "We sued 'em and they were shocked . . . beyond belief. South Carolina has been very hospitable to these folks. But I think the hospitality has probably gone too far." Eventually, the Energy department acceded to the cleanup demand and assured the state that the plant would cool its water before discharge and would allow the state to monitor compliance.

Since the mid-1970s, there has been increasing awareness in the South that environmental objectives and economic development can be compatible, that an unheeding prosperity would be short-lived if ecological issues were ignored. The North was an unenviable model in this latter regard. As Florida Governor Reubin Askew noted in 1975: "The economic development of the South need not result in the degradation of our land or the deprivation of our people. We cannot separate the future of our economy in the South from the future of our environment." Askew's South Carolina counterpart, Dick Riley, echoed this sentiment in his 1979 inaugural address: "It is not unreasonable to envision a South Carolina of great natural beauty and great economic strength at the same time." This attitude has not only become a matter of public policy but of popular culture as well, especially through the auspices of *Southern Living* magazine. The magazine, in keeping with its primary mission of touting Southern distinctiveness, stresses the beauty and fragility of the regional landscape. The editors seek to maintain "our landscape in its beauty and order," while absorbing "the growth and density of a more concentrated culture." The South, in other words, can accept, even pursue, its economic bounty while maintaining its own attitude toward it.

Preserving the Urban Landscape

One of the contributions of *Southern Living* magazine has been to demonstrate that urban life need not obscure the Southerner's connections to the land. And if, as the 1980 Commission on the Future of the South concluded, "the Future of the South cannot be separated from the future of Southern cities," an urban lifestyle compatible with regional traditions is as essential for the survival of those traditions as is the preservation of the natural landscape. Again, the South was fortunate that the period of most rapid metropolitan development in the 1970s coincided with national concerns about the quality of life in these sprawling, automobile-oriented landscapes. This was especially so in the South, where metropolitan areas seem more sprawling and disorderly than elsewhere, cluttered with unsightly haphazard development, a tribute to the regional penchant for inalienable property rights. The community focal point is no longer the church, the town hall, or the courthouse, but the highway. Arlington, Texas, midway between the Dallas-Ft. Worth metroplex is, according to urbanist Paul Geisel, "three highways in search of a city." Downtown is a jumble of gas stations, fast-food emporia, and car dealerships. Civic consciousness is nonexistent; the average turnout for municipal elections is 10 percent of the eligible electorate. The "older" neighborhoods, erected in the 1950s, are going to seed, and traffic jams mar access to declining commercial strips. In a generation, Arlington has gone from nothing to nowhere.

Of course, the problems of most instant suburbias on the metropolitan fringe are not as severe as Arlington's, though more because of less rapid growth than from planning. But the nature of regional economic development—service and high-tech functions—favors suburban locations because of their proximity to the work force and lower taxes and land costs. So growth is likely to continue to spiral outward. Indeed, the typical commuting pattern in Southern metropolitan areas is cross-suburban rather than suburb to city.

The vital metropolitan fringe implied a series of negative

consequences for Southern cities, even those, such as Houston and Dallas, that have been able to incorporate the rapidly sprouting periphery. Those cities that have been mere spectators to the suburban boom, whether through stiff annexation laws or through the rapid incorporation of these proto-communities, continue to experience a "noose effect," resulting in an increasingly poorer population, a stable or declining economic base, and a segregated school system; in short, it is a reflection of what Northern cities had become in previous years. In the Atlanta area, for example, 80 percent of new jobs between 1975 and 1984 were located in the suburbs. The new subway system, designed radially from the center, is irrelevant to the typical suburban commuter. So while the city caters to poor blacks and transients, whites have evolved an affluent, isolated civilization, particularly in the northern suburbs. Though this overstates the case somewhat—white upscale enclaves, such as Inman Park and Ansley Park, flourish, as do solid, middle-class black neighborhoods—it reflects a general trend that has not yet found a counter.

But those Southern cities heretofore immune from the impact of peripheral development primarily because of annexation are now reaping the results of their territorial voracity. And Houston has become the epitome of what might happen to other land-happy metropolises. All-day rush hours; frequent breaks in overtaxed water lines; an overextended police force requiring merchants and some wealthy residents to employ their own private corps; overpumping of underground aquifers, causing the gradual sinking of the city; the increased possibility of severe flooding; and in November 1983, in obvious Biblical judgment, a plague of locusts signify that the past is finally catching up with this city of the future.

Despite this bleak catalog and a similar, though less dramatic, array of growing-pain problems in other cities, there are hopeful indications that the built environment may be rescued by the same forces that are struggling to maintain the South's distinctive natural ecology. The attention of Houston, Dallas, and other cities to servicing and embracing ever-larger chunks of metropolitan territory had left inner-city neighbor-hoods neglected. Moreover, since these districts were typically residences of poorer black and Hispanic households, tradi-tional patterns of racial and ethnic discrimination reinforced their invisibility. In more affluent urban neighborhoods, the pressure of traffic spilling over and cutting through from out-lying areas, as well as the declining quality of services, ex-panded the constituency of discontent. But even in those cities not preoccupied with territorial gain, the decay of older neigh-borhoods seemed beyond the control of a financially strapped urban administration or a local government, whose priorities extended finite resources more to the business community than to neighborhoods. So neighborhood groups began to coalesce around these issues and, by the early 1970s, four external events catapulted the neighborhood into a major political force in Southern cities as an important counterweight to the devel-opment community.

First, the national historic preservation movement shifted priorities from the conservation of single structures to groups of buildings *and* the contextual environment. This implied that even mundane architecture held certain intrinsic values as a reflection of community life. Second, the changing demo-graphic (more singles and adult-oriented couples) and eco-nomic (higher energy costs and suburban lot and home prices) trends enhanced urban living. Third, and more peculiar to the South, in the aftermath of the Voting Rights Act federal courts began to dismantle the local electoral apparatus to improve the prospect of minority officeholding. Specifically, at-large elections, which tended to dilute black voting strength, as black voters were concentrated in certain areas of the city, received harsh scrutiny from judges, who ordered either a combination district-at-large representation system or a straight district sys-tem. While enhancing minority strength, the district system also reinforced neighborhood influence, since district lines often coincided with existing neighborhoods.

Finally, in 1974, the federal government made a major philosophical alteration in its urban policy, first evident in

President Johnson's Model Cities program in the late 1960s, by reducing emphasis on new housing in favor of preserving the existing stock. The Community Development Act provided block grant funds for these conservation efforts. Further, the law required local administrations to solicit the opinions of citizens' groups before undertaking projects with federal funding involved.

All of these made the neighborhood a major factor in local politics as a voice for directed or limited growth. The potency of the neighborhood was illustrated early in Atlanta when a group of predominantly white neighborhoods banded together in 1973 to block the construction of I-485 in the city, a project advocated by downtown businesses and the development community. At roughly the same time, several east-side Atlanta neighborhoods—Inman Park and Ansley Park among them—were being rediscovered by young middle-class urbanites, who demanded an upgrading in urban services, a chronic complaint of the city's black neighborhoods. The neighborhood and racial coalition helped to elect the city's first black mayor, Maynard Jackson, thus ending for the time being the domination of urban government by a narrow elite with ties to the financial-mercantile interests and northside residential areas.

The ascendancy of neighborhood interests improved not only service and social inequities in Southern cities, but structural stability as well. The neighborhood movement coincided with renewed interest in the South's built heritage, manifested not only in the rehabilitation of the stately plantation homes in Natchez or the classical residences along Charleston's famed Battery, but in less prestigious locales as well. The Fan District in Richmond, a seedy collection of late-nineteenth-century row houses west of an equally decayed downtown, underwent a revival in the 1960s and 1970s, spurred by low interest loans and new lifestyle preferences for urban living. Charlotte's Fourth Ward, an erstwhile middle-income residential community in the downtown area, was a series of overgrown, empty lots strewn with refuse and dotted with an occasional dilapidated structure. In 1976, through the vision of entrepreneur

Dennis Rash and the NCNB Community Development Corporation, in cooperation with the city and federal governments, existing structures were saved, and others were trucked into the area from elsewhere in the city. And through judicious infill (construction of architecturally compatible dwellings), the principals recreated a late-nineteenth-century urban neighborhood that became a favorite location for so-called yuppies in the early 1980s.

But even long-neglected poorer residents of Southern cities are participating in the structural revival of close-in neighborhoods. Gentrification—a British term connoting the displacement of a lower socioeconomic group by a higher one—had become a problem in several Southern cities, with inevitable racial overtones. Speculators were rapidly buying up historic structures, home to a primarily poor black tenant population, evicting these long-time residents, rehabilitating the buildings and selling them at a profit as high as 100 percent. City officials have been reluctant to interfere with this process, since the salvaging and upgrading of the housing stock translates into a higher tax base. There are some indications, however, that cities are seeking more equitable solutions to the preservation of historic inner-city neighborhoods. Savannah has become a pioneer in this respect.

Just south of Savannah's revitalizing downtown stands a forty-five block neighborhood known as the Victorian District, replete with distinctive wood-frame, gingerbread-style houses erected between 1870 and 1900. Once a fashionable area, the district had fallen into disrepair by the early 1970s, the homes subdivided into rental properties. As part of Savannah's renewed interest in its rich history, it was likely that the general rehab fever in the city would eventually affect even this neighborhood. The residents were predominantly black, poor, and elderly renters who would be unable to withstand a speculative onslaught. In 1977, investment banker Leopold Adler II brought together an interracial group of neighborhood leaders, bankers, architects, and preservation specialists to form a nonprofit development corporation, the Savannah Landmark Rehabilitation Project. The objective of the firm was to rehabilitate roughly one-third of the 800–odd homes in the district without displacing their low-income residents. Financed initially by federal subsidies and more recently by private syndicates taking advantage of historical-structure tax benefits, Savannah Landmark attained its goal in 1984. In addition, it constructed forty-four infill units. The renaissance has stimulated middle- and upper-income rehabs in other parts of the Victorian District, providing a unique mixture of race and income in this inner-city neighborhood.

A prevailing notion in city planning circles in recent years is that "small is beautiful," a professional revulsion from the large housing and road projects of the past that created even larger urban problems. The notion fits well with the Southern urban ambience. Northern cities happened upon "small is beautiful" primarily because that was all they could afford in their new austerity; Southern cities embraced the concept because their residents demanded it and, moreover, it comported well with regional culture. Church barbecues, neighborhood festivals, home tours, and concerts and crafts fairs in the park may be what passes as the most common form of culture and entertainment in today's medium-sized Southern city, but they also reflect the small-town heritage of the region and the desire to keep it that way.

These are encouraging signs that the Southern landscape— metropolis and countryside—may survive the Sunbelt and continue to serve as the wellspring of regional culture. In fact, the better-educated, more cosmopolitan work force of the transformed Southern economy possesses the leisure, affluence, and influence to insist upon maintaining the environment. The South can afford the luxury of preservation. Removing the burden of poverty and its accompanying ailments has enabled the Southerner, native or transplant, to renew the bond to the land.

There was, of course, a direct historical connection between the exploitation of the land and the exploitation of people, especially of black people. It is doubtful whether environmental sensitivity would have flourished long in a biracial society. Lifting the burden of race enabled Southerners not only to see each other, but to value their common land as well. As race relations continue to improve, so will Southern ecology.

Southern Opportunities for Blacks

Race relations continue to improve despite the role of "outside agitators" from Washington threatening affirmative action programs, electoral processes, and desegregation agreements. The symbols and realities abound. In 1983, the white mayor of Jackson renamed a street after Medgar Evers, the slain civil rights leader. Over in Alabama, one can drive into Montgomery on the Martin Luther King, Jr. Expressway or read that in December 1983 a jury of eleven whites and one black convicted a Klansman of murdering a black teenager. Or one could walk over to the State House to hear the Rev. Jesse Jackson address the legislature, as he did in May 1983. And was it not appropriate that the first black man in the United States to run for president from a major party was a black Southerner? Despite Jackson's failure to secure his party's nomination, he offered inspiration and hope to black Southern youngsters who in another time, early in their young lives, were taught by parents or experience to have no hope or spin no dream.

The symbols reflected broader currents in regional race relations. In the 1982 elections, Southerners elected more blacks to public office than any other region of the country. Two years later, 85 percent of new black officeholders elected were Southerners. The percentage of black elected officials in the South increased from 2 percent in 1975 to 8 percent in 1984, though still lagging behind the proportion of blacks in the region's population (24 percent). There were also encouraging indications that at least some of these black officials received modest support from white voters. In 1983, Charlotte's black mayoral candidate, Harvey Gantt, a local architect and the first black student at Clemson University, defeated a white candidate and received nearly 40 percent of the city's white vote. Two years later, he extended that proportion to 46 percent. Black voters comprised only one-fourth of Charlotte's eligible electorate. In 1983, the Rev. I. DeQuincey Newman, a longtime civil rights activist, became South Carolina's first black state senator in ninety-five years. While a milestone itself, equally notable was the fact that 64 percent of his district's eligible voters were white. A year later, he stood up in the Senate to join his colleagues in a rousing rendition of "Dixie." And why not? A good rebel should enjoy a good rebel song. The emergence of fresh, competent black leadership in the South during the 1980s seemed to be fulfilling the 1968 prophecy of black journalist Chuck Stone, when he predicted that "the black South is going to be the leading force among black people and . . . spawn a race of brilliant and articulate black men."

While Southern politics had provided blacks with their most visible and rewarding indication of regional racial parity, it has also been the source of great frustration during the 1980s as blacks have pushed against the limits of political possibility. An early inkling of the gap between black political potential and real policy occurred during the Carter administration. Of the region's black voters, 94 percent supported the Carter candidacy during the 1976 presidential election, enabling him to sweep the Deep South. As president, he appointed more blacks to significant federal offices than any other previous administration, but his inability to cope with inflation and economic stagnation inhibited innovative social or economic legislation that might have helped the vast numbers of poor blacks. Moreover, his always-tentative relations with Congress probably could not withstand a major policy assault, especially on an agenda for which Congress had little enthusiasm. Julian Bond complained bitterly that "we voted for a man who knew the words to our hymns, but not the numbers on our paychecks."

There was also a growing disappointment with the performance of black leaders in office. Successful black office-holders, i.e., those who secured some policy victories as well as their own reelection, quickly understood that at least lipservice to the traditional white political and corporate leadership, locally and statewide, was a necessary part of engaging in politics. Productive local leaders, such as Atlanta's Andrew Young and Charlotte's Harvey Gantt, have learned this lesson. Atlanta banker Robert Strickland, head of that city's Chamber of Commerce, said of Young in 1982: "He's attentive, he's thoughtful—listen, we just plain like him." Two reasons for this admiration were Young's support of a sales tax increase—a levy that is most burdensome to the poor—and his aggressive efforts to attract new, especially foreign, investment to the city.

The regional prosperity in the 1980s further constrained black leaders and their white allies from major socioeconomic policy adjustments, even assuming such measures would have received official approbation at any time in the generally conservative South. The era of Great Society-type legislation at the federal or state levels had passed and experts disagreed on the effectiveness of these programs in any case. There was a growing feeling that the legislation aimed at eliminating discrimination was already on the books and working and that the roots of black poverty in the South had little to do with race prejudice anymore. Black spokesmen, such as journalist William Raspberry and political scientist William Julius Wilson, pointed to factors such as the alarming rise in black female-headed households, teenage pregnancy, high crime rates among young blacks, illiteracy, and drug abuse as the results of the vicious cycle of poverty. But these problems are not amenable to the usual legislative ministrations even in the most sympathetic of times. As Wilson noted: "I suspect that any significant reduction of joblessness, crime, welfare dependency, single-parent homes and out-of-wedlock pregnancies would require far more comprehensive social and economic change than Americans have generally deemed appropriate or desirable. It would require a radicalism that neither the Republican nor the Democratic Party has been bold enough to espouse."

This latter point was especially so for the two-party South in the mid-1980s. For the Democrats, the tightrope act continued, buffeted by crosswinds from Washington and a regional prosperity that took the edge off populist-style appeals. Demographic trends seemed to favor the Republicans. Blue collars turned to white and white lightning to Blue Light specials. There were simply fewer rural working-class whites. Also, some white voters came to perceive the Democratic party as the party for blacks, a perception encouraged by Republicans. Despite these inauspicious developments, Democratic candidates have maintained their balance in the region by hewing to the socioeconomic formula worked out in the mid-1970s. Such successful Democratic politicians as Virginia's Chuck Robb, Albert Gore of Tennessee, Bob Graham of Florida, and Texas Governor Mark White have pursued fiscally conservative and socially moderate policies. The formula seems to be winning growing acceptance among the independent Southern electorate. In the 1985 Virginia gubernatorial election, voters elected Democrats to the top three state offices, including Robb protegé Gerald Baliles as governor, black state senator Douglas Winder as lieutenant governor, and Mary Sue Terry as attorney general. This result occurred in one of the South's most staunchly Republican states and the former province of the ultraconservative Byrd machine. The point is that race and gender may be increasingly less important in the South's political future than policies combining economic development and social equity. If so, then reports of both the Democratic party's eclipse and the dwindling influence of a captive black electorate may be premature. The situation may even move Southern Republican candidates to renew appeals to black voters. North Carolina Republican Governor Jim Martin has demonstrated the success of this approach.

Indeed, as more blacks in the South "make it," their political behavior may move toward the regional norm, shifting from candidate to candidate, with a party label of diminished importance. And more blacks are "making it" in the South.

For an American black today, the economic and lifestyle opportunities are probably greater in the South than in any other region, a situation inconceivable a short two decades ago. Taylor Wilson, a black electrician from Chicago whose father had left Mississippi a generation earlier, joined a growing remigration movement: "I'm moving South for the same reasons my father came here from Mississippi. He was looking for a better way of life." Darenda Mason, a Charlotte employment agency supervisor who left that city for New Jersey in 1968, was astounded "at how much difference fifteen years has made." She cited "changes in housing and employment opportunities, professional association, and civic and political leadership" as some of the differences that convinced her to return to the South. Some middle-class blacks are moving into the region for the first time, like Bobby Wilson, a Brooklyn-born sociologist at the University of Alabama in Birmingham, who finds the city a pleasant place to work and raise a family. The visibility of blacks in professional positions in the South, even in high administrative and executive positions, has increased significantly during the 1980s, where one estimate claims that 10 percent of the black work force in the region held higher-status white-collar employment (banking, commerce, education, law, and medicine) in 1982, compared with less than 3 percent as late as 1975.

The Persistence of an Older South: Another Perspective on Race and Economy

The racial progress in the South (especially in comparison with problems elsewhere) and the prevailing economic prosperity are conditions conducive to smugness and complacency. Southerners, above all Americans, should know from bitter historical experience that prevailing winds have scarcely ever blown in one direction for long. There is even this historical reminder from historian George B. Tindall that "if experience is any guide, the South will blow it." The case for humility persists in the Southern midst. While some blacks in the South participate in the regional economic prosperity, a persistent black underclass remains outside the economy. The hard-fought victories in school desegregation are slipping away. By 1980,

Atlanta's public schools were more than 80 percent black, thus rendering busing almost irrelevant. In response to the erosion of white support for public schools, some jurisdictions, such as Norfolk and Little Rock, are purposely resegregating some of their schools to keep white children in the system. Even some black leaders are now questioning the old verities of an integrated education. Durham school superintendent Cleveland Hammonds, a black, stated that "quality education—not integration—is the top priority." Also, the struggle for voting rights is not yet won, despite favorable signs to the contrary. Selma officials shut down a voter registration office in the black community in 1985, and white political leaders, encouraged by the silence of the Reagan administration, still engage in the abstract art of gerrymandering.

As far as the prosperous economy is concerned, the unevenness that was evident as the Sunbelt burst forth in the early 1970s persists, though some of the locations of economic despair have shifted. The oil boom has gone bust for Texas and Louisiana. Textiles are reeling from the effects of cheaper imports, slipshod management, and tardy mechanization. Factory closings, layoffs, and four-day workweeks became commonplace in the Carolina Piedmont after 1982. The nature of the textile industry—labor intensive and typically located in small communities—compounded the impact of its decline. Between 1975 and 1985, roughly one-fifth of the half million textile workers in the Piedmont had lost their jobs. These were people with few skills beyond mill work and with poor educational backgrounds, the legacy of decades and generations of families revolving their lives around the mill. Closing a plant, frequently the only major employer in the community, reduced and blighted merchants. Young people move away, the Greyhound bus no longer stops, decreasing the mobility of the elderly, and the town slowly dies, another black patch in the Sunbelt quilt.

State development agencies provide some assistance to these fallen communities, attempting to recycle old mill buildings into other manufacturing or commercial enterprises. But a poorly educated and aging work force in an isolated semi-rural setting are difficult selling points, and, in truth, state development efforts and resources are mostly directed elsewhere. The "elsewhere" is usually in the high-tech and service fields, but even here there are some sobering questions. Service employment, while usually more stable these days than manufacturing positions, includes low-paid workers—waitresses, motel maids, and hospital orderlies, for example—and they usually do not draw in money from out of state, an important factor for a region that remains a net importer of capital. While high-tech employment is more remunerative, such activities tend to be equipment-intensive, meaning they provide fewer jobs, and given the lagging quality of the Southern work force and educational systems, these positions tend to go to individuals from outside the region.

Even high-tech is not immune to economic decline—California's troubled Silicon Valley is a prime example. The Sunbelt phenomenon itself may be changing as well. During the 1980s, some cities that flirted with economic disaster in the 1970s—Pittsburgh, Baltimore, and New York—staged surging comebacks, successfully adapting to the transforming American economy and taking advantage of educational and communications attributes already in place. New England, once a region of skeleton industrial communities, now enjoys a reputation as a high-tech haven. In short, the affair of corporate America with the South may be in jeopardy because of other suitors.

These caveats to the South's racial and economic conditions not only present a good case for humility, but also may reflect the fact that the South is merely becoming like the rest of the country. The statistics, from per capita income to urban demographics, indicate a convergence with national patterns. But does this convergence imply that we can at last write the epitaph for Dixie? The question has much more than academic importance, because the cultural elements possessed by the South—the sense of past and place, faith, manners, and the importance of kin—have the potential for acting as an important leaven in the impersonal, self-centered, and rootless life-style of postindustrial America.

Prospects for a Distinctive South: Promised Land or Another American Region?

There is some pessimism that the South has already been taken in by the late-twentieth-century version of the American Dream; that it survived a civil rights revolution with its culture intact, even stronger and more functional in fact, only to succumb at last to the siren song of a material world. Journalist H. Brandt Ayers compared the South to Sisyphus, "fighting for years to push the rock of ignorance, poverty, and prejudice up the hill." Then, Ayers complained, "Sisyphus got a job in real estate, moved to the suburbs, and voted Republican." Some fellow journalists agreed, such as Marshall Frady, who lamented that "the South is becoming etherized in all those ways a people are subtly rendered pastless, memoryless, blank of identity, by assimilation into chrome and asphalt and plastic."

But the South was always more than appearances, much richer in its personal values than its chronic poverty would have one believe, and possessing a deep strain of kindness born of rural life and strong faith that belied the visible tragedy of its racial system. And, in the past, the end or change of appearances did not necessarily result in the demise of the inner South. As George Tindall has noted, "The Vanishing South . . . has staged one of the most prolonged disappearing acts since the decline and fall of the Roman Empire."

The empirical evidence of Southern distinctiveness is clear enough. John Shelton Reed has confirmed that Southerners still are "more likely than other Americans to think of their region, their states, and their local communities, as *theirs*, and as distinct from and preferable to other regions, states, and localities." But polls are not necessary to sample distinctive Southern speech inflections, foods, music (from country to Southern rock to blues), and sports. While it is true that college football, for example, is played throughout the country, it has special meaning in the South. As Alcorn State (Mississippi) University football coach Marino Casem explains, "In the East, college football is a cultural attraction. On the West Coast it is a tourist attraction. In the Midwest, it is cannibalism. But in the South, it is religion." There is also a religious fervor about stockcar racing, an indigenous regional sport allegedly owing its existence to lead-footed moonshiners making fast getaways from revenue agents over winding mountain roads.

If the Southern sports world is populated with religious icons (the late Paul "Bear" Bryant's hats), shrines (Legion Field, Talladega), and saints (Bryant, Junior Johnson), it is merely a reflection of the general religiosity of the region. Southerners remain the most Protestant and most church-going (regardless of religious affiliation) people in the nation. The persistence of religion in the South is important for two reasons. First, it demonstrates that the region's assimilation into America may be more statistical than cultural, and second, it demonstrates, as educator David Mathews noted, that "our traditions are two-sided coins, and that the very tendencies that have made Southerners reactionary could, indeed, have at times made them progressive." A major result of the civil rights movement was to expose this "two-sidedness" in religion and in other regional cultural elements; the contemporaneous economic prosperity, by lifting the veil of ignorance and poverty, facilitated the emergence of the "progressive" side of that culture.

Southern Religion as a Cultural Microcosm

The New Religious Right is a national phenomenon, of course, but its headquarters, if anywhere, are with Jerry Falwell and the once-modest Thomas Road Baptist Church in Lynchburg, Virginia. The origins of this revival in the mid-1960s in the South coincided with the civil rights victories and rapid economic development. The transformation to an interracial, urban, postindustrial society evoked frightening prospects, not only for those who resisted becoming part of the new society, but also for those swept along by its currents to become the first college-educated generation or the first white-collar worker from a long line of farmers or mill workers or grocery clerks. The pressures, the newness, cried out for a certainty, and the religious revival delivered the security of simple answers to an increasingly complex life. The look of the audience of the TV evangelists is not the look of the downtrodden, the displaced sharecroppers, the urban reprobates, but of well-scrubbed, relatively affluent people trying to look the part of middle-class America. And in the parking lots of the fundamentalist megachurches on Sunday morning, the custom vans, Cadillacs, and Mercedeses indicate the old insecure materialism of a newly affluent people not quite sure yet of what has happened to them and their region.

Security bred exclusivity, eliminating a good portion of humanity from the purview of the new-old religion. The weak support of new right Baptists for their sect's historic mission and social service work, as well as a general indifference to the poverty around them, emanates from this clubby atmosphere of the saved and the damned. As historian Donald Mathews has noted: "The terrible insistence on universal sin and guilt did not dictate a common fate for all men; but cast in bold relief the distinction between those who would not escape their just condemnation and those who could. The result was a radical cleavage between Evangelicals and worldlings . . . there could be no middle group or lingering devotion to old ways or friends." The exclusivity also tended, accordingly, to limit debate and discourse, to establish an orthodoxy of thought that characterized the old South where deviation was not only sinful but dangerous. Wilmer C. Fields, director of public relations for the Southern Baptist Convention, analyzed the limits of fundamentalist dogmatism by noting that "truth, like knowledge, has nothing to fear from ruthless examination. . . . The unenlightened and the insecure shun inquiry, no less than do the prejudiced and the fearful." He concluded that "Our malady may be too much religion and too little faith, and not enough wisdom to know the difference."

The strident materialism of some of the new right churches

and television ministries reflects these insecurities and the importance of material accumulation in the lives of the congregants themselves. As Charlotte evangelist Jim Bakker said in defense of his plush surroundings, "God doesn't like junk." The problem, as theologian Langdon Gilkey has noted, is that "Being a Christian thus becomes merely the operation of expanding itself." The same exaggerated boosterism and inflated rhetoric that characterized the South's numerous economic false starts characterizes the new religious right. And the stridency has extended into the political arena, reinforcing Republican advances in the region, ironically shunning the first self-professed "born again" Christian to run for the presidency. But the political influence of the new religious right is on the wane in the South; the 1985 gubernatorial election in Virginia is a recent example. The other side of Southern faith is now ascendant, benefiting from the excesses of its opponents and from the fact that increasing numbers of Southerners are more comfortable with the racial and economic changes in the region. This "settling in" has not paled Southern religious distinction; it has merely brought to the forefront a more constructive strain, as exemplified by the leadership exercised by the South's progressive clergy in a variety of issues.

The Rev. Charles Milford of Charlotte's Park Road Baptist Church founded the Humility Club to remind fellow Baptists that self-righteousness is not a Christian trait. He has led his parishioners to adopt a nuclear arms freeze resolution and sponsored a Charlotte delegation to a Hiroshima and Nagasaki memorial service. In fact, in every major Southern community, ministers are the leading forces in the contemporary peace movement and keep that issue before their parishioners. In June 1983, ministers and delegates to the Western North Carolina Conference of the United Methodist Church passed a freeze resolution and affirmed the right of women to have abortions. This is not to say that these positions are "correct," but they recognize the pluralism of Southern, indeed of American religion, that there can be numerous viewpoints and shades of opinion on a variety of issues. James E. Wood, executive director of the Southern Baptist Joint Committee on Public Affairs, in 1980 voiced "strong theological objections to the New Religious Right for its list of issues to constitute the nation's moral agenda, its moral criteria used to evaluate candidates for public office, its assumption that human beings can know with certainty the will of God on particular political issues." Even in national church circles, such as in the recently reunited Presbyterian Church, Southern ministers are playing leading roles. When Presbyterians prepared a report on "The Christian Faith and Economic Justice," they turned to Charlotte's Rev. Doug Oldenburg to write the study. In it, he chided his fellow Christians for neglecting the "gross inequalities and the gross suffering in the world today."

The Gatekeepers of Tradition

The broader view expressed by Rev. Oldenburg reflects the expanded horizons opened up by racial amelioration and economic change. The South is a cosmopolitan region now in many respects. Rather than being damning in two senses, first as further proof of a regional cultural lobotomy and second as an example of decadence, the cosmopolitan mind of the South is an indicator that a distinctive region will survive. As Southern poet and literary critic Allen Tate put it, "Provincialism is that state of mind in which . . . men lose their origin in the past and its continuity into the present, and begin every day as if there had been no yesterday." Because the stock "good ole boy" seems so thoroughly Americanized now, observers have falsely taken that as evidence of a vanishing South. As author Paul Hemphill noted in graphic agreement, this Southern type is "out in the suburbs now, living in identical houses and shopping at the K-Mart and listening to Glen Campbell (Roy Acuff and Ernest Tubb are too tacky now) and hiding their racism behind code words. They have forfeited their style and spirit, traded it all in on a color TV and styrofoam beams for the den." But he is a vestige of the older South, before

1965, even before 1945. In whatever way he embodied Southern culture, it was the underside of that culture.

The insights of Tate and Hemphill are supported by the empirical research of John Shelton Reed. He found that cosmopolitan Southerners serve to strengthen rather than obliterate regional distinctions, especially since the Southern way of life corresponds to our changing concept of the "Good Life." As Louis D. Rubin, Jr. noted in 1980, "the South has long had a habit of incorporating seemingly disruptive change within itself, and continuing to be the South." The changes have not merely left the region at status quo, but rather, have opened up the promise and possibilities of the regional culture to greater numbers of Southerners, many of whom were trapped rather than liberated by that culture.

The South is still fresh and exciting, not necessarily in the heedless pioneer mentality of yore, though there is that as well as a self-congratulatory tone about regional progress; but rather in how a society that still adheres to traditions that are regrettably moribund in most other places can use that culture in a modern world to forge a better civilization. Bob Hall, editor of *Southern Exposure* magazine and more prone to point out the region's shortcomings than to blindly herald its attributes, makes a similar point. "There's nothing pure about the South," he writes, "but the possibilities that the South offers for us are a lot better than the possibilities in a lot of other places. Because the possibilities in the other places have been eliminated, rooted out." Southerners, like the ancient Hebrews, fought among themselves and engaged in a battle of will against their God, but like the Israelites they forged a land of promise out of the conflict itself, and the South may yet be that redemptive region foretold as the first settlers encountered its incomparable beauty and promise.

BIBLIOGRAPHICAL ESSAY

General Works

Two books are essential for placing the dramatic changes that have occurred in the South since 1945 in their proper perspective. One is W. J. Cash's *The Mind of the South* (New York, 1941). The writer, an editor with the *Charlotte News,* portrays the South as a distinctive region burdened by its history of poverty, ignorance, racism, and defeat. The region's leaders traded on myths that bore little relation to the harsh realities of life in the South, and brooked no dissent from prevailing religious, racial, economic, and political beliefs. There was a frustration in Cash's eloquent writing that somehow a good people and a well-endowed land had succumbed to a terrible fate from which there was no escape. The second book is Howard W. Odum's *Southern Regions of the United States* (Chapel Hill, NC, 1936). Odum, a sociologist at The University of North Carolina, presents a statistical profile of a region burdened by rural poverty and its social and economic consequences. Cash fashioned his cultural explanations largely on the empirical data presented by Odum.

Together, the two books provided substantial evidence that the South was a region that was backward and proud of it; that it excluded a sizable portion of its population from meaningful participation in regional life; that it possessed both abundant natural resources and a depressed economy; and that it seemed ill-equipped to meet the challenges of first depression and then world war. The South, of course, not only met those challenges, but benefited from them, and were Cash and Odum writing today, their profiles would be startlingly different, even if the cultural underpinnings may have stayed in place.

Cash and Odum were not, of course, the first Southern writers to analyze their region, though the comprehensiveness and frankness of their works was unusual. In fact, attempting to explain the South is a major theme of Southern history. Fred Hobson chronicles this penchant in *Tell About the South: The Southern Rage to Explain* (Baton Rouge, LA, 1983). The penchant became more earnest in the decades after World War II, when change inundated the region. Journalist Harry Ashmore's *An Epitaph for Dixie* (New York, 1957) sensed that racial and economic changes were making the South less distinctive. By the mid-1970s the verdict was in, according to John Egerton in *The Americanization of Dixie, The Southernization of America* (New York, 1974), which, as the title implies, agreed that region-mixing in terms of culture, race, and politics had become rampant.

But Egerton far from settled the debate over Southern distinctiveness in the midst of change. Indeed, scholarship before and since has provided periodic assessments of the vitality of Southern distinctiveness through time. George B. Tindall's "Beyond the Mainstream: The Ethnic Southerners," *Journal of Southern History* XL (February 1974), 3–18, was among the more forceful reminders that change need not upset culture. Other examples of the persistent distinctiveness of the region are available in John Hope Franklin, "The Great Confrontation: The South and the Problem of Change," *Journal of Southern History* XXXVIII (February 1972), 3–20, and Sheldon Hackney, "The South as a Counterculture," *American Scholar* 42 (Spring 1973), 283–293.

The search for Southern identity (or explication of its demise) is not limited to individual writers. Groups of scholars have gathered at periodic conferences called to celebrate, search, or eulogize post-World War II Southern distinctiveness and have published several helpful works that assess change and its impact on the regional culture. Among the earliest of this genre was Avery Leiserson, ed., *The American South in the 1960s,* (New York, 1964), whose contributors argued for a transformed region in all senses. John C. McKinney and Edgar T. Thompson, eds., *The South in Continuity and Change* (Durham, NC, 1965), concurred, though they warned that certain parts of the South, especially rural areas, were outside the forces of change. A few years later, another collective assessment, H. Brandt Ayers and Thomas H. Naylor, eds., *You Can't Eat Magnolias* (New York, 1972) was a liberal manifesto that exuded confidence in a changed region, though it warned that these changes should not destroy the blessings of regional life and traditions. Ernest M. Lander and Richard J. Calhoun, eds., *Two Decades of Change: The South since the Supreme Court Desegregation Decision* (Columbia, SC, 1975), takes a similar perspective—heralding the change, but hopeful that the region is not swallowed by it.

Collective works since the mid-1970s have taken a more combative tone and have proclaimed that the distinctive region flourishes amid the changes. Representatives of this viewpoint are Fifteen Southerners, *Why The South Will Survive* (Athens, GA, 1981), and William C. Havard and Walter Sullivan, eds., *A Band of Prophets: The Vanderbilt Agrarians After Fifty Years* (Baton Rouge, LA, 1982).

These later works reflect a general trend over the past decade of reaffirming the distinctiveness of the Southern region. Three works in particular stress the continuity of Southern differences over time: Carl N. Degler's *Place Over Time: The Continuity of Southern Distinctiveness* (Baton Rouge, LA, 1977); Dewey W. Grantham's *The Regional Imagination: The South and Recent American History* (Nashville, 1979); and Stephen A. Smith's *Myth, Media, and the Southern Mind* (Fayetteville, AR, 1985).

Journalists as well, in recent years, have dissented from Egerton's amalgamation hypothesis. Their accounts, often undertaken after extensive travels in the region, reveal that the economic and social transformations have not occurred uniformly throughout the South and, even when they have, local distinctions remain intact. Typically, these chronicles are optimistic, if guarded, about the region's future. The most helpful examples are Neal R. Peirce's two books, *The Deep South States of America: People, Politics, and Power in the Seven Deep South States* (New York, 1974), and *The Border South States: People, Politics, and Power in the Five Border States* (New York, 1975), both of which include extensive interviews with leading public figures in a state-by-state analysis. Fred Powledge, working for the *Charlotte Observer,* undertook a personal as well as a journalistic odyssey through the South in the mid-1970s, finding a spirit of racial reconciliation and the persistence of Southern hospitality that he wrote about in *Journeys Through the South: A Rediscovery* (New York, 1979). Also helpful in evoking the flavor of the region from the perspective of a returning native son is Marshall Frady's collection of essays, *Southerners: A Journalist's Odyssey* (New York, 1980). More impressionistic, though not entirely about the South is William Least Heat Moon's *Blue Highways* (Boston, 1982). Among the most recent and thoughtful journalistic compilations is John B. Boles, ed., *Dixie Dateline: A Journalistic Portrait of the Contemporary South* (Houston, 1983), whose contributors discuss the persistence of past and place, the extent of change, and the dangers of complacency.

Compare these accounts with earlier reporters' assessments of the state of the South. Such works as Pat Watters *The South and the Nation* (New York, 1969) and Peter Schrag, "A Hesitant New South: Fragile Promise on the Last Frontier," *Saturday Review* 18 (February 12, 1972), 51–57, were hopeful that the South could save itself and the nation through its racial trials, but also noted the persistence of a darker strain of adherence to white supremacy and intellectual conformity. Later works were less hesitant about the South's place in national leadership as far as race relations and economic development were concerned.

The journalistic studies provide valuable insights and evoke well the atmosphere of the region. But they treat history in a perfunctory manner. Historians have not yet dealt with the postwar era in its entirety. Charles P. Roland, *The Improbable Era: The South since World War II* (Lexington, KY, 1975), provides a lively overview that stresses the themes of continuity and change, but ends his chronicle in the early 1970s. There are also no state surveys of this period, aside from Neal Peirce's chapters. Numan V. Bartley's *The Creation of Modern Georgia* (Athens, GA, 1983), though it covers a longer time span, is a model of what historians could accomplish with an interpretive work on the impact of change on a Southern state.

Culture

The preceding books are starting points for the discovery of the postwar South. But the initiation would be incomplete without some grounding in the regional culture: literature, music, and religion. These cultural elements have persisted through the upheavals of civil war and civil rights and are among the more obvious reminders of a distinctive region. The South, of course, has generated some of the most prominent twentieth-century writers. The so-called Southern Renaissance began in the early 1920s with Robert Penn Warren, Thomas Wolfe, William Faulkner, and Ellen Glasgow. Some observers believe that this literary flowering has wilted. Walter Sullivan, in two works, *Death by Melancholy: Essays on Modern Southern Fiction* (Baton Rouge, LA, 1972), and *A Requiem for the Renascence: The State of Fiction in the Modern South* (Athens, GA, 1976), is the leading exponent of this view. Others disagree and claim that a new generation of prominent Southern literary figures is emerging. Richard H. King, *A Southern Renaissance: The Cultural Awakening of the American South, 1930–1955,* (New York, 1980), provides an introduction to the postwar era that includes other aspects of regional culture in addition to literature. Three books advocate the persistence of a Southern literary tradition over the past generation. Louis D. Rubin,

Jr., *The Faraway Country: Writers of the Modern South* (Seattle, 1963), is an early proponent of this view. More recent works are Ben Forkner and Patrick Samway, S.J., eds., *Stories of the Modern South* (New York, 1977), and Philip Castille and William Osborne, eds., *Southern Literature in Transition: Heritage and Promise* (Memphis, 1983).

The serious historical literature on Southern music has not been extensive, but Bill Malone provides good, if not interpretive, surveys in *Country Music, U.S.A.: A Fifty-Year History* (Austin, 1969), and in *Southern Music-American Music* (Lexington, KY, 1979). On the more specific regional folk music form, the blues, the leading analysis is William Ferris's *Blues from the Delta* (New York, 1979). On Southern rock, particularly since the 1970s, see Courtney Haden, "Dixie Rock: The Fusion's Still Burning," *Southern Exposure* V (Summer/Fall 1977), 37–43.

Religion, especially evangelical Protestantism, is one of the most pervasive of the South's cultural elements, coloring social and political perspectives even as the region has undergone significant change. Historians are only beginning to recognize the historical dimensions of this phenomenon and, indeed, the most useful works are those by trained theologians who have moved into the field. The leading practitioner is Samuel S. Hill, and his numerous works are essential starting points for understanding Southern religion. Hill denoted the close relationship between religion and culture in "The South's Culture-Protestantism," *Christian Century* LXXIX (September 12, 1962), 1094–1096; on the social implications of Southern theology, see his collection of essays, *Religion and the Solid South* (Nashville, 1972); and on the persistent distinctiveness of Southern religion compared with that of the rest of the country, see *The South and North in American Religion* (Athens, GA, 1980). Other helpful overviews include Kenneth K. Bailey, *Southern White Protestantism in the Twentieth Century* (New York, 1964), and David Edwin Harrell, Jr., ed., *Varieties of Southern Evangelicalism* (Macon, GA, 1981).

Southern Baptists comprise the region's largest denomination, and there are numerous journal articles written by prominent Baptist lay educators. Leon McBeth, in "Southern Baptists and Race since 1947," *Baptist History and Heritage* 7 (April 1972), 155–169, depicts the gap between pulpit and pew, between regional organizations and individual churches, on racial perspectives. Walter B. Shurden makes a similar point, though the gap seems to have produced others during the ensuing years, in "The Southern Baptist Synthesis: Is it Cracking?" *Baptist History and Heritage* 16 (April 1981), 2–11. James E. Wood, Jr., discusses a major reason for this cracking synthesis in "The New Religious Right and Its Implications for Southern Baptists," *Foundations* (Apr.–June 1982), 153–166. J. Wayne Flynt supports the continuity-within-change thesis for Southern Baptists who are now more urban and wealthy, but who remain connected to beliefs derived from their rural heritage, in "Southern Baptists: Rural to Urban Transition," *Baptist History and Heritage* 16 (January 1981), 24–34.

Much of the recent literature on religion in the South has been critical of what the authors perceive as an overweening emphasis on self-aggrandizement and dogma as opposed to good works. They view the trend as antithetical to evangelical principles. In this vein, see Jim Sessions, "A Mighty Fortress: Protestant Power and Wealth," *Southern Exposure* IV (1976), 23–103; Ernest Kuntz, "The Tragedy of Southern Religion," *Georgia Historical Quarterly* 66 (Summer 1982), 217–247; and E. Glenn Hinson, "Neo-Fundamentalism: An Interpretation and Critique," *Baptist History and Heritage* 16 (April 1981), 33–42. For an early example of this critique, see Marshall Frady's sensitive essay, "God and Man in the South," *Atlantic Monthly* 219 (January 1967), 37–42.

Other works combining several aspects of Southern culture include a collection of essays by *Charlotte Observer* editor Frye Gaillard, *Race, Rock and Religion: Profiles from a Southern Journalist* (Charlotte, NC, 1982) that is helpful in removing the stereotypes from these cultural elements, and Jack Temple Kirby's *Media-Made Dixie: The South in the American Imagination* (Baton Rouge, LA, 1978) which deals with popular perceptions of Southern life and culture as conveyed on film, in books, and on television.

If the reader remains unconvinced of the South's persisting distinctiveness by this point, then the work of John Shelton Reed, a sociologist at Chapel Hill, will provide the clincher. In his first major book *The Enduring South: Subcultural Persistence in Mass Society* (Lexington, MA, 1972), he used polls to develop a profile of a region that perceived itself as distinctive and whose characteristics, from attitudes toward place to churchgoing, are, in fact, different from those of the rest of the nation. During the next decade, Reed expounded on a number of these themes, and he collected the essays in *One South: An Ethnic Approach to Regional Culture* (Baton Rouge, LA, 1982). His most recent book, *Southerners: The Social Psychology of Sectionalism* (Chapel Hill, NC, 1983) expands on his earlier surveys and offers the conclusion that the changes that have occurred in the region over the past generation have actually reinforced Southern culture.

Many of these works on Southern society and culture since World War II touch upon, if only implicitly, the current raging Southern historiographical debate on whether there is a continuity or a discontinuity to Southern history. Cash is probably one of the most forceful proponents of the continuatarian philosophy. This philosophy is challenged by C. Vann Woodward, who in numerous essays and in *The Strange Career of Jim Crow* (New York, 1955) argued that change has been a major constant in Southern history. Actually, the general works surveyed here, collectively, indicate that both views are correct, hence the artificial nature of the controversy. The Civil War, World War II, the massive migrations of blacks and whites from South to North, from farm to city, and the various forms of race relations and economies support the notion of change or discontinuity in Southern history. On the other hand, Southern culture has remained remarkably resilient. As Reed's surveys indicate, the sense of place and past, strong family ties, faith, and manners remain regional characteristics, not to mention accents, food, music, and literature as distinctive cultural elements as well. It is also important to keep in mind that although many authors, including myself, write about "The South," there are, in fact, many Souths, and that the strength and nature of culture varies with location within the region.

Race

The general and cultural studies provide both overview and context for learning about the South since 1945. Concerning the specific changes themselves—race, politics, and economic development—there is an extensive literature devoted to each of these aspects. The literature on race in the postwar era is particularly extensive, so I will include those works that I found especially helpful in developing insights about this aspect of regional life. There is one introduction and two readable overviews to recommend in setting the boundaries for racial change in the South. The introduction is Aldon D. Morris, *The Origins of the Civil Rights Movement: Black Communities Organizing for Change* (New York, 1984), which stresses the planned rather than spontaneous nature of early movement activities. The two general works are Manning Marable, *Race, Reform and Rebellion: The Second Reconstruction in Black America, 1945–1982* (Jackson, MS, 1984), and Harvard Sitkoff, *The Struggle for Black Equality, 1954–1980* (New York, 1981). Sitkoff's is the more useful survey, though both take a national perspective without elaborating on the particular cultural context of the South and how that context shaped the movement. In addition, Marable's Marxist rhetoric occasionally intrudes and confuses his narrative. The history of the civil rights movement in the South remains to be written.

More helpful for establishing the Southern context of the movement are works by black and white participants or observers. There are two collections that offer a variety of observations by Southern civil rights leaders: William R. Beardslee, *The Way Out Must Lead In: Life Histories in the Civil Rights Movement* (Atlanta, 1977), and the more comprehensive work by *New York Times* reporter Howell Raines, *My*

Soul is Rested: Movement Days in the Deep South Remembered (New York, 1977). Individual blacks have provided detailed reminiscences that enable readers to gain insight into the psychological impact of the movement and its aftermath along with the better-known narratives of the events themselves. Among the most enlightening of this genre are Anne Moody, *Coming of Age in Mississippi* (New York, 1968) and Maya Angelou, *I Know Why the Caged Bird Sings* (New York, 1969). Though Angelou's book does not deal with the civil rights movement per se, it relates very well the extent of racial separation and the onus of segregation for blacks. In addition, Albert Murray's *South to a Very Old Place* (New York, 1971) provides an interesting contrast with the Moody and Angelou autobiographies, since Murray recounts his return to the South in the late 1960s, a very different place than it had been during the childhoods of the two black women. Murray acknowledges that certain cultural customs remain despite the outward changes. White Southerners have also offered their reminiscences of the 1940s, 1950s, and 1960s. Willie Morris's formative years in Yazoo City during the early stages of the civil rights movement are recounted in his autobiography, *North Toward Home* (Boston, 1967). Frank E. Smith, a Mississippi congressman deposed by his constituents because he suggested compliance with federal civil rights legislation, offered his assessment of the failures of regional leaders during the late 1950s and 1960s in *Look Away from Dixie* (Baton Rouge, LA, 1965). Perhaps the most sensitive white eyewitness account of the movement's impact on the South was by a Northerner. Yale psychiatrist Robert Coles, in *Children of Crisis: A Study of Courage and Fear* (Boston, 1964), reports the heroic, yet unassuming, roles carried out by black children pioneering the desegregation movement. A later book by Coles, *Farewell to the South* (Boston, 1972), is a more general work touching upon service inequities and the changes that occurred as a result of the civil rights legislation during the 1960s.

Southern whites not only functioned as chroniclers of the movement but also as partisans. The regional tradition of oratory and written advocacy was renewed during the troubled postwar decades. James McBride Dabbs, an official with the interracial Southern Regional Council and an Episcopal lay leader, wrote an eloquent, learned attack on the South's biracial society, pointing to racial commonalities, in *Who Speaks for the South?* (New York, 1964). Though more cautious than Dabbs, *Atlanta Constitution* editor Ralph McGill was an effective voice for compliance in the decade after 1955 and earned great respect within and outside the South. His editorials, columns, and articles are collected in two volumes and edited by Calvin M. Logue, *No Place to Hide: The South and Human Rights* (Macon, GA, 1984). Finally, there is the perspective of a white woman involved deeply in the civil rights struggle. Hollinger F. Bernard has edited the reminiscences of the remarkable Virginia Foster Durr, an Alabama matriarch, in *Outside the Magic Circle* (University, AL, 1985).

There are numerous secondary works dealing with white Southerners who advocated a range of actions from moderate to radical in order to effect racial reconciliation. Morton Sosna presents a fine overview of this group and places them in historical perspective in *In Search of the Silent South: Southern Liberals and the Race Issue* (New York, 1977). As the title implies, outspokenness did not come easily to this group, which is not surprising given the cultural strictures on dissent. Irwin Klibaner notes an exception to this reticence in "The Travail of Southern Radicals: The Southern Conference Educational Fund, 1946–1976," *Journal of Southern History* XLIX (May 1983), 179–202. But the price of speaking one's mind was ostracism and loss of influence. Anthony P. Dunbar provides some historical background for this group in *Against the Grain: Southern Radicals and Prophets, 1929–1959* (Charlottesville, VA, 1981).

Studies of individual liberals include John A. Salmond, *A Southern Rebel: The Life and Times of Aubrey Willis Williams, 1890–1965* (Chapel Hill, NC, 1983); David W. Southern, "Beyond Jim Crow Liberalism: Judge Waring's Fight Against Segregation in South Carolina, 1942–1952," *Journal of Negro History* (Fall 1981), 209–227; and Charles W. Eagles, *Jonathan Daniels and Race Relations: The Evolution of a Southern Liberal* (Knoxville, TN 1982). Eagles's biography is particularly interesting because it depicts a frequent pattern among Southern journalists who were very liberal in the 1930s yet became increasingly conservative as the civil rights debate heated up.

In fact, the designations conservative-moderate-liberal-radical, when applied to Southern whites, had different meanings at different times. Thus, conservatives might end up advocating immediate integration for practical reasons—a city's image or the loss of investments—while liberals might espouse an incremental approach, fearful of provoking extreme segregationists and therefore eroding gains already made. The subtleties of these distinctions are illustrated very well in Elizabeth Jacoway and David R. Colburn, eds., *Southern Businessmen and Desegregation* (Baton Rouge, LA, 1982), and also by Virginia H. Hein, "The Image of 'A City Too Busy to Hate': Atlanta in the 1960s," *Phylon* XXXIII (Fall 1972), 205–211. The Jacoway and Colburn book is especially effective in sorting out why some cities integrated relatively easily and others resisted. A great deal depended on the historic role of the business community. Even so, a clever and image-conscious leadership could obstruct meaningful desegregation for years, as William H. Chafe relates in *Civilities and Civil Rights: Greensboro, NC, and the Black Struggle for Freedom* (New York, 1980).

There were few subtleties with respect to the so-called Massive Resistance against desegregation that developed after the *Brown* decision in 1954. The definitive work on this subject is Numan V. Bartley, *The Rise of Massive Resistance: Race and Politics in the South in the 1960s* (Baton Rouge, LA, 1969). Bartley analyzes the success of massive resisters in using the Southern political process and its traditions to their advantage. On a more particular aspect of this resistance, see Neil R. McMillen's *The Citizens' Council: Resistance to the Second Reconstruction* (Urbana, IL, 1971). Contemporary accounts of white resistance generally lack the historical perspective of these two books, but capture the frenzy and fear of the era. Mississippi was often most synonymous with the worst excesses of resistance, and the atmosphere is evoked by a victim, James W. Silver, in "Mississippi: The Closed Society," *Journal of Southern History* XXX (February 1964), 3–34; and by an anguished native son and novelist, Walker Percy, in "Mississippi: The Fallen Paradise," *Harper's* 232 (Apr. 1965), 166–172. Journalist John Bartlow Martin compiled an extensive survey of white resistance sentiment at is height in the mid-1950s, *The Deep South Says "Never"* (New York, 1957). Among the more genteel resisters of the period was South Carolina politician William D. Workman, who attempted to fashion a legal and cultural brief for segregation, or at least for allowing the South to work out its own problems, in *The Case for the South* (New York, 1960).

Workman's abhorrence of federal intervention was widespread among white Southerners. Historically, such intrusions had portended ill for the South. William Faulkner raised this concern, even as he acknowledged the need for change, in his first postwar novel, *Intruder in the Dust* (New York, 1948). There is little doubt that the federal role was a crucial one. Merl E. Reed chronicles federal efforts during World War II in "FEPC and the Federal Agencies in the South, *Journal of Negro History* LXV (Winter 1980), 45–56. Reed's account is one of great hope and few results. Monroe Billington, "Civil Rights, President Truman and the South," *Journal of Negro History* LVII (April 1973), 127–139, finds more substantive results, though not particularly in the South. The use of the civil rights issue as a political weapon is apparent in Harvard Sitkoff, "Harry Truman and the Election of 1948: The Coming of Age of Civil Rights in American Politics," *Journal of Southern History* XXXVII (November 1971), 597–616. The Eisenhower administration, currently undergoing a general reassessment, has elicited a mixed review on civil rights support from Robert Frederick Burk, *The Eisenhower Administration and Black Civil Rights* (Knoxville, TN, 1984), who argues that the Eisenhower administration institutionalized certain aspects of the federal response to civil rights as well as the limits of that response. The role of the federal judiciary in advancing civil rights was less equivocal. Two useful studies are Jack Bass, *Unlikely Heroes* (New York, 1981), on the Fifth Circuit Court of Appeals, and Tinsley E. Yarborough, *Judge Frank Johnson and Human Rights in Alabama* (University, AL, 1984), on the noted federal district court judge who defied a governor and public opinion in his native state.

There is considerable literature on specific aspects of the civil rights movement and its aftermath. Two recent overviews are, first, a liberal lament on the status of school desegregation, especially in the North, George R. Metcalf's *From Little Rock to Boston: The History of School Desegregation* (Westport, CT, 1983), and, second, a conservative critique, especially of the federal courts' role, Raymond Wolters's *The Burden of Brown: Thirty Years of School Desegregation* (Knoxville, TN, 1984). On one of the most notable milestones along the road to school desegregation see Tony Freyer, *The Little Rock Crisis: A Constitutional Interpretation* (Westport, CT, 1984), which approaches this issue from a legal perspective.

The Montgomery bus boycott has its definitive history in J. Mills Thornton III's "Challenge and Response in the Montgomery Boycott of 1955–1956," *Alabama Review* XXXIII (July 1980), 163–235, in which he places the boycott within its political context and notes the general failure of the boycott itself as well as important lessons King learned from the experience. Catherine A. Barnes places the Montgomery incident in the broad context of transit desegregation in *Journey from Jim Crow: The Desegregation of Southern Transit* (New York, 1983). She stresses the role of the federal government in ending segregated transit facilities. For background on the Freedom Riders, see August Meier and Elliott Rudwick, "The First Freedom Ride," *Phylon* XXX (Fall 1969), 213–222.

Voting rights shared center stage with desegregation as the focus of movement activities, particularly during the early 1960s. John R. Salter, a leading participant, chronicles the year prior to the Mississippi Freedom Summer of 1964, culminating in the assassination of NAACP leader Medgar Evers, in *Jackson, Mississippi: An American Chronicle of Struggle and Schism* (Hicksville, NY, 1979); he also analyzes the divisions among black leadership. Mary Aickin Rothschild, *A Case of Black and White: Northern Volunteers and the Southern Freedom Summers, 1964–65* (Westport, CT, 1982) also focuses on internal dissension, especially the sexual tensions that resulted from the introduction of Northern white women into the Mississippi voting rights campaign. The culmination of these efforts was the Selma-Montgomery march in March 1965, and David J. Garrow evokes the spirit of the march as well as chronicling the calculation of black leaders that whites would react violently in *Protest at Selma: Martin Luther King, Jr. and the Voting Rights Act of 1965* (New Haven, 1978). Anne Nall Stallworth, in *Go, Go, Said the Bird* (New York, 1984), depicts the Selma march in novel form, using a mulatto protagonist to relate the conflicts generated by the voting rights demonstrations in a society that perceived well-defined roles for blacks and whites.

As many of these authors have observed, the civil rights movement not only struggled against an external enemy but also contended with differences from within. Generational, gender, personal, and philosophical conflicts plagued the movement from the outset, but the acceleration of blood-letting in the early 1960s and, ironically, the successful culmination of the movement's initial objectives as embodied in the 1964 Civil Rights Act and the Voting Rights Act of 1965 worsened the schisms. Adam Fairclough provides an overview of the decline and fall of Martin Luther King's organization, the Southern Christian Leadership Conference, in "The SCLC and the Second Reconstruction, 1957–1973," *South Atlantic Quarterly* (April 1981), 177–194. Not surprisingly, much of the work on divisions in black leadership has centered on the controversies surrounding King's steadfast adherence to nonviolence in the face of growing white intransigence and violence, and his pronouncements on issues seemingly far afield from civil rights, such as nuclear disarmament and the Vietnam War. David Halberstam relays King's response to mounting criticism in "The Second Coming of Martin Luther King," *Harper's* 235 (August 1967), 39–51, while Carl Rowan, a black syndicated columnist, chastises King for his opposition to President Johnson's foreign policies in "Martin Luther King's Tragic Decision," *Reader's Digest* 91 (September 1967), 37–42. Two general biographies of King deal extensively with the issue of leadership, generally favoring King's perspective: David L. Lewis, *King: A Critical Biography* (New York, 1970), and Stephen B. Oates, *Let the Trumpet Sound: The Life of Martin Luther King, Jr.* (New York, 1982). The best defense of King, and the most eloquent, are the speeches of the civil rights leader and his early exposition, *Stride Toward Freedom: The Montgomery Story* (New York, 1958).

There is no postmovement assessment of civil rights in the South. Several scholars have written about persisting problems within Southern black communities that legislation has not ameliorated. Residential segregation, compounded by urban renewal and inadequate housing, is one such problem. Robin Flowerdew has surveyed research on this situation in "Spatial Patterns of Residential Segregation in a Southern City," *Journal of American Studies* 13 (April 1979), 93–107. For a historical perspective focusing on one city, see Barry J. Kaplan, "Race, Income, and Ethnicity: Residential Change in a Houston Community, 1920–1970," *Houston Review* 3 (Winter 1981), 178–202.

Joel Williamson offers a pessimistic view of contemporary race relations in the South in the last two chapters of *The Crucible of Race: Black-White Relations in the American South since Emancipation* (New York, 1984). Though he admits that "things are better," the white elite has relinquished little real power. A more general treatment that does not focus specifically on the South is Michael V. Namorato, ed., *Have We Overcome? Race Relations since Brown* (Jackson, MS, 1979). The contributors generally answer the question in the negative.

There are a few dissenters to the pessimism of these writers. Foremost among them is a black University of Chicago political scientist, William Julius Wilson. In *The Declining Significance of Race: Blacks and Changing American Institutions* (Chicago, 1978), Wilson argues that even in the South race is no longer a significant problem; the situation of blacks today is due less to discrimination than to structural changes in the American economy, and solutions must be economic, not race-specific. And, in fact, economic opportunities for blacks in the South may be greater than elsewhere. A reflection of this is the movement to the South after generations of migration in the other direction. See Rex R. Campbell, "Return Migration of Black People in the South," *Journal of Politics* 39 (February 1975), 129–162. Finally, Alice Walker's three novels, *The Three Lives of Grange Copeland* (New York, 1970), *Meridian* (New York, 1976), and *The Color Purple,* (New York, 1982), represent an odyssey of attitudes on civil rights and Southern blacks. The first novel is filled with hate and rage that is ultimately self-destructive. By the second novel, Walker's characters (except for the title character) display a listlessness and a resignation. In *The Color Purple,* Celie, the protagonist, discovers an inner strength rooted in her faith and in the land. Whites are only shadows in this novel.

The civil rights movement was above all, a religious phenomenon. Aside from the works on and by Martin Luther King, scholars have not explored this connection. Julia K. Blackwelder discusses the reaction of white fundamentalist denominations in "Southern White Fundamentalists and the Civil Rights Movement," *Phylon* XL (December 1979), 334–341. The best analysis of the religious meaning of the movement for white Southerners in particular is James Sellers, *The South and Christian Ethics* (New York, 1962).

If the religious dimension of the movement is an area for future research emphasis, so is the connection between civil rights for blacks and for Southern women. Lillian Smith was among the earliest writers to suggest this link in *Killers of the Dream* (New York, 1949). Sara Evans, "Women's Consciousness and the Southern Black Movement," *Southern Exposure*

IV (1976), 10–18, provides firsthand evidence of the distinctions between black and white women in the movement and the potential of these differences to split the ranks along racial lines. Sisterhood was still a goal to be attained.

Other works on Southern women do not deal explicitly with the impact of the movement on women's rights, but it is clear from this literature that it heightened the consciousness of Southern white women in particular, who were constricted by layers of myths that effectively cut them off from meaningful participation in regional life as much as other strictures excluded blacks. Rosemary Daniell's *Fatal Flowers: On Sin, Sex, and Suicide in the Deep South* (New York, 1980) is an autobiographical account of a painful breaking from regional mores that in itself becomes an aberration. Shirley Abbott's *Womenfolks: Growing Up Down South* (New Haven, CT, 1983) is a less wrenching personal breakthrough that concludes hopefully: ". . . thankful for a changing South yet grateful that past, place, and family remain as constant as ever." A more whimsical perspective on Southern female stereotypes is Florence King's *Southern Ladies and Gentlemen* (New York, 1975).

Politics

The Southern political scene has historically fascinated scholars, perhaps because of its colorful nature and its occasional extremism. The literature on the changes in Southern politics since World War II is consequently extensive. V. O. Key's *Southern Politics in State and Nation* (New York, 1949) is still the first step in learning about contemporary Southern politics; it not only establishes the foundation of the region's political culture and its state-by-state varieties, but it is also a useful benchmark to measure how far the South has moved from a political culture dominated by the race issue. Key's influence is so great that two subsequent political surveys of the region adopted his state-by-state organizing framework and consciously sought to update his assessments. Jack Bass and Walter De Vries, *The Transformation of Southern Politics: Social*

Change and Political Consequence since 1945 (New York, 1976) focuses on how the amelioration of race has worked in the political arena. The Republican party became a beneficiary of the backlash from racial accommodations, as Alexander Lamis points out in *The Two-Party South* (New York, 1984). He also argues persuasively that the Democrats, with appropriate candidates, can maintain at least parity in the region. For a brief overview of the political transformation, see William C. Havard, "Intransigence to Transition: Thirty Years of Southern Politics," *Virginia Quarterly Review* 51 (Autumn 1975), 497–521.

The realignment, or more specifically, the dealignment in party affiliation in the aftermath of the 1965 Voting Rights Act has generated several useful studies. William C. Havard, "Protest, Defection, and Realignment in Contemporary Southern Politics," *Virginia Quarterly Review* 48 (Spring 1972), 161–184, traces the weakening of Democratic party identification back to the 1930s. Paul Allen Beck, "Partisan Dealignment in the Postwar South," *American Political Science Review* 71 (June 1977), 477–496 stresses the changes in presidential voting in the South. The best state case study on dealignment is Patrick R. Cotter, "Southern Reaction to the Second Reconstruction: The Case of South Carolina," *Western Political Science Quarterly* 34 (December 1981), 543–551. Another state case study, Tip H. Allen, Jr. and David A. Krane, "Class Replaces Race: The Reemergence of Neopopulism in Mississippi Gubernatorial Politics," *Southern Studies* 19 (Summer 1980), 182–192, emphasizes the attempt of Mississippi Democrats to seize upon class issues in order to maintain their traditional white working-class support.

Of course, the reason for this significant electoral shift has been the participation of large numbers of blacks in the political process as a result of the 1965 Voting Rights Act. The two books that most effectively chart the application of the act to secure black voting rights are by Steven F. Lawson: *Black Ballots: Voting Rights in the South, 1944–1969* (New York 1976), and *In Pursuit of Power: Southern Blacks and Electoral*

Politics, 1965–1982 (New York, 1985). By the 1980s, Lawson concludes, compliance with the act was institutionalized, but the act itself has mainly psychological as opposed to economic benefits for blacks. This latter assertion complements an early assessment by Chandler Davidson's *Biracial Politics: Conflict and Coalition in the Biracial South* (Baton Rouge, LA, 1972). More recently, Davidson has gathered a fine collection of essays relating to the various devices Southern jurisdictions have employed to reduce black participation in *Minority Vote Dilution* (Washington, DC, 1984). The moral is the necessity of continued vigilance at the federal level. The uneven federal enforcement record, according to Howard Ball, Dale Krane, and Thomas P. Larth in *Compromised Compliance: Implementation of the 1965 Voting Rights Act* (Westport, CT, 1982), offers little comfort to those concerned about compliance in the future. For historical background on federal involvement in voting rights in the South, see Allan Lichtman, "The Federal Assault Against Voting Discrimination in the Deep South, 1957–67," *Journal of Negro History* LIII (October 1969), 346–367.

There have been few profiles of political leaders who have emerged in the South since 1965; the previous generation of leaders is better represented in the literature. For a fine profile of Alabama's "Big Jim" Folsom, see Carl Grafton, "James E. Folsom and Civil Liberties in Alabama," *Alabama Review* 32 (January 1979), 3–27. For two decades after World War II, editor Ralph McGill prepared numerous profiles of regional politicians. Calvin M. Logue collected many of these essays in *Southern Encounters: Southerners of Note in Ralph McGill's South* (Macon, GA, 1983).

Future works may well concentrate on the emergence of black leaders, especially at the local level, such as Atlanta's Andrew Young, Jr., and Birmingham's Richard Arrington. In fact, the presence of black elected officials is probably the most visible result of the Voting Rights Act. F. Glenn Abney and John D. Hutcheson, Jr., discuss the impact of Atlanta's first black mayor, Maynard Jackson, on local politics in "Race,

Representation, and Trust: Changes in Attitudes after the Election of a Black Mayor," *Public Opinion Quarterly* 45 (Spring 1981), 91–101. The dramatic increase in black voter participation provided the balance not only in urban areas, but in rural jurisdictions as well, especially in Black Belt districts. In the best state survey to date, Neil R. McMillen dctails the early years of black enfranchisement in Mississippi and their impact in "Black Enfranchisement in Mississippi: Federal Enforcement and Black Protest in the 1960s," *Journal of Southern History* XLIII (August 1977), 351–372.

The expanded black electorate has not only succeeded in electing blacks to office, but black voters have also influenced white legislators at state and national levels to moderate, even liberalize, their voting record on social issues. Charles S. Bullock quantifies this view in "Congressional Voting and the Mobilization of a Black Electorate in the South," *The Journal of Politics* 43 (August 1981), 662–682. For a survey of black voting power in rural areas, see David Campbell and Joe R. Feagin, "Black Politics in the South: A Descriptive Analysis," *Journal of Politics* 37 (February 1975), 129–162.

But there are limits to black voting power, as Bullock indicated in an earlier article, "The Election of Blacks in the South: Preconditions and Consequences," *American Journal of Political Science* XIX (November 1975), 727–739, in which he argues that black elected officials often face empty treasuries and uncooperative whites. Chandler Davidson's *Biracial Politics* demonstrated the limits of black voting patterns and influence in Houston.

The Houston situation brings up another factor in contemporary Southern politics, the growing influence of Latin voters. Raymond A. Mohl's soon-to-be published book on Miami will be a prototype for such analysis. In the meantime, F. Arturo Rosales's "Mexicans in Houston: The Struggle to Survive, 1908–1975," *Houston Review* 3 (Summer 1981), 24–48, provides a useful background of Chicano politics in that city. Houston has also experienced a significant in-migration of Northerners, as have several other Southern metropolitan areas. William Lyons and Robert F. Durant have studied the impact of such migration on Tennessee politics in "Assessing the Impact of Inmigration on a State Political System," *Social Science Quarterly* 61 (December 1980), 473–484, and have concluded that the newcomers are generally "more affluent, more liberal, and more Republican" than natives. Here is another area that demands further study.

Economic Development

The economic transformation of the South after World War II was as momentous as the political and racial changes and, in fact, the three were closely interrelated. It is important to begin the study of the Southern economy with agriculture. Changes on the farm precipitated a chain reaction through the rest of the Southern economy as early as the 1930s. It is fortunate to have two excellent overviews of the agriculture transformation. Gilbert C. Fite, *Cotton Fields No More: Southern Agriculture, 1865–1980* (Lexington, KY, 1984), is an upbeat account of the demise of King Cotton and the agricultural prosperity that followed. In *Breaking the Land: The Transformation of Cotton, Tobacco, and Rice Culture since 1880* (Urbana, IL, 1985), Pete Daniel presents a less optimistic view, charging that federal policies, especially in the cotton sector, destroyed the independence of the small farmer, threw the tenant off the land, and severed the strong psychic ties to the soil. This scenario was less applicable to tobacco- and rice-growing areas. There is also a helpful collection of essays on the decline of the plantation system, *Proceedings: Tall Timbers Ecology and Management Conference* (Tallahassee, FL, 1982), as well as a fine study of the transition to alternative cultivation patterns (the so-called Green Revolution), Harry D. Fornari, "The Big Change: Cotton to Soybeans," *Agricultural History* 53 (January 1979), 245–253.

As Daniel's book argues forcefully, the shift took its toll, and accompanied by changes in other sectors of the regional economy, it changed the rural landscape and its people. A sensitive collection of essays depicting these changes is Robert L. Hall and Carol B. Stack, eds., *Holding on to the Land and the Lord: Kinship, Ritual, Land Tenure, and Social Policy in the Rural South* (Athens, GA, 1982). Anthony M. Tang's *Economic Development in the Southern Piedmont, 1860–1950: Its Impact on Agriculture* (Chapel Hill, NC, 1958) discusses the differential impact of industrialization on rural counties in terms of services and development.

Perhaps the major impact of these changes on the farm has been the drastic reduction in the farm labor force, a Southern version of the enclosure movement. Mechanization accelerated rural depopulation, as depicted by Charles R. Sayre, "Cotton Mechanization since World War II," *Agricultural History* 53 (January 1979), 105–124. Paul Good, *The American Serfs* (New York, 1968), relates the impact of federal policies and mechanization on black farm laborers, and Janet K. Wadley and Everett S. Lee, in "The Disappearance of the Black Farmer," *Phylon* XXXV (September 1974), 276–283, quantify the phenomenon. And many of these blacks moved to the city, as John D. Reid calculates in "Black Urbanization of the South," *Phylon* XXXV (September 1974), 259–267.

The agricultural transformation was merely the beginning of Southern economic development in the postwar era. Several observers foresaw a prosperous region during the war years, and their accounts offer a good perspective on an economy about to "take off." Rupert B. Vance, in *All These People: The Nation's Human Resources in the South* (Chapel Hill, NC, 1945) analyzes the potential and liabilities of the region's abundant human capital and proposes policies designed to develop it. *Fortune* magazine reporters noted hopeful signs in a wartime tour of the South, though they observed that "economic change coexisted with white supremacy," in "The Deep South Looks Up," *Fortune* 28 (July 1943), 95–98, 100, 218, 220, 223–224. By the late 1950s it was evident that something extraordinary was afoot in the regional economy even in the midst of racial strife, and Walter Prescott Webb chronicles the region's advantages in "The South's Call to Greatness: Challenge to All Southerners," *Texas Business Review* 33 (October 1959), 5–8.

World War II was clearly the economic watershed for the South, but scholars have yet to study this vital period in a comprehensive way. George B. Tindall's *The Emergence of the New South, 1913–1945* (Baton Rouge, LA, 1967) includes a useful chapter on the war in the South, especially on economic and racial developments. John R. Skates, Jr., "World War II as a Watershed in Mississippi History," *Journal of Mississippi History* 37 (May 1975), 131–142, indicates the potential for research on other states during this period.

But did the economic changes portended by the war imply equally fundamental changes in Southern culture? William H. Nicholls, in *Southern Tradition and Regional Progress* (Chapel Hill, NC, 1960), contends that the persistence of agrarian values, the rigid social structure, and the closed political system would inhibit significant economic development: the culture needs to change before prosperity can occur. James C. Cobb, in two well-reasoned books, *The Selling of the South: The Southern Crusade for Industrial Development, 1936–1980* (Baton Rouge, LA, 1982), and *Industrialization and Southern Society, 1877–1984* (Lexington, KY, 1984), contends that Southerners continued their exploitation of land and labor and maintained their interlocking directorate of business, political, and clerical leadership while successfully attracting outside investment.

Indeed, the South remains the least-unionized region of the country. Robert B. Cooney, in "The Modern South: Organized Labor's New Frontier," *American Federationist* 68 (May 1961), 15–19, admits difficulties in organizing Southern workers, but remains hopeful of the future. By 1980, this hope was not fulfilled, as Robert Emil Botsch contends in *We Shall Not Overcome: Populism and Southern Blue Collar Workers* (Chapel Hill, NC, 1980). Robert J. Newman's *Growth in the American South: Changing Regional Employment and Wage Patterns in the 1960s and 1970s* (New York, 1984) also notes the persistence and advantages of nonunion labor in attracting

BIBLIOGRAPHICAL ESSAY 249

investment. For a historical survey of Southern unionization, see Merl E. Reed, Leslie S. Hough, and Gary M. Fink, eds., *Southern Workers and Their Unions, 1880–1975* (Westport, CT, 1981). And despite the myth of the Southern lady, women have historically comprised a sizable portion of the work force. As Betsy Mahoney points out in "The Facts Behind the Myths," *Southern Exposure* IX (Winter 1981), 6–8, Southern working women are less unionized and paid less than male workers or than working women elsewhere in the country.

So even amid the Sunbelt hyperbole, Southern labor remains exploited to some extent. There is also poverty, as J. Wayne Flynt points out in *Dixie's Forgotten People: The South's Poor Whites* (Bloomington, IN, 1979). And the South remains, in some areas, in a colonial position with respect to the North, as Joe Persky contends in "The South: A Colony at Home," *Southern Exposure* I (Summer 1973), 14–22, though this is less accurate today. The increasing concern among other regions about the South's favored status is unwarranted. The concern was generated in part by media attention to the Sunbelt and in part by scholarly documentation of the shift of the American economy from the North to the South. See, for example, Robert Estall, "The Changing Balance of the Northern and Southern Regions of the United States," *American Studies* 14 (December 1980), 365–386, and, especially, Bernard L. Weinstein and Robert E. Firestine, *Regional Growth and Decline in the United States: The Rise of the Sunbelt and the Decline of the Northeast* (New York, 1978). Thoughtful Southerners confronted two dilemmas—first, to defuse sectional antagonism that could eventually translate into national policy, and second, to address the very real economic shortcomings of the South.

Debunking the Sunbelt was relatively easy, as George B. Tindall demonstrated in "The Sunbelt Snow Job," *Houston Review* 1 (Spring 1979), 3–13. More difficult was preparing a regional agenda for broad and equitable economic development. Thomas H. Naylor and James Clotfelter's *Strategies for Changes in the South* (Chapel Hill, NC, 1975) was an early attempt at such agenda setting. The Southern Growth Policies Board has been especially active in promoting progressive economic development. In two publications in particular, the board first analyzes the Southern economy in detail, baring faults and potentials, and then prescribes specific remedies. See E. Blaine Liner and Lawrence K. Lynch, eds., *The Economics of Southern Growth* (Research Triangle Park, NC, 1977), and Pat Watters, ed., *The Future of the South: Preliminary Report* (Research Triangle Park, NC, 1981).

Despite these careful efforts, the impression of federal favoritism persists, especially in the realm of military expenditures. See, for example, James Clotfelter, "The South and the Military Dollar," *New South* 25 (Spring 1970), 52–56. The most comprehensive work on the subject, though not limited to the South, is the fine collection of essays assembled by Roger W. Lotchin in *The Martial Metropolis: U.S. Cities in War and Peace* (New York, 1984).

It is a tall order to fend off Northern adversaries, avoid the seduction of Sunbelt rhetoric, develop strategies to broaden regional economic development, and maintain the elements of Southern culture all at the same time. It is to be hoped that the latter two objectives will merge and reinforce each other. A recent novel by Peter La Salle, *Strange Sunlight* (Austin, 1984), disturbingly suggests that acting out Sunbelt fantasies would hollow out the personal South, leaving a shell encrusted with crass materialism.

It is a vision conjured up by William Faulkner as well, in *Go Down, Moses* (New York, 1942), in which it is Southern man's desecration of land and nature that ultimately leads to destruction of both. Indeed, the natural environment has a sacred place in Southern culture. The most thorough survey of the destruction and attempted resurrection of the natural South is Albert E. Cowdrey's *This Land, This South: An Environmental History* (Lexington, KY, 1983). A similar sequence affecting the region's timberlands is eloquently told in Thomas D. Clark's *The Greening of the South: The Recovery of Land and Forest* (Lexington, KY, 1984). Unfortunately, some parts of the South may be beyond redemption. For the story of how Florida was lost, the most poignant work is a novel by Patrick D. Smith, *A Land Remembered* (Englewood, FL, 1984). An excellent scholarly perspective is Nelson M. Blake, *Land into Water—Water into Land: A History of Water Management in Florida* (Tallahassee, FL, 1980). On the pollution of the Gulf by the petrochemical industry, see Joseph A. Pratt, "Growth of a Clean Environment? Responses to Petroleum-related Pollution in the Gulf Coast Refining Region," *Business History Review* LII (Spring 1978), 1–29; as Pratt notes, legislation and citizen resolve are attempting to reverse the cycle of pollution. The erosion of the Atlantic and Gulf coasts accelerated by coastal development, as well as by industrial pollution, is the subject of a series in *Southern Exposure* X (May/June 1982), 90–120. Again, recent movements in the regulatory field as well as increased public awareness are challenging the free-wheeling developmental mentality long characteristic of a beautiful region. But government cannot always be counted on as a preservation ally; note, for example, the deliberate flooding of farm lands for hydroelectric power generated by the Tennessee Valley Authority. Robert Penn Warren chronicles one such event in his novel *Flood* (New York, 1964). The TVA, in fact, has become a frequent target of environmentalists, especially for its mining activities in Appalachia, as noted by Osborn Segerberg, Jr., in "Power Corrupts," *Esquire* 77 (March 1972), 138–142, 192–195, and Jim Overton, "Taking on TVA," *Southern Exposure* XI (January/February 1983), 22–28. On the social costs of TVA, see Michael J. McDonald and John Muldowny, *TVA and the Dispossessed: The Resettlement of Population in the Norris Dam Area* (Knoxville, TN, 1982).

The South, however, has been fortunate to experience its major spurt of growth in an era of increased environmental consciousness. Linda Liston discusses the beginnings of the protective movement in the region in "The Southeast: Economic Imperatives Bow to Environmental Integrity," *Industrial Development and Manufacturers Record* 140 (September-

October 1971), 6–21. On more recent efforts, focusing on the South's fragile wetlands, see Ray Jones, "Saving the Wild South," *Southern Living* 18 (January 1983), 83–89.

The Appalachian subregion has attracted a number of studies on the environmental impact of unbridled economic development. Five works in particular capture the tragic history of Appalachia and its people. There are three excellent overviews of the subregion that stress the transition from farming to industry. Harry M. Caudill's two works, *Night Comes to the Cumberlands* (Boston, 1963), and *Theirs Be the Power: The Moguls of Eastern Kentucky* (Urbana, IL, 1983), detail the economic exploitation of the area in a poignant, forceful manner. A more quantitative, though complementary, survey is *Who Owns Appalachia? Landownership and its Impact* (Lexington, KY, 1983), by the Appalachian Land Ownership Task Force, which analyzes land and mineral ownership patterns in eighty counties in six states. Local and federal agencies have been cognizant of the poverty and the colonial economic conditions, though policies designed to alleviate these conditions have generally failed. See David E. Whisnant, *Modernizing the Mountaineer: People, Power, and Planning in Appalachia* (Boone, NC, 1980). The best insight into the people of this troubled region and how they slid into dependency is Ronald D. Eller, *Miners, Millhands, and Mountaineers: Industrialization of the Appalachian South, 1880–1920* (Knoxville, TN, 1982).

Although Appalachia has generated everything from songs to subsidies, the rural South in general has receded in regional consciousness as the South's economy and its people have moved to the cities. David R. Goldfield, *Cotton Fields and Skyscrapers: Southern City and Region, 1607–1980* (Baton Rouge, LA, 1982) is an overview of Southern urbanization that places the city in its regional cultural context. Chapel Hill regionalists Rupert B. Vance and Nicholas J. Demerath edited a collection of essays, *The Urban South* (Chapel Hill, NC, 1954), that was the first major scholarly acknowledgment of the rise and importance of the Southern city, though the essays are mostly descriptive rather than analytical. Other early recognitions of Southern urbanization and its potential include Walter J. Matherly, "The Emergence of the Metropolitan Community in the South," *Social Forces* 14 (March 1936), 311–325, and Robert Earl Garren, "Urbanism: A New Way of Life for the South," *Mississippi Quarterly* X (September 1957), 65–72. These last three works hail urban growth and predict that it would alter regional life. Goldfield's book contends that it did not work out that way, a thesis implied in several essays in an anthology edited by David C. Perry and Alfred J. Watkins, *The Rise of the Sunbelt Cities* (Beverly Hills, CA, 1977).

By the 1960s the urban trend was unmistakable and policy discussions were commonplace on how to deal with this relatively new phenomenon without repeating mistakes made elsewhere. The policy focus is effectively addressed in the proceedings of a conference held in Atlanta in 1967, the Southern Regional Conference on Urbanization, *Proceedings* (Athens, GA, 1967).

The scholarship on Southern cities is beginning to catch up with the demographic and economic realities of the region. Scholars are studying individual cities, as a collection of essays edited by Richard M. Bernard and Bradley R. Rice indicates, *Sunbelt Cities: Politics and Growth since World War II* (Austin, 1983). Book-length studies include Christopher Silver, *Twentieth-Century Richmond: Planning, Politics, and Race* (Knoxville, TN, 1982), Michael J. McDonald and William Bruce Wheeler, *Knoxville, Tennessee: Continuity and Change in an Appalachian City* (Knoxville, TN, 1983), and Don H. Doyle, *Nashville since the 1920s* (Knoxville, TN, 1985). Silver uncovers the race and class biases of city planning and, in the latter two works, the authors depict the control of the cities by the business elite. Though more specific, in terms of focusing extensively on politics, David M. Tucker, *Memphis Since Crump: Bossism, Blacks, and Civic Reformers, 1948–1968* (Knoxville, TN, 1980), presents an intriguing analysis of one of the most rigid of the South's biracial cities.

The historiography of elites is enjoying a resurgence nationally and Southern urban elites will doubtless attract attention before long, aside from more general city surveys. Floyd Hunter has worked in the field for nearly four decades, his most recent contribution being *Community Power Succession: Atlanta's Policymakers* (Chapel Hill, NC, 1980), though his connection between power and reputation is questionable. Harold H. Martin presents an adequate, if a bit too complimentary, biography, *William Berry Hartsfield: Mayor of Atlanta* (Athens, GA, 1978). Among the best elite studies to date is Edward F. Haas, *DeLesseps S. Morrison and the Image of Reform: New Orleans Politics, 1946–1961* (Baton Rouge, LA, 1974).

Urban residents have challenged the booster mentality in recent years. Historic preservation, in particular, has been a popular activity that complements regional reverence for the past. Michael Fazio, "Architectural Preservation in Natchez, Mississippi: A Conception of Time and Place," *Southern Quarterly* 19 (Fall 1980), 136–149, and Don H. Doyle, "Saving Yesterday's City: Nashville's Waterfront," *Tennessee Historical Quarterly* 35 (Winter 1976), 353–364 are two essays that deal with this movement, though more needs to be done in this area as well as in the neighborhood preservation field.

Southern cities reflect what may be the future American city: sprawling, suburban, and automobile dependent. Writers have not specifically addressed the implications of this configuration for the metropolitan South, though some work has appeared that demonstrates the importance of such study. Bradley R. Rice, "Urbanization, 'Atlantaization,' and Suburbanization: Three Themes for the Urban History of Twentieth-Century Georgia," *Georgia Historical Society* LXVIII (Spring 1984), 40–59, and parts of Dana F. White and Timothy J. Crimmins, "How Atlanta Grew: Cool Heads, Hot Air, and Hard Work," *Atlantic Economic Review* 28 (January-February 1978), 7–15, discuss the expansion of that city, but Atlanta's difficulties with suburbs and its inability to annex freely are atypical of the metropolitan South.

Aside from race relations, the historiography on other topics of the modern South remains relatively thin compared with the work undertaken by other humanities and social science disciplines. Economic development, urbanization, politics, conservation, and culture contain numerous topics to occupy future scholars. Analyses of race—especially since 1965—are also necessary. As the South emerges as the nation's most affluent and populous region, it becomes important for historians to explore how and why this came about, as well as how and why the South can retain its distinctive culture.

INDEX

Promised Land: The South since 1945 was copyedited by Anita Samen. Production editor was Brad Barrett. Elizabeth Rubenstein and Martha Kreger proofread the copy. The map of the southern states was rendered by Sarah Park Stuart. The text was typeset by Impressions, Inc., and printed and bound by Edwards Brothers, Inc.

Book and cover design by Roger Eggers.